Feminist Security Studies

This book rethinks security theory from a feminist perspective—uniquely, it engages feminism, security, and strategic studies to provide a distinct feminist approach to security studies.

The volume explicitly works toward an opening up of security studies that would allow for feminist (and other) narratives to be recognized and taken seriously as security narratives. To make this possible, it presents a feminist reading of security studies that aims to invigorate the debate and radicalize critical security studies. Because feminism is a political project, and security studies are, at their base, about particular visions of the political and their attendant institutions, this is of necessity a political intervention. The book works through and beyond security studies to explore possible spaces where an opening of security, necessary to make way for feminist insights, can take place. Although it develops and illustrates a feminist narrative approach to security, it is also intended as an intervention that challenges the politics of security and the meanings for security legitimized in existing practices.

This book provides and develops a comprehensive framework for the emerging field of feminist security studies and will be of great interest to students and scholars of feminist IR, critical security studies, gender studies and IR, and security studies in general.

Annick T.R. Wibben is Assistant Professor of Politics and International Studies as well as Chair of the interdisciplinary Bachelor Program in International Studies at the University of San Francisco (USF). From 2001 to 2005, she was the Co-Investigator of the Information Technology, War and Peace Project at the Watson Institute for International Studies at Brown University.

Series: PRIO New Security Studies
Series Editor: J. Peter Burgess
PRIO, Oslo

The aim of this book series is to gather state-of-the-art theoretical reflexion and empirical research into a core set of volumes that respond vigorously and dynamically to the new challenges to security scholarship.

The Geopolitics of American Insecurity
Terror, power and foreign policy
Franois Debrix and Mark J. Lacy, eds.

Security, Risk and the Biometric State
Governing borders and bodies
Benjamin Muller

Security and Global Governmentality
Globalization, governance and the state
Miguel de Larrinaga and Marc G. Doucet

Critical Perspectives on Human Security
Rethinking emancipation and power in international relations
David Chandler and Nik Hynek, eds.

Understanding Securitisation
The design and evolution of security problems
Thierry Balzacq, ed.

Feminist Security Studies
A narrative approach
Annick T.R. Wibben

Feminist Security Studies

A narrative approach

Annick T.R. Wibben

Routledge
Taylor & Francis Group

LONDON AND NEW YORK

First published 2011
by Routledge
2 Park Square, Milton Park, Abingdon, Oxon OX14 4RN

Simultaneously published in the USA and Canada
by Routledge
270 Madison Ave, New York, NY 10016

Routledge is an imprint of the Taylor & Francis Group, an informa business

© 2011 Annick T.R. Wibben

The right of Annick T.R. Wibben to be identified as author of this work has
been asserted by him in accordance with sections 77 and 78 of the
Copyright, Designs and Patents Act 1988.

Typeset in Bembo by
Book Now Ltd, London
Printed and bound in Great Britain by
CPI Antony Rowe, Chippenham, Wiltshire

British Library Cataloging in Publication Data
A catalog record for this book is available from the British Library

Library of Congress Cataloging in Publication Data
Wibben, Annick T.R.
Feminist security studies: a narrative approach/Annick T.R. Wibben.
     p. cm.
1. Security, International—Social aspects. 2. National security—Social aspects.
3. Feminist theory. 4. Women's rights. 5. Women and war. I. Title.
JZ5588.W53 2010
355′.03300082—dc22   2010025338

ISBN13: 978–0–415–45727–9 (hbk)
ISBN13: 978–0–415–45728–6 (pbk)
ISBN13: 978–0–203–83488–6 (ebk)

Contents

Acknowledgments   vii

Introduction   1

1   Feminist interventions: the politics of identity   10

2   Challenging meanings   27

3   Toward a narrative approach   43

4   Security as narrative   65

5   Feminist security narratives   86

6   The future of feminist security studies   107

Appendix   115
Notes   117
Bibliography   131
Index   150

Acknowledgments

The journey to completing the book has been a long one and many people and institutions need to be acknowledged for their support of this project and its author. To begin, I want to thank Cynthia Enloe, Vivienne Jabri, Christine Sylvester, and J. Ann Tickner. They, along with other feminist scholars, have not only made it possible for young scholars such as myself to consider security from a feminist perspective but have also provided encouragement for this project in concrete ways by commenting on my work and ideas. I also need to thank Andrew Humphrys at Routledge, who had faith that the book would be written eventually, and Peter Burgess at PRIO for selecting the book for inclusion in the New Security Studies series.

When I began working on these topics at the University of Wales in Aberystwyth in 1998, my research was supported by the British Economic and Social Research Council and an Aberystwyth Postgraduate Studentship. Jenny Edkins and Michael C. Williams had the task of helping me to figure out what exactly the PhD project was going to be and how I could possibly tackle it, making a contribution to the field of International Politics while at the same time questioning its very foundations, and they did so with much patience. Given that this was also the start of a process of coming to voice—of "carving out the intellectual and political space that would enable me to be heard" (Collins 2000: xii), the Department of International Politics at the University of Wales, with its excellent faculty, varied research groups, and a continuing flow of speakers and inquisitive students, provided an ideal environment for these explorations. I am especially grateful for the continued friendship of Jenny Edkins and of Maja Zehfuss—your work is an inspiration and our conversations keep me sane.

From 2001 to 2005, I had the opportunity to work with James Der Derian on the Information Technology, War and Peace project at the Watson Institute for International Studies, funded by the Ford Foundation. I will forever be grateful for the intellectual stimulation and supportive atmosphere that characterized the Watson Institute under the leadership of Thomas J. Biersteker, who personally ensured that everyone was able to do their best work. Working on a rapid response to the events of September 11, 2001, with my colleagues at the Watson Institute (see http://www.infopeace.org) has profoundly shaped not only this book but also my thinking about the limits of the discipline and its politics.

James—your ongoing encouragement and steadfast support can only be repaid by paying it forward, as you once said, and I am working on that.

In the fall of 2003, I spent a semester as a Rockefeller Humanities Fellow for Human Security at the National Council for Research on Women and the Center for the Study of Women and Society at CUNY in New York City. I would like to acknowledge the support of these organizations for my work on human security. Although the examination of privilege was already a concern of mine, participation in the weekly seminars and conversations with the other fellows, Ratna Kapur and Uma Narayan, made the struggle with imperial tendencies within feminism a central concern in my work. Thank you!

As an assistant professor at the University of San Francisco since 2005, it has been much harder to find time to write but not for a lack of support. Weekend Writing Retreats, sponsored by the College of Arts and Sciences under the leadership of Jennifer Turpin and run, impeccably, by Pamela Balls-Organista, have provided space for rethinking the research as a book. A sabbatical in 2008–9 allowed time for large parts of the book to be composed. The ongoing support of colleagues in the Friday Writing Warriors, especially the original members Tracy Seeley, Stephanie Sears, and Shawan Worsley, has made the completion of the manuscript possible. I also owe thanks to my student assistants, Erika Carlsen, Mary Solon, and Maggie Boyle who spent many hours collecting materials and entering bibliographic data into Endnote. My colleague and friend, Keally McBride, commented on several parts of the final manuscript, and Kerry Donoghue provided editorial assistance and pep talks through the very end. I could not have done it without you!

Last, and most importantly, I need to acknowledge the support from my family, especially my mother, Sabine. Although sometimes puzzled by the path I have chosen and wishing I were writing in German, so that it would be easier for her to read my research, she always tries to support my endeavors. I am dedicating this book to my husband, Ted, who does his best to keep our lives balanced, and to our daughters, Klara and Luise, whose vocabulary included "mommy—work?" almost as soon as they could talk. They have lived with this project for too long, and if anyone could be happier than I that this book has been completed, it would be them.

Introduction

I always turn the news on, and I'm not ever watching it, I'm just hearing it. Really, I'm listening for the weather, OK? And I remember that being on there [the first plane crashing] and not even associating it as being live. You know, I walked by, "C'mon girls. We gotta get up," or whatever. I come back, and I am doing what I'm doing, got out of the shower, and it's still there. "Oh. OK." And then, when I seen the second plane hit, that made me stop for a second. Though, not like "Wow!" but it made me stop. "Oh. OK, what's going on?" And then, that's when it sunk in that what was going on was actually happening in present time. And for some reason, once that hit, I was paralyzed. I didn't want to leave the television, although my younger children had no idea what was going on. And they're ready to, generally it's me going, "C'mon girls, I've got to comb your hair," and all that. They're knocking at the door going, "Mom, you've got to comb our hair. We're ready." I did manage to break away long enough to do their hair and walk them to daycare.

(Moira, quoted in Mattingly *et al.* 2002: 746)

This narrative, recounting Moira's experience of the events of 9/11, is quite familiar. Against the backdrop of what seemed to be an ordinary New York morning in September 2001, the crashing of two planes into the World Trade Center and the immediate access to this event provided by the media constituted a breach of normality. Almost everyone in the United States, provided they were old enough at the time and had some access to media, remembers where they were and what they were doing when they heard "the news." Moira's narrative is of interest because it reveals what is considered normal, that is, "accounts of times when the expected is flouted, or when things somehow go awry, rely on a shared understanding (between narrator and audience) of what the normal and expected look like" (Mattingly *et al.* 2002: 745). What happens when such a shared understanding does not exist? What if the breach that constitutes an event as notable is not considered an exception because the vision of normality from which it deviates is that of only a privileged few?

The question of a shared understanding, or normality, is central to feminist interventions in international politics, generally, and in security studies, specifically. Because feminist theorizing starts from women's experiences of everyday life, it has to accommodate the varied contexts of women's lives while also remaining attuned to the contextual nature of "normality." What is more, as feminist theorizing has become more sophisticated over time, the intersections of gender with class, nationality, race, and other markers of identity have come to inform conceptualizations of women's experience and subjectivity. Staying attuned to varied everyday experience, through the telling of women's stories in this case, is central to feminists' resistance to abstraction. It provides a corrective to the generalizing and universalizing tendencies in traditional science that work to institute bias and obscure responsibility. Insisting on specificity also reveals how there is always more than one point of view and more than one story to be told. The choice to privilege one perspective over another is never innocent or obvious but always intensely political. What is more, the insistence on a singular narrative is itself a form of violence.

Narratives are essential because they are a primary way by which we make sense of the world around us, produce meanings, articulate intentions, and legitimize actions. "Narrative ordering makes individual events comprehensible by identifying the whole to which they contribute [...] thereby attributing significance to individual actions and events according to their effect on the whole" (Polkinghorne 1988: 18). Narratives, as such, are sites of the exercise of power; through narratives, we not only investigate but also invent an order for the world. They police our imagination by taming aspirations and adjusting desires to social reality (though narratives can also be disruptive when they do not "fit" into a particular social, political, or symbolic order). As Cheryl Mattingly, Mary Lawlor, and Lanita Jacobs-Huey argue, personal narratives are especially interesting because they "allow us to attend to the collective and the personal, the intersubjective and the individual" (Mattingly *et al.* 2002: 745). The choice of genre, character, plot, and other elements in a particular narrative reveal much about the teller's location, hinting both at shared cultural meanings and marking where the personal and the collective deviate. As such, both the *content* and the *form* of a narrative are crucial.

Moira's narrative resonates with the dominant US narrative of 9/11 (which marks the events as an unthinkable attack on an innocent victim and neatly divides time into a pre- and post-9/11 world), while simultaneously challenging this account by ending with a return to the normal activities of doing the children's hair and dropping them off at daycare. The African American mothers whose stories Mattingly *et al.* have collected quickly mark the difference between their personal stories and the collective US narrative. In comparison with the daily challenges they face, the events of 9/11 are rather insignificant. Consider the following story:

> But the September 11 thing didn't really bother me. It affected my family more than me. My children were asking me questions like, "Why would somebody kill those people?" I can't explain it. I said, you know, "Something is wrong with him [bin Laden]. Nobody didn't show him love or something." You know, it's something that's really wrong with that whole

family for them to be plotting that kind of stuff. I just told my children that they need to love each other as a family and don't worry about him, because we can't do nothing about it. And that [terrorist attack] scared my mom. I have my mom now... she's handicapped. Her whole point, she can to everything for herself, she just don't want to be by herself. She said, you know, she don't want to wake up bombed without her family. But her being in my house, she's much calmer. At first she was screaming and hollering. You'd call her on the phone, and she was saying, "Please, come get me. Please come get me." She just didn't want to be by herself. And now, she say, ah, she talk to bin Laden, like, she saying, "Now you can't get me, I'm with my family" [Delia laughs, and the group joins in], ... which I really appreciate. It's making me feel stronger. It didn't really affect me.

(Delia, quoted in Mattingly *et al.* 2002: 747)

Indeed, considering that Delia's life "had recently been marked by the fight to keep alive a critically ill infant who then died, the death of her mother-in-law, her husband's stroke, and a violent armed robbery by neighbors" (Mattingly *et al.* 2002: 747–8), the events of 9/11 and the subsequent move of her mother are minor additional challenges. What is more, many of the women in the group also felt that they recognized that the United States was not an innocent nation. They had more empathy for the people who were going to suffer as a result of the US response because they had experienced oppression as members of a marginalized group.[1]

Moira and Delia's 9/11 narratives, as well as some of the other stories collected by Mattingly *et al.*, allude to several insights that are crucial to feminist security studies (FSS). They illustrate the complex subject positions and allegiances that are the result of intersections of class, gender, and race. They locate the events of 9/11 on a continuum that stresses continuities within their everyday lives and make connections with others that seemingly share their marginal positions. They exhibit a cautionary approach to violence as the appropriate response, and even a preference for nonviolence, based on their own familiarity with violence and its destructive consequences. They also present a different version of normality and, consequently, of security influenced by their location in terms of class, gender, and race. For them, fear and vulnerability are common enough to make the events of 9/11 appear as simply "more of the same." As such, their 9/11 narratives do not begin on September 11, 2001, nor do they mark this moment with enough significance to divide the world into a pre- and post-9/11 world as the dominant US 9/11 narrative does. Indeed, Mattingly *et al.* found that some of the women in their ongoing collective narrative group were annoyed to even be asked about the events because they had more important topics to discuss.[2]

The framing of events in a particular narrative always has implications for action because it includes and excludes options and actors, while also limiting what can be thought or said, thus eventually imposing silences. The framing "decides, in a forceful way, *what we can hear*, whether a view will be taken as explanation or exoneration, whether we can hear the difference and abide by it" writes Butler (2004: 5). The dominant framing of 9/11 by the George W. Bush administration as "'uncaused' cause" (Zehfuss 2003: 521) consequently "works both to preclude certain kinds of questions, certain kinds of historical inquiries, and to function as a moral justification for retaliation" (Butler 2004: 4). Drawing on traditional, militarized security framings, the Bush administration quickly set the stage for perpetual war, eschewing any alternatives like the humanitarian framing proposed, among others, by Kaldor (2001).[3] In what ways could listening to 9/11 narratives such as Moira and Delia's impact the US response to the events of September 11, 2001? How might it challenge the way we imagine and study security?

Questioning international politics

Feminists have challenged core concepts of International Relations (IR), as well as the study of war, for decades. Their writing on issues of peace, war, and violence, much of it in the form of historical and cross-cultural case studies, has highlighted women's roles in peacemaking, war-fighting, and the in-between. Some of the more theoretical work, much of it initially in peace research, has focused on militarization and its effects. In the early 1990s, feminists began to explicitly frame their concerns in terms of "security." Tickner published *Gender in International Relations: Feminist Perspectives on Achieving Global Security* in 1992, and a year later, Betty Reardon wrote *Women and Peace: Feminist Visions of Global Security*.[4] Besides the fact that both of these feminists focus on global security, rather than national security, they also draw on a long tradition of feminist engagement with security issues.

Within IR, Tickner's work is the most common starting point for elaborations of feminist thought in security studies.[5] In *Gender in International Relations*, she outlines a set of questions and concerns that feminist scholars need to address to challenge the prevailing notion that national security should be the highest good. Unlike much of security studies at the time, she explicitly includes economic and environmental concerns as part of this broader notion of security. In line with these concerns, her definition of violence includes a physical, a structural, and an ecological component. Reviewing feminists' attempts to redefine national security, she notes that although there are varying positions on what constitutes security, agreement exists that "security meant nothing if it was built on other's insecurity" (Tickner 1992: 55). Furthermore, in addition to the absence of war (negative peace), feminist approaches include a concern with eradicating violence and a commitment to social and economic justice (positive peace).[6] Throughout her analysis, Tickner also stresses the need to examine power as it shapes gendered hierarchies.

Enloe (1983, 1990b, 1993, 2000, 2007) has probably been the most prolific writer of FSS in IR. Her comparative, mostly case-study-based writing on the linkages between militarism, masculinities, and women's lives is exemplary of feminist concerns. She takes the feminist slogan "the personal is political" to the international realm and reveals how much power it takes to make IR appear as though women are not in it (Enloe 1990b: 195–8). She has consistently shown how starting from women's everyday experiences, whether they are diplomatic wives, prostitutes, or plantation workers, can provide insights into matters of peace, war, and violence; her work has inspired many others to do the same (cf. Katharine Moon's study of Korean–US relations discussed in Chapter 4). What is more, she never loses sight of the linkages between economic and security interests, showcasing the relationship between structural and other forms of violence. All that is needed, according to Enloe (2004: 3), is a "feminist curiosity" where one takes *all* women's lives seriously, "listening carefully, digging deep, developing a long attention span, being ready to be surprised."

Much of the writing that might be considered FSS has its roots in peace research, where, in the 1960s, feminists constituted a significant presence in the field (Boulding 1992). By the late 1960s, feminist peace researchers were analyzing power, emphasizing empowerment over coercion. In the 1970s, these researchers moved on to developing notions of common security that stress commonalities with an adversary, while also broadening the notion of security to include security against want, security of human rights, the security of an empowered civilian society, ideas that are central to the more recent human security concept. By the 1980s, they focused on the linkages between war and patriarchy, which, in various guises, remain important components of FSS and one of its most fruitful areas of research (e.g., Enloe 1983, 1993, 2000; Reardon 1985, 1993).[7] A flurry of edited collections at the turn of the century (e.g., Jacobs *et al.* 2000; Lorentzen and Turpin 1998; Meintjes *et al.* 2001; Moser and Clark 2001) attests to the fact that feminist perspectives continue to emerge in peace research.[8]

Overall, feminists have played an important role in proposing alternative conceptions of power and violence that go beyond the traditional military configurations of the discipline of IR, including ideas of common and cooperative security arrangements, and non-state-centric perspectives on security (initially by Brock-Utne 1985, 1989; Reardon 1985, 1993; Ruddick 1983, 1989b; Stiehm 1982, 1983). However, this accumulation of research has generally been ignored both within peace research and IR, even though much of it addresses issues that are central to security studies.[9] Even so, feminist insights have entered the field of security studies through debates in critical security studies.[10] Largely, though falsely, seen to arise as a consequence of the breakdown of the bipolar world order, attempts at revising the security agenda have been widespread and multifarious since the early 1980s.[11] These attempts reflect a multiplicity of scholars working within and without various IR traditions. Some scholars want to add new issues to the existing list of threats (e.g., Mathews 1989; Ullman 1983). Others, in contrast, are concerned with the notion of security more directly, asking what it means (e.g., Huysmans 1998; Rothschild 1995), how it operates (Buzan and Herring 1998; Huysmans 2006; Wæver 1995a, 1995b), and for whom security is provided (e.g., Bilgin *et al.* 1998; Booth 1991a, 1997; Tickner 1992, 1995; Wyn Jones 1995, 1999).

Much of this scholarship is reformative in nature, aiming for a revision and reorganization of the study of security studies, so that it reflects the current state of affairs more accurately; most accounts do not review feminist work. Furthermore, some thinkers are considered too radical and far-reaching because they question whether security studies have ever contributed to an understanding of issues or whether they have been reinforcing, if not inventing, the security dilemma we face (e.g., Burke 2002, 2007; Campbell 1998a, 1998b; Constantinou 2000; Der Derian 1995; Dillon 1996; Peterson 1992b).

The reassessment of security studies has received quite a different reception in the United States than it has in Europe or Canada (the more prolific sites of activity). Although a slight move away from the traditionally military-focused strategic studies can be observed in the United States (mostly using constructivist tools, e.g., Katzenstein 1996; Weldes *et al.* 1999), Canadians, in particular, have pushed a human security agenda (e.g., MacLean *et al.* 2006; McRae and Hubert 2001), and European IR has embraced a set of critical approaches to security studies (e.g., Behnke 2007; Betts 1997; Bilgin *et al.* 1998; c.a.s.e. collective 2006; Ceyhan 1998; Krause 1998). Notwithstanding the broader scope of their approaches and analyses, even the European debate has remained limited by insisting on parameters that arguably constitute a new orthodoxy, that is, although a broadening (to include more types of threats) and a deepening (to include referents and agents beyond the state) of the security agenda are encouraged (Krause and Williams 1996), an opening, which would imply a discussion of the meaning(s) and, thus, the politics of security, is considered potentially dangerous.[12] As Hansen (2000: 288) notes, one of the major European reformulations of security studies, the Copenhagen School, has been successful "through the formulation of a 'solution' which allows for widening, as well as deepening, without opening the concept to unlimited expansion which would render it meaningless."[13]

However, it is precisely this third axis of inquiry, an opening, that is needed to challenge the way IR has conceptualized security and to make room for the types of feminist narratives and concerns mentioned earlier (Wibben 2008). This third axis of inquiry investigates: why appeals to security are so powerful (Der Derian 1995; Deudney 1990; Edkins 2002a), why particular formulations remain meaningful whereas others have withered over time (Burke 2002; Constantinou 2000; Dillon 1990; Dillon 1996; Neocleous 2000; Rothschild 1995), and, most importantly, how meanings might be challenged (Huysmans 1998, 2006). Der Derian (1995: 25) argues, "We have inherited and *ontotheology* of security, that is, an *a priori* argument that proves the existence and necessity of only one form of security because there currently happens to be a widespread, metaphysical belief in it." An opening of the agenda, thus, needs to begin by understanding how security has traditionally worked (e.g., Campbell 1998b; Dillon 1996) and how meanings of security are fixed in certain narratives that make up security studies (cf. Huysmans 1998, 2006; Wæver 1995b).

Although there has been much critical examination of security studies in the past three decades, the work is united mainly by its rejection of the narrow framework of traditional (neorealist) approaches (c.a.s.e. collective 2006; Krause 1998). Even as the *content* of some critical security narratives shifts considerably, they share much of their *form* with more traditional security studies narratives. Such security narratives include the following elements: (1) threats that locate danger; (2) referents to be secured; (3) agents charged with providing security; and (4) means by which threats are contained and, so the tale is told, security provided (cf. Chapter 4, Wibben 2002). What is more, they are tied to an epistemology where, "(a) everything can, in principle, be known; and (b) if it is known its truth does not change over time" (Huysmans 1998: 245). Security narratives that do not conform to the above structure (especially those that might challenge its epistemological or ontological assumptions) are not recognized as security talk. The two axes of reformulation identified by Krause and Williams (1996)—broadening and deepening—fit this structure more easily.[14] They simply exchange one or another threat or actor (whether referent or agent) without disturbing the overall structure too much. On the other hand, the third axis—opening—does not readily add to this existing framework. This has been a major obstacle to alternative formulations of security whose narrative form diverges more significantly.[15]

Calls for feminists to "add" their insights to the effort of some scholars at the critical end of security studies are a fairly recent development arising out of the more general attempt to widen the debate on security, briefly described earlier. "Adding" their insights, however, is problematic for feminists because it tends to take place on the terms laid out by the dominant discourse (cf. Harding 1986).[16] Consequently, the more innovative (and often more radical) inventions and interventions cannot be brought to bear on the field (Weber 1994). As Smith (2005: 48) has realized, "looking at security from the perspective of women alters the definition of what security is to such an extent that it is difficult to see how any form of traditional security studies can offer an analysis."

Besides these problems, calls for a feminist engagement with (critical) security studies neglect the fact that feminists have actively debated issues of peace and war, of which debates about security form a part.[17] They have, however, rarely been noticed. The difficulty of being heard does not lie in a failure to provide alternatives, but in feminist alternatives not being perceived as contributing to the debate on security. For one, until fairly recently, they have rarely been framed in terms of security (or strategic) studies and are, thus, dismissed as irrelevant. Second, feminists have difficulties placing their work strategically in contexts where it might reach larger audiences, both because they might prefer informal or nongovernmental settings and because they often lack access to other forums.[18] Third, mainstream IR and security studies, in particular, have not made much of an effort to seek our feminist contributions by reading feminist writings or partaking in their activism.[19]

This book addresses these issues by explicitly working toward an opening of security studies that would allow for feminist (and other) narratives to be recognized and taken seriously as security narratives. To make this possible, it presents a feminist reading of security studies with the aim of invigorating the debate and radicalizing critical security studies. Because feminism is a political project, and security studies are, at their base, about particular visions of the political and their attendant institutions, this is by necessity a political intervention. It is about time that the insights garnered in feminists' long-standing engagement with issues of peace, war, and violence make an impact on the field of security studies.

Outlining the structure

This book is composed similar to a patchwork quilt; although each piece is individually crafted in detail, it is the eventual sewing together of the pieces that provides the overall image. At the same time, the stitch pattern that covers the entire quilt indicates the continuation of the argument and showcases reappearing questions and insights. Each chapter, then, presents a crucial piece of the overall pattern. The common thread is the development of a feminist narrative approach to security through an opening of security studies.

Chapter 1 introduces the reader to feminist concerns and approaches as a basis for developing an appreciation for feminist approaches to security. It begins with a discussion of ongoing debates within the feminist movement, focusing specifically on the consequences of identity politics. The following section addresses the feminist attempts to infuse IR with their insights, from adding women to the field's purview to questioning its underlying assumptions about gender, knowledge, and power. The last part of the chapter hones in on the varied feminist contributions to security debates that the field of security studies tends to ignore.

The second chapter challenges the reader to consider how the world is made meaningful. It begins by examining the emergence of modern science as a response to particular historical events during the Enlightenment era and proposes other modes of knowledge production that are appropriate to the current historical context. The next section uses philosophical hermeneutics to take a closer look at the ways in which meaning is produced in the process of trying to understand and explain phenomena. Finally, the insights developed in these discussions are applied to the field of security studies to point to the contextual nature of security meanings and their effects.

In Chapter 3, a feminist narrative approach to social and political inquiry is developed. Starting with a discussion of narrative theory, it explains how narratological tools can be used to gain insight into the production of meaning in narrative. Following this overview, these tools are applied (and further specified) in an analysis of September 11, 2001 and George W. Bush's *Address to the Nation* that evening. On the basis of these elaborations, the chapter proposes that narratives are inherently political as they create particular versions of normality.

Chapter 4 presents a reading of approaches to security as narrative, using the feminist narrative approach developed in the preceding chapters. The first part traces the development of security studies from the postwar era through the Cold War and illustrates how a shifting, yet enduring combination of narrative elements gives meaning to security and organizes social relations in a particular manner. The following section focuses on the broadening and deepening of the security studies agenda, as expressed in critical security studies, pointing to both continuities and departures from the accepted security narrative. In the final section of Chapter 4, the emergence of human security is examined as potentially opening security.

In the next chapter, three exemplary feminist security narratives are presented to illustrate how meanings of security are contextual. Drawing on personal narratives, these accounts showcase how state security practices often produce insecurity for marginalized populations. The narratives presented here complicate the relationship between identity, marked by the intersecting oppressions that shape the lives of women (and men), and security, which shifts alongside them. Chapter 5 ends with a discussion of the larger implications of a narrative approach to security, including how it provides an opening to discuss the meanings and politics of security.

The book works through and beyond security studies to explore possible spaces where an opening of security, necessary to make way for feminist insights, can take place. Although it develops and illustrates a feminist narrative approach to security, it is also intended as an intervention that challenges the politics of security and the meanings for security legitimized in existing practices. The following interrogation of security from a feminist perspective, therefore, is, like all feminist projects, inherently political.

1 Feminist interventions
The politics of identity

Besides, one does not simply add the idea that the world is round to the idea that the world is flat.

(McIntosh and Minnich, quoted in Sheridan 1990: 49)

On November 17, 2001, Laura Bush, then first-lady of the United States, used the weekly presidential radio address to try to persuade the public that "the fight against terrorism is also a fight for the rights and dignity of women" (2001). She goes on,

> Afghan women know, through hard experience, what the rest of the world is discovering: The brutal oppression of women is a central goal of the terrorists. Long before the current war began, the Taliban and its terrorist allies were making the lives of children and women in Afghanistan miserable.
>
> (Bush L. 2001)

This is one of the examples of the George W. Bush administration's repeated references to women's rights in its propaganda supporting the US-led so-called "war on terror." By suggesting that ousting the Taliban would liberate Afghan women, the Bush administration managed to receive the backing of a number of feminists, including the Feminist Majority Foundation, a US-based organization that had been lobbying on behalf of Afghan women since the late 1990s. These feminists hoped, against all odds, that something good would come of the war. Barbara Ehrenreich mused, "women's rights may play no part in US foreign policy, but we should perhaps be grateful that they have at least been important enough to deploy in media mobilization for war" (Ehrenreich 2001). Other feminists disagree. Krista Hunt (2006) argues, that this type of "embedded feminism" has proved divisive among feminists. Indeed, the "feminist focus on women under the Taliban rang with superior tones of enlightenment and righteousness, singling out the most exotic and distant situations, and representing the women of Afghanistan as passive victims" (Young 2003: 230).[1] What is more, the appeal to women's rights has now become associated with foreign invasion, so that conservatives in Afghanistan and elsewhere commonly refer to them as an outside imposition to be resisted.

> The oppression of women serves a dual function—it works as a demonstration of political might and as a convincing rejection of the West. What better way to show your defiance of the United States than by symbolically cloistering your female population from the 'corruption' of the sexually liberated American woman, as seen in movies, advertising and TV?
>
> (Brown 2001a)

Embedded feminism, at least in this particular case, clearly weakens rather than strengthens women's rights. As such, appealing to women's rights as a justification for military intervention is controversial within feminist circles.

The concerns voiced by feminists—and the reactions to them—are always contextually specific, that is, although feminists are generally concerned with making the world a better place for women, what is better for whom is always subject to debate:

> A feminist perspective results from the conflict and contradictions between dominant institutionalized definitions of women's nature and social role [...] and our experience of these institutions in the context of the dominant liberal discourse of the free and self-determining individual.
>
> (Weedon 1987: 5)

What is more, feminist debates have only begun in earnest during the twentieth century, even though the term feminism was first used in the early nineteenth century when it appeared in the writings of Charles Fourier (quoted in Brockhaus 1990: 188) who "proposed the idea that the degree of liberation for women is the touchstone of every society and the standard measure of general human emancipation."[2] Feminisms contain both normative and descriptive elements: they have a vision of how the world ought to be organized that contrasts with the way it is currently structured to the disadvantage of women. What follows as a consequence of the contrast between a normative ideal and the description of a current economic, social, and symbolic order is prescriptive, articulating a particular political vision.

Feminisms are, thus, always political, as are all approaches to thinking and being in the world, even if they fail to acknowledge this. Contrary to other scholars in International Relations (IR), feminists are not afraid to make their political goals explicit and to publicly debate the differences within the movement. Besides showcasing feminism's reflexive nature, however, this also makes them more vulnerable to attack. Especially within the context of IR, and also that of security studies, feminists have often been sidelined as a political rather than a scientific project (i.e., feminists tend not to embrace a positivist model of science that is supposedly apolitical). A series of engagements between IR scholars and feminists revolve around this issue (cf. Carver *et al.* 1998;

Ehrenreich 1999; Fukuyama 1998; Jones 1996, 1998; Keohane 1989, 1991, 1998; Marchand 1998; Peterson 2004; Pollit 1999; Tickner 1997a, 1997b, 1998; Weber 1994; Wibben 2004). Some of these engagements are more sophisticated than others, but they exhibit an overall tendency of either not reading (much) feminist work or only assessing it according to the parameters of a privileged approach (or a particular topic) to which its insights might be added. Overall, it is, thus, possible to observe a still widespread ignorance of, and reluctance to engage with, feminist work in IR.

Characterizing feminisms

What then, is the political project of feminism? As noted in the introduction, feminists question what is assumed to be normal. Cynthia Enloe, one of the most prolific writers of feminist IR, has made it her task to continually question what is considered normal, often under the guise of "nature" or "tradition." She urges researchers to become curious but warns that being curious takes a lot of energy:

> Take, for instance, the loaded adjective 'natural'—generals being male, garment workers being female—it saves mental energy. After all, what is deemed natural hasn't been self-consciously created. No decisions have to be made. The result: we can imagine that there is nothing we need to investigate. We can just feel sympathy with women working in sweat shops, for instance, without bothering to figure out how they got there and what they think about being women sewing there.
>
> (Enloe 2004: 1)

Many feminists have been curious. They have refused to accept tradition or nature as explanation and sought to create their own accounts of how things came to be. They have chastised others for their lack of curiosity when it comes to women's lives and the power arrangements that shape them. They have understood that to develop alternative visions, existing accounts need to be engaged: "We must work through them, understand them, displace them in order to create space of [our] own, a space designed and inhabited by women, capable of expressing their interests and values" (Gross 1990: 60). Over time and across space, the idea of what is considered normal and which power arrangements are considered natural has undergone great transformations. Feminists have adapted their activism and research accordingly.

Starting from the perspective of women's everyday lives, feminists challenge the idea that one can presume a shared understanding of the world in theorizing about it. Feminists have, for the most part, resisted making a distinction between theory and practice and instead assumed an integral relationship between them. Its evolution through practice infuses feminism with an appreciation of the impact of perceptions and representations on lived experience. Feminists start with "the politics of the personal, in which women's subjectivities and experiences of everyday life become the site of the redefinition of patriarchal meanings and values and of resistance to them," writes Chris Weedon (1987: 5–6), to then generate "new theoretical perspectives from which the dominant can be criticized and new possibilities envisaged."

Although feminists in the 1960s and 1970s in particular embraced the idea of a global sisterhood, this notion came under scrutiny when international conferences (such as the 1975 United Nations conference in Mexico or the 1995 meeting in Beijing) revealed the different concerns of feminists from around the world. Although Western feminists tended to be preoccupied with combating sexism and gender discrimination, feminists in Africa, Asia, Latin America, and the Middle East were paying greater attention to the ways in which the lives of women are often profoundly shaped by additional, intersecting forms of oppression based on gender and sex, as well as class, nationality, race, or religion. What is more, the legacy of colonialism, which also implicates Western women (cf. Pettman 1996), influenced the concerns and suspicions of postcolonial (or Third World) feminists.[3] Feminists in Latin America, for example, have a long history of being involved in revolutionary struggles and have met with their Caribbean counterparts on a regular basis since the early 1980s. Their regional *encuentros* (encounters) have revealed the different agendas on the continent. They have also provided forums for the negotiation of resentments as well as the discovery of connections. Feminists in the former communist countries of Eastern Europe and the Soviet Union again have a unique history of feminism—having had access to education and full-time jobs as a consequence of the revolution, yet facing a double-shift at home. Already in 1909, Russian feminist Alexandra Kollontai argued "that feminism was not just a matter of political rights, or rights to education and equal pay; the real problem was the way the family was organized and imagined" (Walters 2005: 135). The themes are similar, but the time and circumstance vary, leading feminists to emphasize different aspects and to develop multiple strategies in response. Clearly, what is considered normal or natural depends on the power relations that shape women's lives in a particular time and place.

Even though it now seems as though demands for women's equality have, at least in principle, been widely accepted, these changes were hard-won—and only very recently. What is more, they are by no means complete at this point, and the continued wage gap between women and men is one example: a 2007 OECD (Organization for Economic Cooperation and Development) country report shows an average wage of 15 percent higher for men in all OECD countries, with some countries having significantly higher disparities.[4] Although one might expect conservatives to challenge demands for women's equality (especially concerning sexual liberation), a major challenge has come from within the movement; Black, Chicana, lesbian, and postcolonial feminists have pointed to the limits of liberal feminism. One critic, bell hooks, finds that the very idea of aiming for equality between women and men reveals the bias in mainstream feminism. She asks, "Since men are not equals in white supremacist, capitalist, patriarchal class structures, which men do you want to be equal to?" (hooks

1984: 18). Lower class and poor women, especially if they are not White, recognize easily that this type of feminism is flawed—equality with men in their communities still leaves them marginalized and oppressed. Lugones and Spelman drive home this point when they question feminisms' attempts to speak in one voice and to propose one solution to women's oppression. They worry that change perceived as making life better for some women might not at all be liberating for women

> whose lives would be better if they could spend more time at home, whose identity is inseparable from their religious beliefs and cultural practices [...] who have ties to men—whether erotic or not—such that to have them severed in the name of some vision of what is 'better' is, at that time and for those women, absurd.
>
> (Lugones and Spelman 1983: 579)

Instead, it is necessary to take into account the multiple visions of differently situated women. Otherwise, feminism becomes part of the problem, rather than the solution.

During the 1960s and beyond, consciousness-raising had been developed as a feminist approach to build knowledge on the basis of personal experiences. The premise of this approach was that "through discussion women would begin to see what they had once been convinced were personal problems are actually political problems" (Kaufman 2001: 28). Indeed, when women began to share their experiences in partnerships, friendships, the workforce, or the marketplace, they discovered systematic patterns of male domination in all of these areas. They argued that these new insights, based on women's experiences, would transform ways of thinking and cultural categories. At the time, however, consciousness-raising groups consisted largely of young, White, middle-class feminists who, in their effort to identify commonalities as women, glossed over the ways that class, race, and religion marked women's oppression in distinctive ways. In the process, a dominant version of feminism (epitomized, in the United States, by the National Organization for Women and the Feminist Majority) emerged. When, in the 1970s and early 1980s, feminists from a variety of backgrounds began to demand that their voices and experiences be taken seriously, the limited scope of existing feminisms became rather obvious.[5] In *This Bridge Called My Back* (1979), a number of radical women of color voice their frustration with their experience in the women's movement:

> We want to express to all women—especially the white middle-class women—the experiences which divide us as feminists; we want to examine incidents of intolerance, prejudice and denial of difference within the feminist movement. We intend to explore the causes and sources of, and solutions to these divisions. We want to create a definition that expands what 'feminist' means to us.
>
> (Moraga and Anzaldúa 1983 [1979]: xxiii)

These interventions lead to a phase of intensified identity politics within the feminist movement. Rather than assuming a shared identity—womanhood—on which to base political action, the feminist movement, prompted also by a new generation of feminists who rejected the separatism of their feminist fore-mothers, began to turn to examine issues of identity itself. Similar to earlier feminists, they were still interested in building knowledge on the basis of women's everyday experience, but this experience was no longer monolithic. To specify variance within the movement, it was not uncommon to find women embrace hyphenated identities such as "Black-lesbian-radical-feminist" or "White-working-class-eco-feminist." The specificity sought here expresses the feminist insight that a shared understanding cannot be assumed (Sylvester 1993). It also aims to show the contextual nature of experience and the necessity to engage the voices of all women. Although hyphenating identities aims to show diversity, it also suggests problematic conceptions of identity and interest, that is, it assumes that identities are the sum of a collection of markers and can be matched like clothing to be taken off when needed or wanted. Such a conception easily turns into a politics of lifestyle that is focused on personal conduct and mirrors the logic of the marketplace if it is not constantly kept in conversation with feminists involved in everyday material struggles. When the focus turns to what people wear, eat, and say individually, rather than what they are doing politically as a social movement, feminists lose sight of the commonalities that are still needed to form a political movement. The commonalities that consciousness-raising sought to discover drift into the background, and the outcome is a culture of political correctness with a focus on personal conduct. Preoccupied with micropolitics and failing to build solidarity based on shared oppression in their attempt to remedy the mistake of speaking for all women, these feminists no longer speak for anyone but themselves.

This trend and the accompanying vision of identity reveal again the privileged (and liberal) nature of much feminist discourse, where choice is both available and safely made. However, "gender, race, and class are, in a sense, hyper-identities that individuals cannot choose to reject wholesale," which means, according to Hekman (1999: 22), that "feminist analysis of identity must not lose sight of the fact that all aspects of identity are not equal: some are frivolous and inconsequential, while others are all-pervasive and life-altering." Given the power relations in any particular circumstance, for many women (some of them feminists), the options are quite limited. "Feminism in the United States has never emerged from the women who are most victimized by sexist oppression; women who are beaten down, mentally, physically, spiritually," notes hooks (1984: 1). For many women, wherever they are located, defiance is dangerous and provokes retaliation from families, communities, or the state (cf. INCITE! Women of Color Against Violence 2006). Feminists, therefore, cannot assume a homogeneous group of women, nor lose themselves in identity politics, and build coalitions only according to what Narayan (2001: 25) calls "an oppressed identity cutoff model of political membership whereby membership in feminist groups is restricted to those how suffer from [a particular kind of] patriarchal oppression." Instead, feminists need to engage in a politics that examines privilege and enter into coalitions around issues rather than identities (cf. Mohanty 1992). This also entails recognizing that some feminists are systematically and structurally more able to engage in social construction:

> women and other 'excluded others' *are* less free within these contexts and within the terms of masculinist discourse itself. But 'less free' does not mean 'unfree'; 'more difficult' does not mean 'impossible.' We need to acknowledge that 'excluded others' participate in social construction to varying degrees [...] they share a responsibility within the system.
>
> (Hirschmann 1996: 60)

Present-day consciousness-raising, therefore, needs to include an examination of privilege and an acknowledgement of complicity in upholding the structures of oppression (cf. Sylvester 2010). Consciousness-raising can no longer be thought of as something that discovers a reality and then changes it but rather as something concerned with representations and actualizations of identity—we discover "a reality that is being created and re-created when practiced and discussed" (Yuval-Davis 1994: 414). To confront power, feminists need to ask (1) "How our identities are represented in and through the culture and assigned particular categories" and (2) "Who or what politically represents us, speaks and acts on our behalf" (Brandt, quoted in ibid.: 415). Only then can feminists (and other activists) strategically inhabit whatever privileged status they may enjoy and change the status quo.

Gendering IR

The debates among feminists are ongoing, but this does not prevent them from also impacting other disciplines as feminist scholars bring their insights to bear on them. The field of IR, similar to many traditional sciences, assumes gender neutrality and does not generally use gender as a category of analysis. Feminists argue that this oversight leads to biased explanations of world politics and limits our understanding of international affairs. Gender neutrality is impossible, because "gender is a socially imposed and internalized lens through which individuals perceive and respond to the world" (Peterson 1992c: 194). As a consequence, concepts and ideas as well as practices and institutions are shaped by gender, where gender is "any social construction having to do with the male/female distinction" (Nicholson 1994: 79). They are gendered insofar as they are associated with attributes designated as feminine or masculine (whereby the latter is valued more highly) and the binary, heteronormative gender order is taken for granted.

IR has been one of the last fields to slowly open up to feminisms. Indeed, compared with other disciplines, the arrival of feminist contributions to IR has been very late. The first major engagement with the topic took place at a 1988 conference on "Women and International Relations" at the London

School of Economics and culminated in a subsequent special issue of the journal *Millennium* (cf. Grant 1991; Grant and Newland 1991). Shortly thereafter, in 1990, a conference on "Gender and International Relations" took place at Wellesley College with part of its proceedings published in the collection *Gendered States* (Peterson 1992a). Both volumes present a variety of groundbreaking arguments and provide a glimpse of the feminist challenge to IR.[6]

To follow up on these initial impulses, feminists follow a manifold research agenda to overcome gender bias and to infuse IR with feminist insights. They begin by uncovering women's presence in IR, showcasing both how they impact IR and how they are impacted by it. The transformative potential of the simple question, "Where are the women?" should not be underestimated as is illustrated in the work of Enloe (1990b) who finds women in the most unlikely places, such as in her classic *Bananas, Beaches and Bases*, but then continues to ask questions about why they are rarely seen in IR. What is it, she wonders, that makes it so hard to notice the gendered nature of militarization (e.g., Enloe 1983, 1987, 2000)? By asking this, she uncovers how much power it takes (Enloe 1996) to make it appear as though IR and security studies is not also populated by diplomats' wives who provide friendly spaces for back-room maneuvers, barmaids and prostitutes who serve military personnel (cf. Moon 1997), and women who fight for their cause, also in combat roles (cf. D'Amico 1998; Feinman 1998; Goldman 1982; Herbert 1998; Solaro 2006; Stiehm 1996). Enloe and other feminists reveal that not only are women present everywhere but also their existence is central to the workings of IR and of security politics. What is more, asking about women also reveals the roles and locations of men and, thus, tells us more about how IR is gendered.

However, asking only about women's lives—without also questioning men's location or examining the intersections of gender with ethnicity, sexuality, or religion among other markers—leads to an impoverished feminism. Part of the feminist research agenda is, therefore, to examine how gender has infused our very ways of thinking. We see the world through gendered lenses—our own experience of gender shapes the way we think about and represent world politics. In IR, which has traditionally been a male-dominated (and great-power dominated) discipline, most of the standard research questions have been those that these scholars have found interesting—questions about the foreign policy behavior of powerful states and, most importantly, about their attempts to achieve (military) security in what is conceptualized as an anarchical world. What is more, what has been considered worthwhile studying has often been male-experience, for example, that of the soldier and the diplomat, as classical realist Raymond Aron (1967) proposed. The male-bias in IR, therefore, is not only limited to the ideas and concepts used in the discipline (cf. Grant 1991) but also extends to the main institutions and practices that IR scholars traditionally study. Because many of them have been dominated by men, whether governments, militaries, or international organizations, their structures and the behaviors they exhibit and reward are often typically masculine. The conception of power in IR has been dominated by masculine-associated power-over rather than feminine-associated power-with or empowerment (Peterson and Runyan 1993). One might say, IR writes "a story of the world that presupposes exclusively male behavior and vantage point" (Peterson 1996).

To reduce such bias, feminists ask that scholars become aware of the context in which the research is conducted by asking two basic questions: what is the location of the researcher in relation to the subject of research and how are the subjects of research selected? Although these might seem like fairly standard questions of research design, for feminists, they introduce the crucial topic of (self-)reflexivity during the research process. For most feminists, this means that only when researchers and researched are placed on the same critical plane "can we hope to produce understandings and explanations which are free of distortion from the unexamined beliefs of social scientists themselves" (Harding, quoted in Tickner 2006: 27). This subjective element, also to be found in feminist attempts to build theory on the basis of personal experience, enhances the objectivity of the research project. The process of self-reflection continues throughout the research process such that methodological or other adjustments can be made where necessary, as is often the case in fieldwork in particular (cf. D'Costa 2006; Jacoby 2006; Stern 2006a). What is more, the feminist commitment to this type of knowledge building, which also actively includes input from the researched, is aimed at improving women's lives through empowerment both during the research process and by the results.

Feminist gender analysis can, thus, yield important, otherwise overlooked, insights and "gender may serve as the bearer of other meanings besides the subordination or emancipation of women" (Jabri and O'Gorman 1999: 14).[7] Some scholars have begun paying more attention to what women's everyday experiences of IR can tell us about nation, race, or religion (e.g., Yuval-Davis 1997; Yuval-Davis and Werbner 1999). Helpful here are postcolonial and poststructuralist efforts to examine inherited frameworks of knowledge that still restrain feminist contributions and remain untouched by approaches that simply "add women and stir," as most early feminisms did. Feminists engaged in these efforts "appear skeptical that we can locate anything morally and politically worth redeeming or reforming in the scientific world view, its underlying epistemology, or the practices it legitimates," (Harding 1986: 29) as they were designed to support a Eurocentric colonial enterprise and are based largely on the ideas of White males whose experience is taken as the ideal to be imposed on all others. Weedon (1987: 7) thus urges, "We should be thinking in terms of transforming both the social relations of knowledge production and the type of knowledge produced." How, where, and by whom is knowledge produced? What is considered knowledge and how is it disseminated?

In traditional science, women "are eliminated from the central focus of the theory and invisible in as much as they don't appear as subjects in their own right" (Thiele 1986: 31). They are invisible because of exclusion, pseudoinclusion, and alienation, as well as other maneuvers such as the appeal to the "natural" discussed earlier, the assumption of universal reach, the division of events in dichotomous fashion, the appropriation and reversal of woman-centered activities, and decontextualization (Thiele 1986). Decontextualization, however, is central to approaches striving for objectivity by presenting only what is seen or perceived—without comment or interpretation. However, in the process, a subtle intervention of value systems and ideology takes place because perception

> is a psychosomatic process, strongly dependent on the position of the perceiving body [...]: one's position with respect to the perceived object, the fall of the light, the distance, previous knowledge, psychological attitude towards the object; all this and more informs the picture one forms and passes on.
>
> (Bal 1997: 142)

Feminists, as women frequently subject to the gaze of others, are often more attuned to the impact of perception and representation, and this shapes their approach to the subject matter.[8] Examining war narratives, Elshtain (1987: 208), for one, finds that a much more nuanced and complicated story emerges when one tells "the story *from the ground up* as a narrative of men's experiences, rather than as an account of strategic doctrines or grand movements of armies and men seen from a birds-eye point of view." A lack of attention to lived experience and the specific context of an event reduces what IR sees: When

> one can concentrate exclusively on states and their 'behavior,' questions of human agency and identity fall to the wayside. No children are ever born, and nobody ever dies, in this constructed world. There are states, and they are what is.
>
> (Elshtain 1987: 91)

Feminist critiques point to the need to reject unitary visions in general and the belief in one truth in particular.[9] Critics of this move often argue that objective means to distinguish right from wrong are necessary because otherwise "might makes right," and women suffer as they have historically had little access to power. When considering that "objective truth" is a reflection of power relations as they are, however, this criticism loses its power. By openly declaring the shortcomings of unitary notions of truth, feminist poststructuralists are noting how truths are relative to context. Although there are feminists who think giving up truth is problematic for feminism as a political project, they are in danger of contradicting themselves if they cling too tightly to traditional science.

> We cannot simultaneously claim (1) that the mind, the self, and knowledge are socially constituted and what we can know depends upon our social practices and contexts *and* (2) that feminist theory can uncover the truth of the whole once and for all.
>
> (Flax 1987: 633)

In other words, the situated character of all knowledge claims makes it impossible to produce a universally valid truth. This also means that, instead of arguing for a unitary feminist project, "certain forms of acknowledged fragmentation might facilitate coalitional action precisely because the 'unity' of the category woman is neither presupposed nor desired" (Butler 1990: 15).

The same applies to other intersecting hierarchies, warns Trinh T. Minh-Ha (1989: 101): "the search and claim for an essential female/ethnic identity-difference today can never be anything more than a move within the male-is-norm-divide-and-conquer trap." This is especially acute in feminist IR when well-meaning, but parochial, Western feminists come to the support of their second- or third-world sisters and "discursively colonize the material and historical heterogeneities of the lives of women in the third world" (Mohanty quoted in Ferguson 1993: 85). Rushing to the rescue of Afghan women, for example, these feminists exhibit an ethnocentric universalism of the worst kind and undermine local feminist activism. Whether Afghan women are wearing a burka should not become the indicator of respect for women's rights. Although some Western feminist regard the burka as a symbol of oppression, this is a point of contention with Afghans such as General Suhaila Siddiq, Minister of Health in Hamid Karzai's government after the Taliban had been ousted. She "sighs with exasperation at Western feminists and their obsession with the burka" (Farrel 2001). Western feminists have to trust that feminists in Afghanistan (or elsewhere) can find solutions that work for them. This does not mean that all Afghan women want to wear a burka, and indeed, the *Declaration of the Essential Rights of the Afghan Women*, adopted at a conference that brought together several hundred Afghan women in 2000, explicitly provides for "the right to wear or not to wear the chadri (burka) or the scarf" (Section III, Art. 9). It also does not mean that the situation is not oppressive for Afghans whose movement is severely restricted without a burka, even if some Afghan women do not find it to be oppressive. It does mean that "American women need a much better understanding of Afghanistan women's religion which is the matrix of their lives," says Riffat Hassan, who goes on to caution, "the paradigm 'you need to be like us' will not work" (quoted in Benet 2001).

It is not just the divisions between women, though the recognition and the overcoming of internalized patterns of oppression (Lorde 1984) in this context are important too, but the impossibility of a unitary self that pushes feminist theory to develop new ways of understanding multiplicity that extend beyond tolerance of difference. If subjectivity is fragmented, even feminist attempts to situate the self and to stress the location of the research project are not quite enough. The researcher and the inquiry are so intermingled that feminists need to adopt dynamic practices of positioning themselves (cf. O'Gorman 1999). They need to become comfortable with the idea that subjectivities are mobile, relational, temporal, and ambiguous. Such "mobile subjectivities," writes Kathy Ferguson (1993:154), "are politically difficult in their refusal to stick consistently to one stable identity claim; yet they are politically advantageous because they are less pressed to police their own boundaries, more able to negotiate respectfully with contentious others." The necessity to articulate feminist political projects in these shifting contexts leads to a productive tension that propels the feminist project in IR.

Challenging security studies

Even though feminist scholars only began to make their mark on the field of IR in the late 1980s, matters of security were always at the top of their agenda. Important early statements of a feminist perspective on security can be found in the work of Jean Bethke Elshtain (1987), Cynthia Enloe (1983, 1990b, 1993), Peterson (1992a), Sylvester (1987, 1989, 1994b), and Tickner (1992, 1995), as well as the writings of some peace studies scholars such as Boulding (1978, 1981, 1992) and Reardon (1985, 1993).[10] What is more, feminists have long been writing about issues of peace, war, and violence (Gioseffi 2003) that are arguably the subject of security studies as well; only their writing has largely been in the form of historical or cross-cultural case studies, often involving ethnographic research (Albrecht-Heide and Bujewski-Crawford 1991; Ardener *et al.* 1987; Boulding 2000; Florence *et al.* 1987; Forcey 1989; Isaksson 1988; Nordstrom 1997; Pierson 1986). As Tickner (2004) points out, feminist theory is largely sociological as well as explicitly normative and emancipatory and is, as a result, unlike much security studies research. What is more, Enloe (1987) reminds us, feminist theorizing on security is not confined to academia but takes place wherever women find themselves confronting militarization, war, and violence.[11]

Telling security narratives from the ground up and thereby adopting a bottom-up approach to security, feminist scholars pay close attention to the impact of security policies, including war, on the everyday lives of people. As such, they challenge the notion that wars are fought to protect vulnerable populations (such as children and women) and show that civilians are often explicitly targeted (Hansen 2000, 2001; Kaldor 2007). Rather than offering security for all their citizens, states often threaten their own populations, whether through direct violence or through the structural violence that is reflected in its war-fighting priorities and embedded in its institutions (Enloe 1993, 2000; Peterson 1992b; Reardon 1985, 1993; Tickner 1992; Tobias 1985; Young 2003). Feminists also point out that the increasing technologization of war, from nuclear strategy to the current revolution in military affairs, depersonalizes killing, offers the illusion of clean warfare, and obscures accountability (Blanchard 2003; Cohn 1988, 1989a, 1989b; Masters 2005; Molloy 1995).

Contrary to idealized notions of women's relationship to security (and IR), where women are likely to be associated with peace or as victims in need of rescue and protection (if they appear at all), feminists are showing that women's involvement in matters of international security is much broader than assumed. Just looking at the narrow conceptions of state and military security, feminists find that governments need their citizens to accept established, gendered discourses about protector and protected and show how they leave women in a very vulnerable position (Elshtain 1982, 1987; Peterson 1992b; Stiehm 1982; Young 2003, 2007). The relationship of protector/protected often resembles a protection racket where the protected loses all autonomy and is dependent on the protector who defines the threat and response to it. The chivalrous protector faces the dangers of the outside world but is also burdened by the need for protection and is liable if it fails. In this case, the protector might direct his anger at those closest to him by limiting their movement and ideas or lashing out violently producing new insecurities in the process (Peterson 1992b; Stiehm 1982; Young 2003).

Feminists also point out how militaries need men and women to function in certain gender-specific ways that both draw on existing cultural norms and structural inequalities and also reinforce them (Chapkis 1988; Cohn and Enloe 2003; Enloe 1988, 1998; Herbert 1998; Whitworth 2005). For example, states mobilize women to support wars, whether by drawing on them as mothers (Bayard de Volo 1998; Collins 1999; Haq 2007; Nikolic-Ristanovic 1998), as keepers of nation or tradition (Yuval-Davis 1997; Yuval-Davis and Werbner 1999), or by having them work in factories while the men are away (Woollacott 1998). When women accept these calls and engage in acceptable female activities, they support war by glamorizing and idealizing men's role as just warriors and by picking up the pieces of societies destroyed by men (Boulding 1988; Elshtain 1982). For most feminists, both women and men "share complicity in warfare and militarism through their participation in the dual mythology of masculinity and femininity" (Burguieres 1990: 8).

More recently, the topic of women as aggressors (Jancar 1988; Stiehm 1988; Sylvester 1987, 1989) has again achieved much attention (Alison 2009; Hamilton 2007; Ibáez 2001; MacKenzie 2009; McEvoy 2009; McKelvey 2007; Naaman 2007; Nacos 2005; Parashar 2009; Sjoberg and Gentry 2007; White 2007). These feminists present evidence to show that many women are violent just as many men are peaceful. Thus, they shatter the easily made correlation between women and peace and point to a need to deepen the analysis to analyze the gendering of violence (i.e., its association with femininity and masculinity, respectively). They point out that women who are violent are treated as outcasts, labeled crazy, and their actions are depoliticized. They tend to be overlooked and considered unworthy of researchers' attention because they do not fit accepted standards of femininity. Meanwhile, other feminists, wedded to the ideal of the "woman of peace" (Ruddick 1998), actively discourage investigation of violent women, suggesting that "violence, armed battle or warlike abstractions are [not] authentic" (Sylvester 1987: 496, commenting on Reardon). The association of women with peace denies women power and devalues what they have to say about security issues. What is more, by simply ignoring that many women are engaged in violence, feminists might miss an important part of the puzzle.

This should not obscure the fact that much of the time women are heavily impacted by war and militarized societies, a topic that has always received a great deal of attention by feminists (cf. Wibben and Turpin 2008). One of the oldest forms of victimization that women have been subjected to is rape, as Susan Brownmiller (1975) outlines in her classic *Against Our Will*. Since ancient times, the rape of conquered women (and often the subsequent integration of them into their own community) has been a widely accepted practice.[12] More recently, rape as a strategy of war has achieved much attention due to its use as a tactic of ethnic cleansing in the former Yugoslavia (e.g., Hansen 2001; Nikolic-Ristanovic 2000; Stiglmayer 1993).[13] It is here also that feminist scholars/activists have observed a phenomenon that is a central concern of Feminist Security Studies (FSS)—the continuum of violence between peace and wartime (Cockburn 2004; Cuomo 1996; Reardon 1993) often identified in (personal) narratives.

A few writers have taken up the challenge to assess the impact of feminist insights on security studies—the first such attempt dates back to 1981 when Elise Boulding surveyed then-active women researchers in the fields of disarmament, national security, and world order.[14] Although only half of the women surveyed even bothered to answer the question of whether being a woman mattered in terms of their approach to security studies (20 of 41), five thought it might be important that they were women, and six explicitly noted that they embraced a feminist perspective in their research. A feminist perspective to them entailed "different skills and different sensitivities because of their social roles as women [which made them] more likely to 'humanize' the data they worked with, attempting more interpretation and trying for more reality testing" (Boulding 1981: 25). As a result, they saw themselves as more likely to see different forms of violence as interrelated, and they were "more aware of the 'ridiculousness of the intense preoccupation with military superiority'" (ibid.).

This basic characterization of feminist perspectives in security studies is still relevant today. What is notable about the version of feminism in Boulding's survey is that it emphasizes women's social roles (i.e., gender), inviting the theorization of masculinity in its relation to security, which has become an important concern of FSS. Exploring the linkages of patriarchal society and aggressive (or hegemonic) masculinities with violence and militarism is an important theme of FSS (Cockburn 2004; Cockburn and Zarkov 2002; Connell 2000; Enloe 1987; Reardon 1985; Whitworth 2004). As feminists move beyond "adding women and stirring" and toward analyzing the gendered character of security studies (and IR more generally), men and masculinity need to be analyzed alongside women and femininity. Cynthia Cockburn (2004: 25) cautions, "we need to observe the functioning of gender as a relation [...] of power that compounds other power dynamics." Why is it that being male augments one's chances of becoming a killer? Although there is much material to suggest that there is a direct relationship between masculinity and violence, its form is culturally specific and always changing because gender hierarchies are exploited alongside intersecting hierarchies of class, nation, race, and religion (cf. Cockburn 1999; Sharoni 1997). Nonetheless, it is possible to say that militaries everywhere rely on male privilege and female subordination to function.

Furthermore, the feminists queried by Boulding adopt a specifically antiwar feminist stance, the merits of which are hotly debated in FSS (cf. Cohn and Ruddick 2004). A survey by Mary K. Burguieres (1990) focuses specifically on the question of whether women are inherently peaceful. Stereotypically, women are seen as peaceful, whether due to biology or their social role as mothers, whereas men are considered the violent sex. Burguieres argues that feminists have adopted three positions with regard to these assumptions: (1) to accept the male and female stereotypes but try to subvert them to a feminist purpose (e.g., getting the vote and arguing for women's involvement in public affairs); (2) to reject the female stereotype and to argue that women should seek to be equal to men by becoming more like men; (3) to reject both male and female stereotype, concluding that they are not historically accurate and the imagery of the peaceful mother and the power-seeking, violent man support patriarchy and militarism (ibid.: 2–9). When feminists subscribing to these different orientations are asked to make recommendations on peace, war, and security issues, they will have different answers:

> Broadly, the goal of the first approach is peace grounded in feminine values; the second has equality with men as its main objective; and the third approach aims at peace based on a new world order centered around new gender relations and structures.
>
> (Burguieres 1990: 9)

Although a feminist anti-war stance could theoretically be located in each of these approaches, the last option would be the most wide-reaching approach.

Burguieres' overview provides a useful example of the ways that feminist conceptualizations of gender (and subjectivity more generally) shape their responses to key questions in security studies; when gender is the main category of analysis, what one sees depends on the type of gender lens one adopts. This multiplicity can be confusing, especially for nonfeminists. However, these differences among feminist security scholars, although certainly subjected to debate, are not considered a failure but provide an impetus for continual engagement in the conversation. The open-ended debate and the continual questioning that are an essential aspect of feminist epistemologies can be in tension with the political goals of security studies, which often aim to create a single coherent narrative of security and solid, unwavering answers.

Although some commitments, such as the liberal feminist goal of achieving equality by integrating women into the armed forces and the anti-war feminist analysis of militaries as a central element of patriarchal control, are directly at odds with one another, most feminists see disagreement as a necessary and productive element of scholarly debate (cf. Flax 1987; Sylvester 1987). What is more, "any feminist perspective would argue that a truly comprehensive system of security cannot be achieved until gendered relations of domination and subordination are eliminated" (Tickner 1992: 23). Furthermore,

feminist opposition to militarism emerges from many sources, many cultural venues, in any number of idioms; it does not have to—and finally,
cannot—speak in a single political idiom, and no grand settling of epistemological accounts has to be required.

(Butler 2004: 47)

Other debates in FSS that reflect some of the differences in assumptions about
gender, coupled with political orientations, are ongoing. Are women (or men)
who mother more peaceful than those who do not engage in mothering/caring
practices (Ruddick 1998; Scheper-Hughes 1998)? Should women join militaries and, if so, on whose terms (Goldman 1982; Isaksson 1988; Solaro 2006;
Stiehm 1996)? Can wars benefit women (Enloe 1987; Sylvester 1993)? Do
women make different security policies, and if so, when and how? Or are the
institutions so deeply masculinized that their structure needs changing? What
exactly are the relationships between masculinity and violence—or patriarchy
and militarism? What can security mean in the midst of intersecting oppressions
of class, gender, nation, race, and religion? Finally, how is the entire framework/
mindset of security studies gendered?

Some answers to these questions are being proposed (cf. Wibben 2002).
Where traditional security studies aims to contain threats, "feminists contest
the possibility of a perfectly controlled, coherent security policy that could han-
dle every international contingency" (Blanchard 2003: 1290). If survival of the
state is seen as the ultimate goal of security efforts, feminists question the quality
of survival from a feminist standpoint, especially because women's relations to
states have been historically complex. When security scholars debate military
capabilities—and how to maintain or achieve peace through war (relying on
"power over")—many feminists advocate for violence as a last resort, instead
looking for common ground and ways to negotiate with the enemy (emphasizing "power with"). As discourses about security make stark distinctions between
peace and wartime and emphasize certain events (e.g., the events of September
11, 2001) as ushering in a new era, feminists locate them within the struggles of
everyday life and on a continuum that spans peace and wartime (cf. Cuomo
1996).

Notwithstanding the rich tradition of feminist work on security issues, IR
exhibits a continuing lack of appreciation or even knowledge of their contributions.[15] This is due, at least in part, to the difficulty of integrating them into the
existing frameworks of security studies. Although some IR scholars are concerned with broadening or deepening the reach of security studies, feminist
contributions generally fall under the category of "opening" security studies,
which implies that the meanings and the politics of security are questioned.
Scholars looking to open security studies aim to understand how security has
worked by producing particular types of security narratives (cf. Huysmans
1998; Wæver 1995a). Feminists, among other critical scholars, are particularly
interested in how these meanings can be challenged by addressing also the political visions that underlie them and find expression in the narrative frameworks

of security studies and IR in particular and modernity more generally. The contingency of feminist approaches and insights is fundamentally at odds with attempts to create certainty through securitization that characterize traditional security narratives (cf. Chapter 4). Starting from the experience of women, as fragmented subjects constantly reconstituted in discourse, feminists combine "a critique of the present order with the desire to transform practices that inscribe women as other" (Jabri and O'Gorman 1999: 4). Theorizing on the basis of (women's) everyday lives, feminists question traditional conceptions of security and begin to develop new ways of thinking security.

2   Challenging meanings

When we began theorizing our experiences during the second women's movement [...], we knew our task would be a difficult though exciting one. But I doubt that in our wildest dreams we ever imagined we would have to reinvent both science and theorizing itself in order to make sense of women's social experience.

(Harding 1986: 251)

Feminist theorizing proposes alternative processes of narration. IR feminists do not just ask, "Where are the women?" but also question the idea that it would be possible to "add women and stir." Instead, they interrogate the way gender, among other markers such as race, nation, or religion, shapes conceptions of our world. Feminists inhabit a discipline; they work through and beyond it and incrementally but radically, (re)think it critically (cf. Colebrook and Buchanan 2000). In the process, they disturb the foundational narratives of IR as well as of modernity and modern science. Through their explorations of various disciplines, feminists have come to note that it is necessary to not only challenge the content but also the processes of knowledge production.

An attempt to open security studies by challenging the meaning(s) of security also has to engage the question of meanings more generally. Meaning is constructed during the process of drawing the unfamiliar into our context to make it intelligible. This process of understanding is intensely political because meanings are possible only within a context, a tradition, a narrative framework: "Context is what makes meaning possible; meaning makes reality" (Hirschmann 1996: 56). Drawing on philosophical hermeneutics, meaning here is understood to emerge in the interplay between prejudgment/ prejudice with which the text is approached and the conversation within it.[1] In other words, meaning is to be encountered at the interstices of the text and the reader through a process of question and answer. Thus, the narrative does not speak for itself but need to be articulated through our reading/ engagement with it. While meanings are encountered, any meaning is always already contingent and the context within which the encounter takes place, in turn, is constituted by different meanings.

> The key is to be aware to the context that one supports and to make a choice between contexts insofar as that is humanly as well as historically possible. This awareness and choice is crucial for women; for 'if the social translation of the human value of being a woman is not done by women, it will be done by men according to their criteria'.
>
> (Hirschmann 1996: 69, quoting Milan)[2]

This, however, is not the way in which modern science approaches knowledge construction. Instead, having emerged in its contemporary form largely as a result of the reorganization of life during and since the Enlightenment era, modernity relies on a particular version of formal science circumscribing what counts as real (ontology) and knowledge (epistemology) as well as how one could access it (methodology). Most importantly, since modern science developed as "a corrective to the revelatory notion that the nature of human existence was primarily spiritual and was governed by a relationship to God rather than by the laws of nature," writes Donald Polkinghorne (1988: 125), it "was based on the notion that reality, including human beings, was ultimately located on a plane consisting of objects whose actions and reactions were governed by stable laws." This definition is overly reductive and fails to account for the realm of meaning that is fundamental to human existence. Thus, where the dominant narrative of modern science maintains the applicability of this approach to all scientific inquiry, a second approach points to the specificity of the *Geisteswissenschaften* (human sciences, also including the social sciences). It proposes that the subject matter (humans and their actions) calls for a different framework and an approach focused on understanding (*verstehen*) should be considered as a corrective supplement.

Revisiting modern science

The Enlightenment era was a time of revolution during which a major reorganization of social/symbolic/political orders occurred in Europe. These changes are mirrored in the emergence of modern science because the manifold relations of power "which permeate, characterize and constitute a social body [...] cannot themselves be established, consolidated nor implemented without the production, accumulation, circulation of discourse" (Foucault 1980: 93). The move from a cosmology with God at its center to one that centers on an atomistic, equal, and free (hu)man subject required the construction of an elaborate narrative—that of modern science.

The myth of modern science maintains that from Copernicus to Galileo and then Newton, the scientific revolution progressed until "at last the crumbling Aristotelian universe was replaced by a comprehensive and coherent world-view, and a new chapter in man's developing conception of nature was begun" (Kuhn, quoted in Harding 1986: 205).[3] Stress is placed on separating political interests and values from the natural order. As the twentieth century positivists of the Vienna Circle propose, "truly scientific justification [establishes] claims about the regularities of nature and their underlying causal determinants to which all relevantly situated observers, regardless of their personal social or political commitments, can agree" (Harding 1986: 205–6). "Naturally" these "relevantly situated observers" did not include everyone, especially not women, leading feminists to wonder whether it is possible to reform such a fundamentally biased endeavor.

However, the main elements of modern science (such as atomism, value-neutrality, and experimental observation) did not develop in a vacuum and neither did the belief in the progressive emancipatory nature of science. Indeed, according to Sandra Harding (1986: 221–22), this belief "emerges only in the projects and meanings of a *prepositive* science, where experimental observation is not yet separable from the historically specific political goals it seemed to advance." Also crucial in the move away from the medieval cosmology centered on a higher, heavenly authority was the renewed legitimacy of subjectivity—an emerging faith in the individual. This version of subjectivity needs the simultaneous demand for political emancipation to which it was coupled during its emergence. Like many features of modern science, it developed as a response to a particular quest at a particular location and, once institutionalized, lost its emancipatory potential.

The reorganization of life during the Enlightenment era illustrates this lost potential. First, the feudal division of labor broke down. It had been characterized by "a hierarchy of personalized, cross cutting relationships among vassals and lords" (Deibert 1997: 80) where some worked on the land and others were engaged in "educated pursuits." The development of capitalism required the skills of artisans, carpenters, foundrymen, mariners, miners, and shipbuilders. They combined the manipulation of instruments and raw materials with educated intelligence, thus, creating the possibility of experimental observation. The emergence of this new class and the growth of an urban bourgeoisie paved the way for "a displacement of political legal power upwards to the 'national' level" (Axtmann, quoted in Deibert 1997: 85). Second, a new political self-consciousness emerged, exemplified in the New Science Movement (NSM) of seventeenth-century England, whose goals bear striking resemblance to that of many feminist projects. Of particular interest is the perception, fundamental also to feminist projects, that "science's progressiveness was perceived to lie not in method alone but in its mutually supportive relationship to progressive tendencies in the larger society" (Harding 1986: 219). Harding identifies six aspects that the NSM and feminist modes of inquiry have in common (Table 2.1).

Table 2.1 Goal comparison, NSM and feminisms

New Science Movement	Feminist projects
• An antiauthoritarian attitude and a reliance on personal experience as the source of knowledge	• Challenge authoritarian attitudes and emphasizing personal experience and self-confidence
• The belief that progress is both desirable and possible	• The belief that it is possible to redefine political and intellectual progress as changeable
• The placement of perception of the senses and "real" things above rhetoric and wit, in a democratic, participatory mode	• Emphasize the analysis of everyday life and the role of human activity as a source of cognition
• An educational reform, which would purify knowledge from prejudice and corruption	• An educational reform that reeducates men to a less biased understanding and infuses feminist perspectives into the mainstream of science
• The furthering of the public good via a humanitarian orientation	• To improve the daily social relations for all by improving sectors of public life where women are particularly affected
• Unity of theological and philosophical truth	• Unity of knowledge, combining moral and political with empirical understanding

Source: Summarized from Harding 1986: 219–21 and 40–1.

During the seventeenth century, a further reorganization of social labor in Europe consolidated modern science. The institutionalization of science, exemplified in the establishment of the Royal Society in London in 1662 and *Académie des Sciences* in Paris in 1666, leads to a new visibility and prestige for science. It also guaranteed the protection of standards and ensured the relative continuity of scientific work. At the same time, however, it instituted a division of labor that divorced science from politics and led to the abandonment of the social reform goals at the basis of much of science at the time: "The destiny of Modern Man was bifurcated: scientists as scientists were not to meddle in politics; political, economic and social administrators were not to shape the cognitive direction of scientific inquiry" (Harding 1986: 223).

This ideal could not and cannot be upheld in practice. The production of knowledge and its modalities (science and scientists) is intrinsic to the social/symbolic/political order and cannot be free from its dimensions. As Foucault (1980: 52) famously said, "the exercise of power perpetually creates knowledge and, conversely knowledge constantly induces effects of power [...] it is not possible for power to be exercised without knowledge, it is impossible for knowledge not to engender power." In light thereof, the division of knowledge from politics, and vice versa, has consequences of a different kind: It *represents* science *as though* it was clearly divided from politics, and thus provides legitimization that seems to rest on a foundation other than authority. This is exemplified in the insistence on value-neutrality. Limiting science to the positive phenomenal world was supposed to ensure that there would be no privileged authorities on matters of morals or knowledge (as the Church had been). Only the so-called primary properties of nature, those that would be measured in the same way by different observers, were considered real. Any secondary qualities (e.g., color, feeling, odor, taste, and touch producing different measurements from one observer to the other) were relegated as subjective and therefore not truly real. The introduction of this hierarchy had dire consequences throughout the next centuries. A large part of life was "left out," was defined as "unreal," when "sensory impressions became less than real, as did politics, morals and the entire world that emotion and feeling pick out" (Harding 1986: 228). Incidentally, many of these "worlds" that became "unreal" were those within which women (or, for that matter, any actual person) are located.[4]

Martin Hollis and Steve Smith provide evidence for the centrality of value-neutrality to IR when discussing Hans Morgenthau's six principles of Realism (cf. Tickner 1988). For Morgenthau, "politics was governed by 'objective laws that have their roots in human nature'" (quoted in Hollis and Smith 1991: 24). He replicates the ideal of a division of labor between science and politics when declaring that Realism believes

> in the possibility of distinguishing in politics between truth and opinion— between what is true objectively and rationally, supported by evidence and illuminated by reason, and what is only a subjective judgment, divorced from the facts as they are and informed by prejudice and wishful thinking.
> (quoted in Hollis and Smith 1991: 24)

In security studies, neorealists also draw on this particular conception of science in an attempt "to anchor the legitimacy of neorealist security studies to a claim of authority within the field" (Krause and Williams 1997b: 38). Furthermore, possibly a remnant of its initial emancipatory impulse, "a series of foundational claims are now presented unproblematically as facts" (Krause and Williams 1997b: 38). Consequently, the centrality of the state as the subject of security is seen as legitimate because we can (now) observe that states *are* the main actors on the international stage and *have* the monopoly of legitimate violence, "forgetting" that this particular social/symbolic/political order emerged alongside the very perception of science that is now seen to authorize it. Placing features of modern science (or of security studies) into the contexts of their emergence, it becomes possible to understand how they are historical responses rather than givens.

In IR, the question of modern science was the topic of the post/positivism debate in the late twentieth century. At this point, the (old) disagreement about the nature of scientific inquiry was brought to the discipline of IR: whether the human sciences (and thus the social sciences), due to their different subject matter, require alternative methods of inquiry. In 1862, Hermann Helmholtz, speaking about the relationship between the two sciences, claimed that there were different ways of arriving at insight in both. He proposed that one draws on the scientific method aimed at observing events (as positivists would) whereas the other follows a hermeneutic method concerned with understanding human action. This perception of a difference in method was picked up by Max Weber who considered "the fundamental task of social science [to lie] in analyzing society as a structure of meaning-endowing actions centered on the human subject" (Swingewood 1984: 142). However, Weber did not dismiss causal analysis entirely and instead suggested one work with probabilities. His development of the ideal type was an attempt to combine it with the hermeneutic concept of *verstehen*, as for him "understanding becomes scientific through its integration into objective, causal explanation" (Swingewood 1984: 145).

In *Explaining and Understanding International Relations*, Hollis and Smith introduce this idea of two distinct approaches to IR. They argue that there are always two fundamentally different stories to tell: one that explains and the other that understands. In their overview of how these two intellectual traditions impact IR, Hollis and Smith maintain that explanation proceeds from the outside and assumes that regularities can be observed, whereas understanding takes place from inside. They argue that in IR, at least after the first great debate with Idealism, "there is a large-scale agreement that the aim is explanation by applying the methods of the natural science" (Hollis and Smith 1991: 43). By publishing their ideas early in the post/positivism debate, they introduce the Weberian version of hermeneutics as a corrective. This version of hermeneutics, which draws Wilhelm Dilthey and Friedrich E.D. Schleiermacher, maintains "that action must always be understood from within" (1991: 72). The classic and romanticist hermeneutics were especially concerned with hermeneutics as a method that could make sure, once and for all, that truth could be discovered by certain ways of approaching the text.[5] It was thought that hermeneutics could help recover what an author had originally felt or thought and with sufficient information, the interpreter could understand the author better than she did herself.[6] Hollis and Smith replicate this move for IR and maintain that "to understand is to reproduce the order in the minds of actors; to explain is to find causes in the scientific manner" (1991: 87). They thus make a clear distinction between an interpretative tradition and a scientific method and claim that although one can either follow the understanding or the explanation path—one will always have to be prioritized over the other.

Precisely, this issue was also the subject of the *Methodenstreit* of Weber and his contemporaries—which failed to fundamentally challenge modern science, since it did not address some basic characteristics of Enlightenment epistemology. A main error of the humanist critique of positivism lies in trying to redefine rather than dissolve Enlightenment dualisms. "Weber's position is an excellent example of this error," writes Susan Hekman, "without challenging the subjective/objective dichotomy of the positivists he argued that the social sciences are subjective but that this subjectivity is their strength, not their weakness" (1990: 5). What is more, the assumption that the natural and human sciences are fundamentally different remains intact. Unquestioningly adopting the Weberian conception of social science, Hollis and Smith's version of the understanding approach also fails to provide a radical alternative for IR. Similarly, many feminist attempts to carve out a space for women fail because they do not wrestle

with the basics of knowledge construction, thus relegating them and their concerns to some "other" realm while trying to maintain that bias is correctable by
using adequate methods.[7]

Any attempt to develop a Feminist Security Studies worthy of the name (i.e.,
not just an adding and stirring of some gender-related materials) consequently
needs to challenge the foundational narratives of the discipline as well as modernity itself. Hekman proposes that poststructuralist approaches, which she con-
ceives as fundamentally hermeneutic, are posing this challenge and thus, also
offering the possibility of a feminist critique. Although poststructuralism has
taken many forms, a significant impact has been made through "the rejection
of the dualisms of Enlightenment thought and the argument that the model
of knowledge embodied in the scientific method of the natural sciences is not
the only paradigm of knowledge" (Hekman 1999: 4). Further, feminists criticize
Enlightenment thought because of its gendered bias as a masculine mode of
thought.[8] Central to a feminist poststructuralist approach is an engagement
with Enlightenment epistemology and a subsequent displacement thereof
because it fails to adequately describe the phenomenon of understanding. Feminist poststructuralists deconstruct modern science and reject its object/subject
opposition as well as the assertion that there is only one valid type of knowledge
construction. Instead of attempting to articulate a singular feminist and/or poststructuralist epistemology, they propose explanations of the processes by which
human beings gain understanding of their world.

Producing meanings

On this journey through modern science, it is important to emphasize that the
different approaches always emerge in particular locations (spatially and tempo-
rally) and in response to particular challenges. The first version of modern science can be represented as a reaction to the existing social/symbolic/political
order of the time (i.e., feudalism and the authority of the church) and the violence it produced (i.e., the Thirty Years' War). At the same time, however, this
approach was also constitutive of a social/symbolic/political order that attempts
to exclude competing (subjective) claims to meaning, relegating them to
another realm. The second version of knowledge production then develops
as a reaction to this overly reductive vision of human existence but maintains
a constitutive split between ideal and material that provokes a third version.
The third tale, discussed in this section, can be seen as a reaction to the violence
of the social/symbolic/political order known as modernity and exemplified in
imperialism, colonialism, the Holocaust, and patriarchy (in its particular modern
form).[9] The hope is that this latter tale might be constitutive of less violent
orders, though I remain skeptical in this regard because any kind of order is pre-
mised on inclusions/exclusions and thus remains violent. "Any discourse constitutes a delusion inasmuch as it administers dimensions of silence as soon as
it begins; it establishes practices which force out other practices" (Shapiro
1988: 19). Fortunately, any social/symbolic/political order not only oppresses

and subjectifies but also offers points of resistance since "the exercise of power itself creates" (Foucault 1980: 51). Finally, by providing standards to which one can appeal for inclusion, an order always sows the seeds of its own deconstruction (cf. Rancière 1999).

While modern science certainly has provided useful contributions, the manner in which science (or, more specifically, the triad of ontology, epistemology, and methodology) is conceptualized has particular effects. Were one to posit material reality as the only valid reality, for example, this would allow for only one type of individual—"the indivisible sample of the human species found in all societies and cultures" (Dumont, quoted in Deibert 1997: 95). The properties located in the realm of meaning, that is "the independent, autonomous and thus (essentially) nonsocial moral being as found in our modern ideology of man and society" (Dumont, quoted in Deibert 1997: 95), become projected onto this individual and consequently are seen as natural. Positing something as natural dismisses it from requiring explanation and is one of the ways in which a theoretical realm that does not include women is created in modern science. Further, abstract theorizing in order to make general statements about what are considered to be the "real" properties of humans, states, security, and the like leads to losing sight of gender and to neglecting the work it does. Conceptions of femininity and masculinity underlying practices as varied as militarization, environmental policies, tourism, and textile production have a fundamental impact on international politics and often are manipulated specifically to achieve desired results (cf. Enloe 1983, 1990b, 1993, 2000; Pettman 1996; Sylvester 1994b, 2002). Paying attention to gender, and to everyday lives, can be a useful reminder that, "science cannot be made value-neutral in the sense of blocking political values and interests from the conceptual schemes and methodologies that direct scientific inquiry" (Harding 1986: 238). Thus, although there may be several possible narratives, which one is told and which ones are deemed acceptable scientific knowledge, is political.

The third tale exhibits continuities with the humanist critique of the positivist approach insofar as is also sees meaning as fundamental to human existence. It does not, however, conceive of this meaning in opposition to something else, something supposedly more real. Hans-Georg Gadamer, on whom this version of the tale draws heavily, redefines hermeneutics as a general concern of philosophy and maintains that the hermeneutic problem—that of the interpretation of meaning—is universal. He criticizes the earlier hermeneutics of Schleiermacher and Dilthey for "isolating the kind of methodical understanding that goes on in the *Geisteswissenschaften* from the broader processes of understanding that occur everywhere in human life" (Linge 1976: xi). For Gadamer, the task of philosophical hermeneutics is ontological rather than methodological. It is an attempt "to throw light on the fundamental conditions that underlie the phenomenon of understanding in all its modes, scientific and nonscientific alike" (Linge 1976: xi). What is more, understanding is considered an event over which the interpreting subject has no ultimate control—meaning, is to be encountered in the interplay between prejudgments/prejudices with which the interpreter approaches the text and the conversation within it. Following Martin Heidegger in maintaining the finitude of Being (*Dasein*), Gadamer sees a final form of truth as unattainable. Any insight gained will always be part of our tradition and thus bound by our *Dasein*.[10] "There is no such thing, in fact, as a point outside history from which the identity of a problem can be conceived within the various vicissitudes of the various attempts to solve it" (Gadamer, quoted in Fairlamb 1994: 113). This is echoed also in feminist writing such as Jane Flax's assertion that a feminist standpoint will necessary be partial as "there is no force of reality 'outside' our social relations that will rescue us from partiality and difference" (1987: 391).

Philosophical hermeneutics maintains that meaning is to be encountered in a process of question and answer. The questions a reader may ask of a text or an interpreter may ask of the world are always embedded in the tradition out of which they arise. More specifically, it is the tradition within which our pre-judgments/prejudices evolve that makes any question and thus any answer (meaning) possible: "Only the support of familiar and common understanding makes possible the venture into the alien, the lifting up of something out of the alien, and thus the broadening and enrichment of our own experience of the world" (Gadamer 1976: 15). When engaging in the process of understanding meaning, we adapt it, through a dialogical process, so as to find answers to our concerns. Gadamer here draws on Heidegger who maintained that understanding is always connected to a quest for understanding of the self or, phrased differently, an encounter with our self. The text will only "speak to us" according to the questions with which we approach it, which, in turn, are shaped (and restricted) by the prejudgments/prejudices derived from a certain tradition. Therefore "to understand a text of the past means to translate into our situation" (Grondin 1991: 150).[11] Understanding is not the reconstruction of meaning, as earlier hermeneutics claimed, but its mediation.

Hence, understanding is "participation in the meaning, the tradition, and eventually the conversation" (Grondin 1991: 153).[12] This conversation is never-ending as statements constantly provoke new questions—they are always part of a conglomerate of narratives that intersect and contradict each other. Meaning is ever unstable and always multiple as we participate in an ongoing conversation that has begun long before our engagement in it and will continue afterwards. Moreover, at any one time, there are countless conversations taking place, emerging out of particular traditions while, at the same time, constituting them. This is Gadamer's reformulation of Heidegger's hermeneutic circle, where tradition makes understanding (and therefore meaning) possible while at the same time being the product of these acts of understanding. This ontological structure of the hermeneutic circle explains why Gadamer endorses its universality: "all understanding is preconditioned by a motivation or a prejudice" (Grondin 1991: 144).[13] Prejudgments/prejudices are the decisive link: they are at once a precondition for meaning and a provision for continuity of the tradition.

This historicity is not perceived as a limitation of understanding but as the principle thereof. When historicity is "an *ontological* rather than a merely accidental and subjective condition, then the knower's own present situation is already constitutively involved in any process of understanding" (Linge 1976: xiv).[14] This is strikingly different from the Enlightenment-informed historicism of the nineteenth century (which Gadamer considers a delusion). The attempt to arrive at objectivity via secure methods that suspend the subjectivity of situated understanding can ultimately only lead to less rather than more objectivity if the role of prejudgments/prejudices for the process of understanding is denied and remains unexamined. This is also one of the criticisms many feminists levy in regard to modern scientific practices. Denying the role of prejudgment/prejudice facilitates decontextualization and abstraction. Furthermore, if those theorizing are men, "what is male becomes the basis of the Abstract, the Essential and the Universal, while what is female becomes accidental, different, other" (Thiele 1986: 35).

An awareness of the interpreter's involvement in all understanding—a consciousness of effective history—allows us to grasp that "understanding is never a subjective behavior towards a given 'object' but part of its effective history and this means: part of the being of what is understood" (Gadamer 1965: xvii).[15] Acquiring this consciousness of effective history makes us aware of our involvement in the production of meaning; we formulate questions and look for answers from a particular standpoint. The consciousness of effective history, rather than appealing to some supposedly preexisting reality or fixed foundations, provides hermeneutic anchors as temporary resting points (cf. Ferguson 1993). This produces a multilayered awareness captured in Ferguson's notion of mobile subjectivities that are

> temporal, moving across and along axes of power (which are themselves in motion) without fully residing in them. They are relational, produced through shifting yet enduring encounters and connections, never fully captured by them. They are ambiguous: messy and multiple, unstable but preserving.
>
> (1993: 154)

It is also reflected in the hermeneutic concept of a horizon of understanding. Such a horizon is not determined but "is something into which we wander and which moves with us" (Bleicher 1980: 112, quoting Gadamer). The encounter of meaning involves a fusion of horizons, widening each horizon to the extent that they can be linked, and a moment of meaning takes place. This continual fusion of horizons is referred to as hermeneutic experience: "There is always a world already interpreted, already organized in its basic relations, into which experience steps as something new, upsetting what has led our expectations and undergoing reorganization itself in the upheaval" (Gadamer 1976: 15). All experience, Gadamer maintains, is hermeneutic. The acknowledgement of this ongoing process of interpretation is key, not to perfect knowledge, but to the acceptance of knowledge as always relative to a tradition.

The feminist critique of science, in combination with other challenges to modernity, takes these insights seriously. To reveal the bias of science and its hidden agendas, feminists read science as a text. "The history of various interpretative codes is examined [...] to remind us of our history of constructing unities and pretending they are discoveries" (Ferguson 1993: 27). Whenever an interpretation is produced, the (feminist) genealogist is ready to question it as a temporary resting point, reworking it as a springboard to another destination. In this case, the fluidity, instability, and ever-changing meanings remain present and any totalizing force can be opposed at its roots. "The genealogist, in short, is a major inconvenience to deal with during and after the revolution, particularly for those who are convinced that there is no echo of their enemies in themselves" (Ferguson 1993: 27).[16] What is more, when the subject on whose behalf the revolution is fought is involved in writing its story, it makes a difference to the path that a revolution takes. Since most feminists are also women, they are always directly concerned by the trajectory of the women's movement, albeit each to a different extent (cf. Harding 1986: 242). This, arguably, gives feminists a greater stake in their endeavor—and propels the feminist movement to continually challenge its own bias.

Entering security studies

The field of "Security Studies" only gained greater acceptance in the late 1980s, specifically since the end of the Cold War. Within the US academy, "strategic studies" has been a more common designation because of the almost exclusive focus on "the military means that actors in the international system employ to gain their political objectives or ends" (Snyder 1999: 3–4).[17] The British counterpart, while agreeing on states as the principle actors and strategic studies as being "the study of the threat, use, and control of military force" (Walt 1991: 212), historically included broader questions of security.[18] The German designation *Sicherheitspolitik* (security politics), in turn, immediately emphasizes the political nature of elaborations of security. Consequently, there is not a single field of security studies that can be straightforwardly named and scrutinized. Security is articulated in multiple locations simultaneously and derives its meaning in context only. Nonetheless, given the dominance of the Anglo-American context in IR, some shared assumptions can be delineated and meanings of security can be traced as they shift spatio-temporally.

I am particularly interested in the meaning of security neither to find "the real meaning" of security nor to necessarily define a feminist notion of security but to explore processes of narrating security and their effects. This requires an opening in the security agenda, allowing for questions about the production and impact of security meanings, as has been provided by approaches conceptualizing security as practice. As Michael Williams suggests, conceptualizing security as practice opens up difficult questions "of the relationship of theory to practice, and of the constitutive place of particular forms of knowledge and conceptions of identity in the political constitution of modern societies"

(1998b: 439). What is more, scholars of security are implicated in the politics of security as their theoretical musings and policy recommendations are themselves security practices (cf. Eriksson 1999a, 1999b; Goldmann 1999; McCormack 2009; Wæver 1999; Williams 1999).[19] How the formation of security meanings is approached, sets the parameters for the particulars of security studies and security policy. This leads Jef Huysmans to claim that "rather than being a tool of clarification serving and agenda, the exploration of the meaning of security *is* the security studies agenda itself" (1998: 233).

Although in security studies, especially with the advent of critical security studies, several concepts of security circulate; they share a basic logic. This modern logic tolerates a multitude of meanings but is based on the assumption that meanings are clearly identifiable and a hierarchy of meanings can be established.[20] In security debates, each possible meaning is treated as coherent and stable in itself—instability, fluidity, or uncertainty of meanings is intolerable. "Much of the talk about 'new concepts' is not really about conceptual issues," writes Wæver. It concerns "empirical or political questions where people actually agree about the concept of security, but differ in their interpretation of what actual threats qualify as security issues" (1999: 339). Similarly, by simply disregarding conceptual issues, traditional security scholars have managed to avoid a broadening. As Baldwin (1995: 134) suggests, "any serious attempt to explicate the concept of security is likely to lead to a broader view—which may explain why traditional security specialists have usually avoided such exercises." This supposes an exorcism by omission—by not talking about the question it disappears?

In those cases where conceptual issues are addressed, three different explorations of security meanings are common: definition, conceptual analysis, and a "thick signifier" approach (Huysmans 1998). The definitional approach searches for unity via a delineation of content. It aims to condense meaning into a statement, usually about the location within a particular research agenda and its purpose. While in principle there is no limit to definitions, in practice they are limited by the context within which they are employed. In IR, they are limited by the security studies community that needs to recognize an utterance as pertaining to a security narrative.[21] In *People, States and Fear*, Barry Buzan styles security as an essentially contested concept, that is "an area of concern rather than a precise condition" which, he goes on, requires "theoretical analysis in order to identify the boundaries of their application, the contradictions which occur within them and the significance for them of new developments" (1991: 8). This is a typical form of conceptual analysis, exploring more extensively what characterizes a security policy or debate. It identifies a common denominator in "the shape of an analytical framework which makes explicit how security analysis does (and should?) be organized" (Huysmans 1998: 231). It also starts from the assumption that meanings for security can be developed and aims to make those meanings explicit. Placing a definitional alongside a conceptual approach, it is striking to see how they complement each other. They illustrate that it is by reference to both the *content* (definition) and the *framing* (conceptual framework) that security narratives are recognized as such. How the relationship between these two works in security studies is precisely what this book seeks to explore and explode.

Given the intervening problem of language, however, it is impossible to posit a "self-evident and unambiguous link between signifier and signified [...] neither subject, object nor concept is comprised of essence" (Dillon 1990: 110). Instead, security is a self-referential practice which, rather than referring to a "reality," establishes a security situation. Huysmans' thick signifier approach studies the particular arrangement of questions and material in security narratives, recognizing "that 'security' is not a universal need nor a universal concept, but a function of discourse, a function within a specific and modern discursive economy of the political" (Dillon 1990: 110). A security narrative orders social relations, it positions people, and it has effects on life and death. The third approach thus asks questions about the modern framework within which security is embedded and drafts a logic of security, "an ensemble of rules that is immanent to a security practice and that defines that practice in its particularity" (Huysmans 1998: 232; cf. Huysmans 2006).

Michael Dillon, in *Politics of Security*, argues that "contemporary continental thought has called the way we traditionally think in the 'West' so profoundly into question that we cannot avoid rethinking the political in response to its questioning of thought itself" (1996: 4). Telling one or another type of security narrative is profoundly political since it shapes the world that we take for granted. What is more, the way we think security is fundamentally shaped by the way we think more generally. Security studies, and IR in general, are "one instance of the pervasive cultural practices that serve to discipline ambiguity. Experience has to be arrested, fixed, or disciplined for social life to be possible" (Campbell 1998b: 17). Dominant approaches to security in IR rely on a fairly closed narrative framework, based on the belief that by identifying and coordinating particular elements, a comprehensive agenda can be developed to deal with security challenges. A thick signifier (or poststructuralist) approach, on the other hand, finds that it is only in the practice of security that an issue becomes a security issue. As such, "'security' is a process of subjectification and not the end of an unproblematical subject" (Dillon 1990: 114).[22] Security practices, therefore, are creative. In his analysis of US foreign policy, David Campbell applies these insights to argue, "just as Foreign Policy works to constitute the identity in whose name it operates, security functions to instantiate the subjectivity it purports to serve" (1998: 199). Security narratives are performative, constituting a particular order and its corresponding subjects (cf. Chapter 5). Narratives—and subjects—that do not fit the confines of this order are relegated to the margins by authorized narratives that conform to and confirm the dominant social, symbolic, political, and economic order.

To imagine alternative security narratives, it is necessary to produce space where different narratives can exist alongside each other; where their intersections and contradictions can be seen as enriching, rather than as a problem to be transcended. The task is

[to] understand the discursive power of the concept, to remember its forgotten meanings, to assess its economy of use in the present, to reinterpret—and possibly construct through the reinterpretation—a late modern security comfortable with a plurality of centers, multiple meanings, and fluid identities.

(Der Derian 1995: 26)

One way of opening space for alternative conceptualizations is by showing that there already are multiple meanings. This can be done by referring to the etymology of security as well as by noting connotations of the noun in various contexts. The Latin noun *securitas*, from which the modern "security" derives, "referred, in its primary classical use, to a condition of individuals, of a particular inner sort. It denoted composure, tranquility of spirit, freedom from care" (Rothschild 1995: 61). *Securitas* derives from *sine cura*, "to be without care, free from cares and untroubled" (Neocleous 2000: 9). It thus entails both a condition without danger, that is a condition of safety, and being "without care" or negligent. In the latter instance, security can become a condition of false confidence or misplaced certainty. Indeed, various scholars have pointed out that security has not always been, and probably should not be, unquestioningly considered a good thing (Constantinou 2000; Der Derian 1995; Dillon 1996; Neocleous 2000; Rothschild 1995; Wæver 1995b). What is of interest, particularly in regard to feminist and other alternative approaches to security studies, is that "one of the principal synonyms for 'securitas' in the *Lexicon Taciteum*, is '*Sicherheitsgefühl*': the feeling of being secure" (Rothschild 1995: 61; cf. Wibben 2008).

Drawing on Greek readings of security, Costas Constantinou develops several versions of security. To begin, the ancient Greek word for security—*asphaleia*—entails "(a) rightness, not to err (*sphallo*) and (b) to remain standing and firm, not to fall (*sphallo*)" (2000: 291). Here, security implies certitude and firmness, whereas in a version drawing on Archilochus, security becomes a struggle to live with one's enemy. Rather than trying to eliminate the danger, one faces danger and tries "to reach a mental state where one is secure in danger, where one can dwell (*katatheis*) next to one's enemy, without surrendering, or dominating, or making friend of foe" (Constantinou 2000: 290). In this version of security, one learns to live with one's own fears for "security is not a rescue from danger but freedom from the care of danger; not a given or permanent condition, but a continuous, spiritual, seafaring agon" (Constantinou 2000: 292). For another spiritual form of security, Constantinou draws on the Apostle Paul to declare that real security is not of this world but is only achievable through posthumous salvation. Finally, in Sufism, security requires sacrificing human certitude:

God's creations are reflected in [the believer], but never dwell in his soul permanently. The believer incorporates the creator without identifying with the created. He bears inside him the boundless but remains empty of idols. Being free from the spell of forms, the Sufi is also free from the care of protecting, maintaining or restoring them.

(Constantinou 2000: 301)

This is precisely what the modern, liberal political agent is not. Here, "in the face of danger, a debt, or an obligation of some kind, one seeks a security in the form of a pledge, a bond, a surety" (Der Derian 1995: 28). Security then becomes some*thing* that individuals can and do get for themselves, whether in a collective or contractual enterprise (cf. Rothschild 1995). Yet, the notion of a contract implies an equality of the contracting parties, rarely a given. Feminist political theorist Nancy Hirschmann criticizes this liberal ideal that "requires that we be 'the same' [when] structural elements guarantee our difference" (1996: 64).[23] What is more, here security becomes some*thing* that one "can have more or less and which [one] can aspire to have in a greater or lesser degree" (Wolfers 1962: 150). This also implies that security is seen as some*thing* "in whose interest individuals give up other goods" (Rothschild 1995: 61)—the trade-off between military and social security, for example, is a scenario all too familiar to most feminists.[24]

The dominant, liberal version of security is captured in the oft-used phrase "freedom from want and freedom from fear." This freedom from attack on one's person or property can be traced back to the eighteenth century (Rothschild 1995; cf. Williams 2005). At this time, the security of individuals was subsumed in the security of the nation and eventually the state. It was linked to liberty and property in the triad of "liberty, security, and property," introduced in the writings of Adam Smith and popularized in various documents of the era including the declaration of the *Rights of Man* (Neocleous 2000: 9). It is the values, or properties, associated with security that are now worth securing (Edkins 2002a). Doubly so in the case of "national," "individual," or lately "human" security, where these labels themselves carry a history with them. It is thus, that "security for individuals cannot be defined so easily. The factors involved—life, health, status, wealth, freedom—are far more complicated, and many of them cannot be replaced if lost" (Buzan 1991: 36). What is more, the perception that the valuable properties can be identified (especially as belonging to someone) is questioned by poststructuralists who maintain that it is through processes of subjectification that the subject and its properties are constituted.

Pointing to tales of security that are "less 'evident,' not merely commuted into accounts of safety and certitude, or in perfect tune with the presence of protection and of knowledge [...] shatters, albeit momentarily, the contemporaneous narrative of security" (Constantinou 2000: 288). Take the events of September 11, 2001 that have largely been communicated as a major breach in the US security narrative. Mattingly *et al.* (2002) provide an important corrective in their study of how African American women experienced and narrated 9/11. While mainstream America emphasized the return to normalcy as "an act of courage, a defiant refusal to live as though time had changed, that is, a refusal to show fear," the women interviewed in their study, "repeatedly emphasize that they knew how to live with fear in a racially charged environment" (Mattingly *et al.* 2002: 747). What is more, they stress that these events were, in comparison to the ongoing violence and struggle of their everyday lives marked by intersecting oppressions of race and class, relatively minor. It is "more of the same," they say, "all those same issues have always been in existence" (Mattingly *et al.* 2002: 746). Telling these and other stories about 9/11 provides "a way to live with and recognize the very necessity of difference" (Der Derian 1992: 198). Narrating security differently makes it possible to question the privileging of certain types of security and to imagine ways to move beyond security (cf. Burke 2007).

3   Toward a narrative approach[1]

It does not seem at all exaggerated to view humans as narrative animals, as *homo fabulans*—the tellers and interpreters of narrative.

(Currie 1998: 2)

As *homo significans* (meaning makers), the world is accessible to us only through interpretations. However, we are also *homo fabulans* because we interpret and tell stories about our experiences, about who we are or want to be, and what we believe. Narratives order our world, they are "the primary way by which human experience is made meaningful" (Polkinghorne 1988: 1). Although our lives begin with us being subject to the stories of our parents and others around us, we soon begin to tell stories of our own about who we might become and where we belong. We take issue with how we have been represented, and we deliberate how we might represent ourselves differently (cf. Hall 1996). Narratives both enable and limit representation—and representation shapes our world and what is possible within it. Narratives, therefore, are profoundly political.

Our image of the world is bound up with modes of representation. Once this is recognized, an inquiry into the processes of interpretation and representation becomes necessary. When "what we accepts as real amounts to our use of various interpretative codes," Michael Shapiro writes, we need "an interrogation of the way that form is imposed on an otherwise unruly world and meaning and value are created" (Shapiro 1988: 8). Narratives organize human experience into meaningful episodes. At first glance, narratives tend to confirm the existing social, symbolic, economic, and political order—"in a single text, very little is new" (Meijer 1993: 368). Grand narratives restrict which meanings are possible (i.e., meaningful, reasonable, and rational) and which are not (i.e., meaningless, preposterous, and irrational). As such, narratives are always also an imposition and a form of violence in their insistence on singular meaning. On the other hand, narratives can be disruptive when they refuse to fit into any particular order, as "counter-discourses, modes of writing which oppose the terms of power and authority circulated and recirculated in discourse" (Shapiro 1988: 19). What is more, traditional science assumes that language is transparent and its significance is easily intelligible, whereas here, language is not simply a mode of communication but part of the being of what is understood.

The link between experience, meaning, and knowledge as it has been imagined in modern (positivist) science can no longer be sustained. To think of experience as narrative captures the interpretative aspect inherent in any recollection of experience. As it is impossible to reproduce lived experience, a characterization that includes the interpretative aspect is necessary. This is crucial for feminists who derive their insights on the basis of women's every-day experience and who, long subject to others' interpretations of their lives, are acutely aware of questions of representation. Thinking of potential inter-pretations as narratives encapsulates many of their aspects. Moreover, thinking of experience as narratively constructed alerts us, on one hand, to the concep-tualization of experience itself as narrative and, on the other hand, to the vari-ety of narratives telling us what kind of experiences to expect (cf. Wibben 1998: 78ff.). "Experience is an integrated construction, produced by the realm of meaning, which interpretatively links recollections, perceptions, and expectations" (Polkinghorne 1988: 16). If experience can only be grasped through retrospective construction through narratives, these narratives warrant close attention.

Security narratives, as traditionally imagined, follow a particular form to impose meaning and create value in what International Relations (IR) considers to be an anarchic world. The continual reproduction of these narratives solidifies historically developed practices—violent practices that insist on the imposition of meanings that privilege state-centered, military forms of security. To chal-lenge these practices, it is not only enough to propose different *contents* but the *form* of security narratives also needs to be tackled. A narrative approach uses tools from narratology and literary analysis to identify similarities in struc-ture. It explains how some narratives seem to make sense when others do not; how the imposition of a particular form becomes a tool to dismiss alternatives, and, more insidiously, how it makes the imagination of any alternative seem impossible. The aim of narrative theory is "to make explicit the operations that produce [a] particular kind of meaning, and to draw out the implications this meaning has for understanding human existence" (Polkinghorne 1988: 6). Although narrative theory used to be confined to literary narratives, it is now "capable of bringing its expertise to bear on narratives wherever they can be found, which is everywhere" (Currie 1998: 1).

Theorizing narrative

Narratology, the theory and systematic study of narrative, evolved throughout the twentieth century. Initially conceived as the art of narrative form and struc-ture, it soon developed dominance as an approach to literary narrative. Some-time in the 1980s, narratology became exceedingly technical and limited in scope, leading many to declare its death. However, Mark Currie proposes that rather than becoming irrelevant, narrative theory only transitioned away from some of the rigidities of its early years.[2] "From discovery to invention, from coherence to complexity, and from poetics to politics: this is the short summary of the transition that took place in narratological theory in the 1980s" (Currie 1998: 2). As a result, it has become applicable to all kinds of cultural artifacts that have narrative elements as well as to accounts of everyday experience (cf. Andrews 2007; Moon 2008; Polkinghorne 1988; White 1980; Whitebrook 2001).

Initially, narratology set out to discover a universal plot in narrative. This idea, prompted by the fact that narrative texts can be found in all cultures and all periods of history, has a long history; Aristotle, for example, proposed that plot is the defining feature of narrative. "Good stories, must have a beginning, middle, and end" writes Jonathan Culler (1997: 85), "they give us pleasure because of their ordering." This pleasure derives from a recognition of narrative form; narrative is not a simple sequence, but its appeal lies in the relationship of its ending back to its beginning. Where narratology postulates the existence of narrative structure independent of any particular representational medium, poststructuralist narrative theory suggests that the reader projects structure onto the work.[3] Rather than discovering narrative structure, the reader has an active role in the construction of meaning—she invents it. Consequently, an interpretation, "although not absolutely free and arbitrary since it does, or should, interact with a text, is in practice unlimited and free" (Bal 1997: x).

Attempting to construct unity, narratology tends to reduce complexity and heterogeneity within the narrative, suppressing any details that contradict the dominant theme. Poststructuralist narrative theorists resist this attempt to discover narrative unity and formal or thematic coherence. Focusing on "process, becoming, play, difference, slippage, and dissemination," writes Currie (1998: 3), they seek "to sustain contradictory aspects of narrative, preserving their complexity and refusing the impulse to reduce narrative to a stable meaning or coherent project." Indeed, a narrative always has more to say than can be captured in analysis, even with the best methods. The question becomes, as philosophical hermeneutics also points out, "what happens beyond our willing and doing" (Gadamer, quoted in Linge 1976: xi). These new developments in narrative theory allow for the reintroduction of historical perspective into narrative theory and highlight the political nature of narrative. Deconstruction, for example, challenges the organization of knowledge in binary oppositions where one term is privileged over the other. This is particularly important for feminist analyses, as the privileged term of a binary tends to be associated with masculinity, whereas the devalued term is feminized. This distinction, found in binaries such as irrational/rational, object/subject, and nature/culture that are all central to the modern cosmology, can be traced back to the Enlightenment and still shapes our thinking today (cf. Hekman 1990). The deconstructive move of reversing the binary—for example, by pointing out how security requires insecurity to become meaningful (cf. Campbell 1998b; Dillon 1996; Huysmans 2006; Stern 2005)—can also reverse the gendered hierarchies.

Furthermore, based on the analysis of the binary as reliant on its supposed opposite, it is displaced making room for alternative (nonbinary) conceptions and new forms of politics.

How does one actually begin to approach a text? How can interpretations be made accessible to allow for comparisons? Mieke Bal, following the structuralist tradition, provides a comprehensive toolbox of narrative theory. A series of generalized statements make it possible to formulate, compare, and contrast different interpretations. Although initially conceived to study narratives, her framework can be applied beyond the study of "purely" narrative texts to look at narrative elements of any text.[4] Its use allows for insight into the ways in which the use of a medium, the ordering of text, and the relationships between fiction and what is perceived as real produce certain (un)desired effects and influence the meanings attributed to the text. Bal (1997: 176) finds resemblances "between fabulas [contents] of narratives and 'real' fabulas, that is between what people do and what actors do in fabulas that have been invented, between what people experience and what actors experience." Others have gone further to argue that what is at stake in the narrative turn is

> a change in the self-understanding that constitutes the field of social and political analysis. Part of what must be rejected is that aspect of the terrain predicated on a radical distinction between what is thought of as fictional and scientific genres of writing.
>
> (Shapiro 1988: 7)

What is important here is the aim of the analysis undertaken with narrative tools. Bal stresses that her theory, despite its instrumental character, is not generated from a positivist desire for absolute knowledge. Instead, as textual analysis, it looks at the conditions of the processes of reception—of producing meaning. Meaning, in narrative, "is a cultural phenomenon, partaking of cultural processes. It is the condition of possibility of these processes that constitute the interest of narrative analysis" (Bal 1997: 9). As such, the analysis cannot provide ultimate truth or decide on quality or value. It can only provide insights into how certain mechanisms are used to encourage one or another meaning. These meanings are "the result of the interpretation by the reader, an interpretation influenced both by the initial encounter with the text and by the manipulations of the story" (ibid.). A detailed analysis can help to elaborate on the actualization of interpretation and its conditions of possibility. In this manner, narrative analysis can clarify or aid a value judgment, but evaluation, ultimately, is outside the scope of narrative theory and always political.

Bal distinguishes three layers of analysis: text (medium), story (presentation), and fabula (content). These three layers are the result of looking at the same material with different lenses; general readers would, in contrast, process the narrative as an undivided whole. On the level of narrative text, the analysis is concerned with the medium in which the story is conveyed. A text is composed of a finite, structured set of language signs, imagery, or sounds. This does not imply, however, "that the text itself is finite, for its meanings, effects, functions and background are not" (Bal 1997: 5). In a narrative text, a narrator, who is not identical with the author of the narrative, tells a story. The narrator's identity shapes the character of the text. Here, the narrator appears on the text level; only it is the agent telling the story. It does not include the point of view, which often provides the shading of the fabula. This is discussed separately as "focalization" because Bal specifically focuses on how narration produces subjectivity. She is interested in "the constitution of the subject required to communicate in the first place" (ibid.: 30). Bal illustrates this by reference to "deixis," that is, the phenomenon wherein understanding the meaning of certain words is only possible in the context of utterance.

> The pronouns 'I' and 'you,' as opposed to 'she,' 'he,' 'they,' and the like, are totally empty in themselves. They do not refer outside of the situation in which they are uttered. Each utterance is performed by an 'I' and addressed to a 'you.' This second person is crucial, for it is that subject that confirms the 'I' as a speaker. Conversely the 'you' becomes an 'I' as soon as the perspective shifts. It is only as potential 'I' that the 'you' him- or herself has the subjectivity to act, hence to confirm the subjectivity of the previous 'I.'
>
> (Bal 1997: 30–1)

It is possible to distinguish broadly between two types of narrators. An external narrator does not refer to itself as a character in the fabula but tells about others. A character-bound narrator tends to be identified as a character in the fabula using the "I" to invoke the telling of "true" facts. The narration can alternate between different types of narrators, who may or may not coincide with particular focalizors. Often these shifts, as well as the relationships between author and narrator, are used to indicate larger points such as the difficulty of remembering a traumatic past (cf. Andrews 2007; Edkins 2003; Moon 2008).

The second layer distinguished in Bal's framework is that of the story and concerns the manner in which the fabula is presented. The story is the result of several ordering processes during which, through various techniques, "suspense and pleasure are provoked, and [...] ideology is inscribed" (Bal 1997: 79).[5] Although the theme "good wins over evil" is common to many narratives, the way in which its elements are ordered produces the aspects of a particular story, provides specific nuances of its meaning, and makes it distinguishable from all others. As the analysis on this level is concerned with the techniques of ordering, many concepts that can be applied to non-narrative texts can be located here. The following provides an overview of such ordering activities (Table 3.1).

Table 3.1 Narrative ordering processes

Elements	Processes at story level
Events	The events are arranged in a sequence that can differ from the chronological sequence.
Time	The amount of time that is allotted in the story to the various elements of the fabula is determined with respect to the amount of time that these elements take up in the fabula.
Actors	The actors are provided with distinct traits. In this manner, they are individualized and transformed into characters.
Locations	The locations where events occur are also given distinct characteristics and are thus transformed into specific places.
Relationships	In addition to the necessary relationships among actors, events, locations, and time, all of which were already describable in the layer of the fabula, other relationships (symbolic, allusive, traditional, etc.) may exist among the various elements.
Points of view	A choice is made from among the various "points of view" from which the elements can be presented. The resulting *focalization*, the relationship between who perceives and what is perceived, produces subjectivity.

Source: Following Bal 1997: 8.

One of the main principles of ordering concerns the ways in which events get presented—such as changing their chronological order by moving back and forth between past, present, and future. These so-called "anachronies" can indicate the motivation or explanation for an act. Of interest here is that a reader begins to assume a correct order because she knows that in "reality," fictitious or not, the events must have happened the other way around. At this point, culturally specific, generalized knowledge begins to enter the interpretation (e.g., a notion of linear time). This also means that events are always presented from within a certain tradition—a particular economic, social, symbolic, and political order. What is more, "a point of view is chosen, a certain way of seeing things, a certain angle, whether 'real' historical facts are concerned or fictitious events" (Bal 1997: 142).

This presentation of events from a particular perspective, discussed as "focalization," is often crucial for the meaning of the fabula as produced in the reading. Focalization, a term used in photography and film, refers to the relationship between the elements presented and the vision through which they are presented. A character-bound focalizor locates this vision with a character in the story, whereas an external focalizor presents a vision from outside the story. When the narrative is told by an external focalizor, the vision it presents tends to be associated with its author. If it diverges from the reader's vision or opinion, it is, thus, likely to be subject to critique.[6] However, "if the focalizor coincides with a character, that character will have an advantage over the other characters," writes Bal. "The reader watches with the character's eyes and will, in principle, be inclined to accept the vision presented by that character" (Bal 1997: 146).

This is especially pertinent in political analysis because narrative makes it possible, both in fiction and life, to express the vision of another. To address this perplexing feature of language, traditional narratological concepts are insufficient because they tend not to "make a distinction between, on the one hand, the vision through which the elements are presented, and on the other, the identity of the voice that is verbalizing that vision" (Bal 1997: 143). However, such a distinction is necessary to draw attention to the power relations inherent in presenting someone else's vision for them, a point crucial also to feminist analyses (cf. Chapter 5). Just as the actor on the text level tells the story, the focalizor sees the fabula. This vision always already entails an interpretation and, thus, shapes the meaning of the fabula considerably, which points to another important layer of focalization: the relationship between the focalizor and that which is seen. An analysis of focalization needs to incorporate the two poles of this relation (the subject and object of focalization) and examine the effects produced through the relation. Paying attention to focalization can help to indicate the subtle infusion of the narrative with particular ideals, be they specific to an academic discipline, a worldview, or a particular author.

Maaike Meijer (1993) demonstrates the effectiveness of focalization in her analysis of textual violence. One of her examples is *Het wonder van Frieswijck*, a Dutch children's book, whose distribution as a free gift during a national holiday lead to heated discussions with regard to possible promotion of racism. Although some considered it to be racist, others felt it was fighting racism by explicitly rejecting it, a view "based on the fact that the book's protagonist, the white girl Alijt, sympathizes with Danga [the black slave] and even succeeds in freeing him from slavery" (ibid.: 375). According to its author, Thea Beckman, the book should be seen simply as an accurate historical description of the racist reactions encountered by a Black child arriving in Holland during the fourteenth century as the slave of a Portuguese merchant. Drawing on Bal's distinction between different levels of a narrative text, Meijer demonstrates that there is indeed cause to suspect racism. She notes that the "ethnocentrism is not to be located on the level of narrative events, the level of 'what happens' (the so-called *fabula*)" (ibid.: 376). The racism of the book is to be found at the story level where events are embedded in the way in which they are narrated and focalized.

> When we look at the network of focalisation we can see how all 'agents' in the story (Alijt, her sister Agnes, her father, the merchant) are at some moment or other focalizing subjects. Thus we often experience their thoughts, views, and feelings on events and fellow- characters from the inside. Danga, however, is never set up in the position of a focalizor. This implies that he always remains an object of other (white) people's view of him. Thus Danga is, on the narrative level, expelled from the community of subjects, a position he shares with—guess who—the dog.
> (Meijer 1993: 376)

Furthermore, the dominant narrator, an external narrator who is also the main focalizor, embraces views that are allegedly only portrayed for historical accuracy. Instead of referring to him simply as Danga, "the narrator herself calls the black boy 'Moorian,' 'little nigger,' 'the slave' and so on" (Meijer 1993: 376). What is more, Alijt, the character-bound narrator, is the main embedded focalizor leading the reader to identify with her (heroic) deeds. However, "at the end of the book she becomes quite patronizing as well, looking down on Danga while protecting him. She exhibits the clammy 'do-good-ism' with which white people so often tend to buy off their guilt feelings" (ibid.). Meijer argues that a reader's strong identification with a main focalizor, in this case Alijt's character, makes it difficult to reject her racist mannerisms. "We are seduced into accepting it, sharing it, not questioning it" (ibid.). This example illustrates how the distinction of different narrative layers produces insightful results. The concept of a focalizor, in addition to the narrator, is particularly useful to uncover unacknowledged bias. What is more, it provides insight into the construction of subjectivity in narrative, specifically regarding its precondition of being able to speak, to have a voice. Given the constitutive role of narrative in matters of identity, Bal's approach can be extremely helpful for a feminist reading of IR.

A narrative's third layer, the fabula, concerns the content of the narrative. As a product of imagination, the fabula, although most obvious to a reader, is the least accessible layer from the viewpoint of narrative theory. Nonetheless, a narrative is produced to convey a fabula. For this reason, narrative analysis mainly engages the fabula. The goal of such efforts has traditionally been the identification of a plot whose structure, it was hoped, would conform to a universal model. Such a structure, on the simplest level, is seen to consist of a beginning, middle, and end. Bal identifies a "narrative cycle" with three phases: (1) possibility/virtuality, (2) realization/actualization, and (3) conclusion/termination.[7] Not every narrative completes all three phases, and it is also possible that a series can be embedded within one another, so that an infinite number of fabulas can be formed. Where narratology proposes that a plot is marked by an initial situation (faced by heroine or hero), a challenge, and a solution that relates back to the beginning, Bal proposes the following trajectory:

> The initial situation in a fabula will always be a state of deficiency in which one or more actors want to introduce changes. The development of the fabula reveals that, according to certain patterns, the process of change involves an improvement or a deterioration with regard to the initial situation.
>
> (1997: 193)

This formulation places less emphasis on progress as viewed from the perspective of a hero or, more seldom, a heroine, than traditional narratology. It allows for greater specificity, an analysis of variously positioned characters and, most importantly, insight into the power relations in the fabula.

On the whole, Bal is less interested in a discussion of whether a general plot exists and warns of the dangers of making universal claims. Although there seems to be some overlap between narrative texts in different cultures, generalizations are highly problematic. Consequently, she prefers not to "refer to *the* structure of a fabula, but to *a* structure [formed by the analyst] on the basis of selected events combined with other data" (Bal 1997: 193).[8] During this process, the analyst's prejudgments/prejudices necessarily shape the structures proposed on the basis of a selection of elements. The choice of a particular combination is always intuitive, maintains Bal, because it is impossible to investigate everything and to make it explicit. "This carries with it the advantage of allowing us to pursue our own interests to a great extent while keeping to the same intersubjectively understandable model of analysis" (ibid.: 195). A disadvantage is that bias might go unexamined, a point of great concern to feminists who find that the selection of problems for inquiry, along with their definition, is a main origin of androcentrism, classism, racism, and sexism in research.

Bal's narratology offers a good basis for comparison because various elements of narrative can be discussed within the confines of one framework. However, her approach involves a great deal of classification, which is necessarily reductive and needs to be balanced in relation to the aim of the analysis. Bal (1997: 218) is well aware of this when she cautions that "its use is instrumental: only when classification helps to provide greater insight [...] is it meaningful in describing the text." Combining her approach with insights from poststructuralist thought can loosen the rigidity of an overly constraining arrangement. Plot is often formulated in extremely rigid terms—"there *must* be, first of all, an initial situation, a sequence leading to a change or reversal of that situation, and a revelation made possible by the reversal of the situation" (Miller 1990: 75, stress added). The resolution is supposed to mark the change in the middle of the narrative as significant and relate back to its beginning. Narrative theorists often asserts that if any of these elements are missing, we fail to recognize a narrative or can perceive it only as one that is lacking.

Feminists are among those arguing against the primacy of a particular plot. In her attempt to encourage a feminist narrative theory, Susan Lanser analyzes a letter written by a woman in coded form to escape a husband's censorship. Its structure clearly does not follow the singular plot outlined earlier. "The units of anticipation and fulfillment or problem and solution that structure plot according to narrative theorists of plot assume that textual actions are based on the (intentional) deeds of protagonists," writes Lanser. "They assume a power, a possibility, that may be inconsistent with what women have experienced both historically and textually, and perhaps inconsistent even with women's desires" (Lanser 1991: 623). This is consistent with observations by a number of critics who, when assessing women's writing, find that they can only talk about a "plotless" story (cf. Eagleton 1986; Hite 1989).

Alternatively, if the traditional definition of plot is inadequate, one might see the telling of the narrative, the act of writing, as the fulfillment of desire associated with narrative. Culler notes:

The pleasure of narrative is linked to desire. Plots tell of desire and what befalls it, but the moment of narrative itself is driven by desire in the form of 'epistemophilia,' a desire to know: we want to discover secrets, to know the end, to find the truth. If what drives narrative is the 'masculine' urge to mastery, the desire to unveil the truth (the 'naked truth'), then what of the knowledge that narrative offers to satisfy that wish? Is that knowledge itself an effect of desire?

(1997: 92–3)

The underlying ideas of progress and linearity, of mastery and truth, which are characteristic of plot as traditionally conceived, are problematic. There might be, after all, "a plot behind women's 'plotless' narrative, the subversive plot of sharing an experience so that the listener may complete the speaker's tale" (Lanser 1991: 624–5). There might be a plot of narration, focused on the narrator, rather than on the reader's assumed desire for a clearly structured fabula. Consequently, a feminist narrative approach needs to "study narrative in relation to a referential context that is simultaneously linguistic, literary, historical, biographical, social and political" (ibid.: 614). When narrative theory is focused on identifying and classifying a singular plot structure, it remains biased; it relies on a limited body of texts with a narrow understanding of narrative and its context. In the case of women's writing, and also more generally in a world of hybrid subjectivities, there is a greater diversity of narratives. Furthermore, no matter what their plot, they are profoundly referential and influential in shaping representation. "Implicating literature in the making of society has a reciprocal implication for literature [...] if literature speaks gender, along with class and race, the critic has to read culture and ideology" (Jehlen 1990: 264).

Here, we reach the limits of narratology. Interpretation always has an aim beyond the reach of structural analysis: to further understanding, to critique representation, or to develop a political argument. As the reader's investment in producing meanings has become more pronounced, the concept of both the narrator and the author has become problematic. Neither author nor reader has the ultimate authority over meaning because each reading will be different and will contain elements beyond the intentions of the author. Although meanings consequently fluctuate more widely, Bal maintains that any particular social, economic, symbolic, and political order imposes limits. Though often unacknowledged, they are decisive to interpretation; "any position that does not assess the political basis of the status quo cannot challenge the established cultural powers" (Bal 1997: 17). She argues for shifting strategic limits of interpretation as replacement for "truth" in order to "to develop a politics of reading that draws its legitimacy from political positions, not from any fictitious 'real' knowledge" (ibid.). All the while, she advises against a radical proliferation of meaning, insisting that some strategic limits to interpretation are necessary to provide an opening for a more diverse and more complex understanding— a point of great concern to feminists.

Narrating 9/11

On September 11, 2001, at 8:45am American Airlines Flight 11 crashes into the north tower of the World Trade Center (WTC).[9] Eyewitness Mark Obenhaus reports:[10]

> As I was approaching the subway, a tremendous roar went over my head and—I looked up immediately, and it was a plane much lower than I've ever seen a plane in lower Manhattan, and it was a large plane. I couldn't identify it as anything specific except that it was a commercial jet certainly. And it—it—my eyes followed it because this is approximately 15 blocks from the World Trade Center, and it- it just slammed right into it and was completely engulfed by the building. It was extraordinary.
>
> (ABC News 2001a)

Shortly thereafter, all major TV stations in the United States have their cameras set up and are trying to make sense of the events. Charles Gibson, on ABC's "Good Morning America" is just beginning to introduce the news:

> We're joined by the entire network just to show you some pictures at the foot of New York City. This is at the World Trade Center. Obviously a major fire there. And there has been some sort of explosion. We don't fully know the details. There is one report, as of yet unconfirmed, that a plane has hit the World Trade Center.
>
> (ABC News 2001a)

Several minutes pass while speculations are in full swing, then the anchors are disrupted:

> 'Oh, my God!'—'Oh, my God! Oh, my God!'—'That looks like a second plane just hit … '—'Terrible!'—'I didn't see a plane go in. That—that just exploded. I … "—'We just saw another plane coming in from the side'—'You did? I was—that was obscured from my view'—'That second explosion, you could see the plane come in just from the right hand side of the screen, so this looks like some sort of a … '—'Oh, my!'—' … concerted effort to attack the World Trade Center that is underway in downtown New York'
>
> (ABC News 2001a)

At 9:03am, United Airlines Flight 175 hits the south tower of the WTC and explodes.[11] The events seem unreal. "We will see that scene again just to make sure we saw what we thought we saw," says Diane Sawyer (ABC News 2001a). Mark Obenhaus remarks, "It reminds you of the worst kind of effects in movies that, you know, you're assured watching a movie that it's an effect. But this is not" (ibid.).[12]

Buildings are burning, debris is falling, and people on the upper floors of the towers begin jumping out of windows.[13] Eyewitnesses report from the scene:

> The screaming was just horrendous [...] every time there would be another explosion, people would start screaming and thronging again [...] we saw people jumping from the tower as the fire was going on [...] the sky went black, all this stuff came onto us, we ran.
>
> (quoted in Schmemann 2001)

Meanwhile, in Sarasota, Florida, at 9:30am, having just learned of the second plane crash, Bush makes a first TV appearance during which he calls the events "a difficult moment for America" and "a national tragedy." He goes on to say that in response to this "apparent terrorist attack on our country," the priorities are "to help the victims and their families" and to "conduct a full scale investigation to hunt down and to find those folks who committed this act." He underscores the latter's importance by saying "terrorism against our nation will not stand."[14] Peter Jennings, who has by now assumed the lead of ABC News Special Report he will maintain all day, comments:

> President clearly shaken, I think [...] the president saying the two things which a president must say in a moment like this, 'Terrorism will not stand,' which is an important thing for him to say but not always necessarily effective, and 'God bless the victims and their families.'
>
> (ABC News 2001a)

Considering that the aim of this book is to question security narratives, it is noteworthy how, for Bush, the crashes are immediately labeled as being about "America," "our country," and "our nation," thus indicating a state-centric framework. Besides reinforcing a particular political, social, symbolic order, this also narrows the scope for interpretations. Considering that the Pentagon has not yet been hit, one might ponder other alternatives. Why was there so little (if any) talk of this being an assault on global capitalism, on New York City or large-scale urban development, or simply a means to another end such as drawing attention to the plight of Tibetans or Palestinians?[15] It seems plausible that some of these were also the targets, even within the narrative as it is developed by the Bush administration, but the events are immediately framed in terms of a (national) security narrative.

Shortly after Bush's remarks, at 9:43am, American Airlines Flight 77 crashes into one of the sides of the Pentagon, consolidating hypotheses of a concerted terrorist attack on the United States. However, in the events' unfolding, nothing is as clear as it seems in retrospect. The confusion expressed in the following ABC report indicates that the process of "making sense," of constructing the narrative of 9/11, is still in progress:

Want to hold our breath here, it seems to me, for a second and—and—and—and not get into a mode that the country is under attack. But we now have two attacks on the Twin Trade Towers Center, US buildings, city buildings completely evacuated in New York City. We have this mysterious black smoke at the southwest corner of the White House which is to say there's something going on behind the old Executive Office Building. We now have a report that fire has been confirmed at the Pentagon.

(Jennings, ABC News 2001a)

Jennings clearly is not yet aware that the fire at the Pentagon is from a plane crashing into the Pentagon. Indeed, this only becomes apparent about half an hour later when an eyewitness phones in to give his account "it looked like a commuter plane, two-engine, come down from the south real low, proceed right on an crash right into the Pentagon" (Wright, ABC News 2001b). This information turns out to also be incorrect; it was American Airlines Flight 77, a passenger jet that crashed into the Pentagon.

Within half an hour of events in Washington, D.C., although rescue efforts are underway in New York City, the situation takes a dramatic turn as the south tower of the WTC collapses at 10:05am:

Abruptly there was an earsplitting noise. The South tower shook, seemed to list in one direction and then began to come down; imploding upon itself [...] 'It looked like a demolition' [...] 'It was about the 70th floor. And each second another floor exploded out for about eight floors before the cloud obscured it all' [...] everything was black. People found their eyes burned. [...] Many of the onlookers stayed put, frozen in horror. Slowly the next thought crept into their consciousness: the other tower would come down too.

(Kleinfield 2001)

Then, at 10:10am, a portion of the Pentagon collapses and United Airlines Flight 93 crashes into a field in Pennsylvania, causing speculations about the intended destination of that plane.

I'm just going to add to the chaos and the trauma of the day by saying that a large plane has now crashed just north, or shouldn't I say just, but crashed about 10:00, in the last 15 minutes, north of Somerset County Airport about 80 miles southeast of Pittsburgh. This is a—this is a—reporting from one of the Pittsburgh television stations as a result of a 911 call from the airport itself. There are no other details on this crash yet. And it's not clear whether the crash was related to anything else that has happened in the country today.

(Jennings, ABC News 2001b)

Various rumors are circulating shortly about the plane that crashed in Pennsylvania, among them that it had been shot down by the Air Force or that passengers on board had managed to overwhelm the hijackers and force the plane down. It has since been confirmed that "Vice-President Cheney [told] the military it has permission to shoot down any airliners threatening Washington" (CNN 2001a). What is more, there are reports of "an explosion of some kind at the capitol [sic]" and that "a car bomb has exploded outside the State Department" (Jennings, ABC News 2001b), amidst conflicting reports about how many planes are actually missing as well as their possible destinations. CNN (2001b) states, for example, "the Associated Press is reporting that federal officials fear that a second hijacked plane or another hijacked plane is headed toward the Pentagon."

On ABC, Jennings is trying to put things into perspective (and to reestablish mastery over events by sorting the "false" and "true"):

> Now we have had, as I said, reports today—there are hundreds of reports flying around and so we beg your indulgence on us saying as often as we do, these are reports, they're sometimes unconfirmed, they're sometimes confirmed. We'll try to make it absolutely clear what we absolutely know and what we're uncertain about.[16]
>
> (ABC News 2001b)

At 10:28am, the north tower disintegrates. Then, as a witness standing at Canal Street expresses it, "there is nothing there" (quoted in Kleinfield 2001). Blakemore describes the scene on ABC:

> Throngs of people have been, of course, moving north. Some of them silent, most of them looking stunned, just saying, 'We're just trying to get out of the area after both towers have collapsed [...] People have now begun to accept, but just barely begun to accept, what's happened. All business at a complete standstill. Nothing but sirens down here as these throngs move further and further north just walking away from what they can barely begin to understand.
>
> (ABC News 2001b)

Not 2 hours after the initial reports of an incident at the WTC, people in the United States are in a general state of fear. "'This is America,' a man said, 'How can this happen in America? How?'" (quoted in Kleinfield 2001).

Many observers wondered the same and suggested, as Don DeLillo does, that a radical break was brought about by the events of the day.[17] He writes, "The Bush Administration was feeling a nostalgia for the Cold War. This is over now. Many things are over. The narrative ends in the rubble and it is left to us to create the counter-narrative" (DeLillo 2001: 34). Counternarratives are not simple contestations of the dominant narratives. Often, what is seen to counter a trend, on close analysis, functions to sustain it, albeit to varying degrees—depending on how it is constructed around an awareness of the importance of framing an event. Counternarratives work through and beyond existing narratives and transform them by drawing on events, ideas, and actions not usually heeded when constructing security narratives. There is no inherent structural cause that, as such, would prevent innumerable narratives from being constructed. Limitations are provided by the event itself, the author(itative) agenda, and, markedly, by the cultural confines in which the construction of the narrative takes place. Choosing to narrate an event in a certain manner, even when relying on eyewitness accounts, is to produce meaning. For one, the various statements are already representations; they contain specific interpretations. Furthermore, it presents a selection of statements placed in a particular relation to one another. Together they produce a somewhat meaningful narrative. What is important here is not a particular meaning, but "the condition of possibility of these processes" (Bal 1997: 9).

On September 11, 2001, at 8:30pm, after a day of traumatic events during which "for hours people lingered uncertain where to go or what to do in a no longer plausible world" (Kleinfield 2001), President Bush provides the authoritative narrative of the events of the day. The purpose of this special *Address to the Nation*, in the words of White House press secretary Ari Fleischer, is to deliver "a message of resolve and reassurance. It will be reassuring that our nation has been tested before, our nation has always prevailed" (Fleischer 2001a). What is more, "in particular tonight [Bush] wants to talk about the tragedy that has befallen people's families, those who have lost their lives" (ibid. 2001b). Bush's *Address* frames the events of 9/11 in a particular way; like any narrative, it orders the events and makes them comprehensible by identifying the whole to which they contribute. In doing so, it not only imposes an authoritative account of the events, but it also shapes the possible responses and limits alternative presentations.

The general fabula of the *Address* is quickly recounted and not surprising in the context of traditional security narratives.[18] The initial situation, seen in retrospect of course, is one of America, "the brightest beacon for freedom and opportunity in the world," where "victims were in airplanes, or in their offices; secretaries, businessmen and women, military and federal workers; moms and dads, friends and neighbors" (Bush 2001b).[19] The challenge comes in the form of "airplanes flying into buildings, fires burning, huge structures collapsing," through which "thousands of lives were suddenly ended." In a more evocative phrasing elsewhere in the speech, these become "evil, despicable acts of terror" and "acts of mass murder [...] intended to frighten our nation into chaos and retreat." The solution to address this challenge, or rather these challenges, remains largely in the realm of projection into the future. With the exception of responding "with the best of America—with the daring of our rescue workers, with the caring for strangers and neighbors who came to give blood and help in any way they could" and a description of the actions already taken, the solution remains a possibility (or virtuality).[20] Notwithstanding, Bush articulates the solution that, it has to be noted, might be due to his task as president of the United States to "at once to calm the nation and declare his determination to exact retribution" (Bumiller and Sanger 2001). Bush assures the public that "the functions of government continue without interruption. [...] Our financial institutions remain strong, and the American economy will be open for business, as well." He goes on to say, "a search is underway for those who are behind these evil acts" and projects grander actions stating that "America and our friends and allies join with all those who want peace and security in the world, and we stand together to win the war against terrorism." He also declares, "we will make no distinctions between those who have committed these acts and those who harbor them" while "we go forward to defend freedom and all that is good and just in our world." This links back to the initial situation of America as "the brightest beacon for freedom and opportunity in the world" and nicely completes the narrative.

Some comparisons between Bush's narrative and events unfolding on the evening of 9/11 will complicate the narrative.[21] According to Bush, the initial situation has moved through the realization (or actualization) phase and is in the conclusion (or termination) segment. At the outset of Bush's fabula, it was "our fellow citizens, our way of life, our very freedom that came under attack." At the end of the speech they are restored: "This is a day when all Americans from every walk of life unite in our resolve for justice and peace. America has stood down enemies before and will do so this time." The second element of the plot, the challenge, is still in the realization (or actualization) part of the process, even while certain aspects of it, such as "airplanes flying into buildings," seem to have entered the conclusion (or termination) phase. Bush shows recognition of this, using the formulations "cannot dent" and "cannot touch," which are more tentative, indicating an expression of hope or resolve rather than of certainty. This seems appropriate as fires are still burning and many people are searching for missing friends or relatives. Numerous deaths are very much still a possibility (or virtuality).[22] It seems then, that also in Bush's narratives of 9/11, various elements of the plot remain in motion. It certainly seems to be the case in New York City, and likely at the Pentagon, where people are just beginning to put up "the improvised memorials [that] are another part of our response" (DeLillo 2001: 35). For weeks and months after the events,

> There are many photographs of missing persons, some accompanied by hopeful lists of identifying features (Man with panther tattoo, upper right arm). There is the saxophonist playing softly. There is the sculptured flag of rippling copper and aluminium, six feet long, with two young people still attending to the finer details of the piece. Then there are the visitors to the park. The artifacts on display represent the confluence of a number of cultural tides, patriotic and multidevotional and retro hippie. The visitors move quietly in the floating candlewax, roses, and bus fumes. There are many people on this mild evening and in their voices, manner, clothing, and in the color of their skin they recapitulate the mix we see in the photocopied faces of the lost.
>
> (DeLillo 2001: 35)

What is more,

> if you lived in New York, you saw (and heard and smelled) the flesh and
> stone of the events themselves, and you recalled (you could not help it)
> imagery from some movie, and then you saw TV footage of the flesh
> and stone events, and then you heard a friend who worked downtown
> describe the ash people walking across the Brooklyn Bridge, which you
> also saw on CNN, by the way, and then you went yourself to the Bridge
> and saw the ghastly footprints, and then you woke up at 3am, afterimaging
> it all—and so on, round and round, on and on, as those eerie, early days
> drifted by.
>
> (Zengotita 2001)

Reality narratives, unlike fictional narratives, can rest temporarily, but never conclude (terminate) as life goes on. Notwithstanding the futility of the attempt already evident, Bush's *Address* endeavors to refute the undecidability of life through a narrative of completed processes.[23] This can be explained, at least in part, by pointing to the purpose of the speech. Commenting on Bush's demeanor and presentational style, Elisabeth Bumiller and David E. Sanger (2001) note in the *New York Times* that "the coming days will require him to master the images of sturdy authority and presidential strength." Accordingly, Bush's remarks are intended to reassure people, to restore certainty "after a day of trauma" (ibid.).[24]

Because the fabula is a product of imagination and as such least accessible to narratology, the reading presented here reflects the bias of this particular study. Furthermore, it is only one element of the process of framing. Of particular interest to an analysis of the framing of a narrative is the story level. It concerns the manipulation of the text through ordering, which produces a perspective or point of view and is decisive for the meaning of the fabula. In any narrative, simply by necessity, some sequential ordering takes place and its use determines, to an extent, the author's narrative "style." It can also provide insight into her view of life. In an analysis of sequential ordering, "the relations are being explored which hold between the order of events in the story and their chronological sequence in the fabula" (Bal 1997: 80). To give an example, generally we have to leave one place before we can arrive at another. However, in a narrative, we might first encounter a description of the arrival and only later find an account of the motivation for this act (or simply infer that the character arriving must have come from somewhere). "The reader assumes this, but such assumptions are narrative effects; they do not imply that there exists, or has ever existed, such a series of events in that order" (ibid.). Different types of sequential ordering can have important effects on the reader and provide insights into the style of the author and/or the meaning she or he wishes to convey.

> Frequent use of punctual anachrony sometimes makes for a businesslike
> style; systematic combinations of punctual and durative retroversions can

create—or at least add to—the impression that a story is developing according to clear causative laws: a certain event causes a situation to emerge which makes another event possible, and so on. If durative retroversions are dominant then the reader quickly receives the impression that nothing particularly spectacular is happening. The narrative appears to be a succession of inevitable situations.

(Bal 1997: 94)[25]

An important element of sequential ordering is the story's rhythm, the back and forth movement between past and present. Rhythm indicates how attention is patterned, but it is difficult to measure because it relies on comparing the "relationship between the amount of time covered by the events of the fabula and the amount of time involved in presenting those events" (Bal 1997: 100).[26] However, because the so-called time of telling is rarely available to us, it needs to be estimated by juxtaposing "the amount of time covered by the fabula with the amount of space in the text each event requires, the number of pages, lines or words" (ibid.). In the case at hand, it is possible to divide Bush's *Address* into three segments (see Appendix). The first segment contains sentences 1–14 and is, broadly, a description of "what happened" on and the initial reactions to the events of 9/11. The second section (sentences 15–27) is a description of actions taken by governments in response to the events. The third segment (sentences 28–35) projects into the future while also referring back to the past and present and contains strong religious references.[27]

Dividing the *Address* is not simply "aimed at precise calculation of the number of lines per event; the amount of text set aside for each event only indicates something about how the attention is patterned" (Bal 1997: 101).[28] How much attention is paid to each element, something that can only be analyzed by comparing attention paid to other elements, helps to paint a picture of the vision communicated by the fabula. Drawing attention to the relationship among elements also provides clues about the connections that are being made. When taking a closer look at the different segments of the *Address*, it is striking that the bulk of the story (sections I and III) is concerned with broad characterizations of the events and the response. In addition, the actors here are varied: from moms and dads to rescue workers, from citizens to strangers, from victims to a power greater than any of us. In contrast, about one-third of the story (section II) concerns rather precise descriptions of actions taken in response to the events of the morning. What is more, all the actions described in this segment are taken by officials connected in one or another way to state institutions, thus emphasizing the state as the adequate agent in charge. By providing more detail, the narration in section II is slower than in section I, with the effect that the actions of various government agencies are emphasized and state agency restored.

With a reality narrative, attention should be paid to omission or ellipsis. Theoretically, "an ellipsis cannot be perceived: according to definition, nothing is indicated [and] we cannot know what should have been indicated either" (Bal 1997: 103). If the *Address* were the only document available to tell us about 9/11, we might be able to infer that information has been omitted, but we could not be certain. What has been omitted can be of great importance, as is the fact that it has been omitted. In this case, the omissions are apparent through what is preserved elsewhere. Paying attention to omission is of great importance to feminists; historically women's lives and their contributions tended to be excluded from dominant (state) narratives. Consequently, one might expect the feminist approach to insist on telling the real story, in an effort to get it right this time. However, feminists often find it more useful to measure silences. By looking at what a story does not say, cannot say, and, most strikingly, refuses to say, the epistemic violence of ellipsis can be pointed to and contested. By "measuring silences," Spivak (1988: 287) suggests, we are "'investigating, identifying, and measuring ... the *deviation*' from an ideal that is irreducibly differential." Postcolonial analyses of imperialism point to the value of this strategy; "the narrow epistemic violence of imperialism gives us an imperfect allegory of the general violence that is the possibility of an episteme" (ibid.). Bal also suggests other reasons why ellipsis might be noteworthy:

> The event about which nothing is said may be so painful that it is being elided for precisely that reason. Or the event is so difficult to put into words that it is preferable to maintain complete silence about it. Another possibility [...] is the situation in which, though the event has taken place, the actor wants to deny that fact. By keeping silent about it, he attempts to undo it. Thus the ellipsis is used for magical purposes, as an exorcism.
>
> (Bal 1997: 103)

The most striking example of ellipsis in the *Address* is that Bush provides little indication that suspects are being discussed. The media, on the other hand, started speculating about possible terrorist groups that might be involved almost immediately after the incidents in New York. Kyle Olson, in an interview on ABC, remarked:

> We've been anticipating for a while—we've wondered why it's been so relatively quiet. The actions and suggestions of Osama Bin Laden's involvement, what has he been doing since Cole. Other—other groups out there with—with a real or imagined grudge against the United States. The nature of the event is shocking. The—the fact that it's happened is not.
>
> (ABC News 2001b)

Later, CNN reported "that US officials say there are 'good indications' that Saudi militant Osama bin Laden [...] is involved in the attacks, based on 'new and specific' information" (CNN 2001c).[29] The official line of the government in the meantime, which can be deduced from documents other than the

Address, is not to speculate on the specific identity of possible suspects. It is exemplified in Fleischer's remarks:

> Information is still being gathered and analyzed. I anticipate that will be an ongoing process for a while. Often at a time like this, information comes in, it turns out not to be true. The proper procedure is to carefully, thoroughly evaluate all information.
>
> (Fleischer 2001a)

Fleischer, in his duty as White House secretary, portrays the image of an administration basing action on solid facts and not lashing out wildly. This increases the authority of the administration, displaying an aura of competence and certainty. It also generates the impression that when action is taken (at some point in the future), it will be incontestable, at least on the basis of evidence (which is secret, of course, and thus cannot be directly challenged). Finally, it covers the topic of an intelligence failure, as a competent administration could not very well be accused of failure (and, indeed, it took 8 months for the topic to reemerge).[30]

Frequency, another feature of rhythm, compares the numerical relationship of events in the fabula with those in the story. A premier example of increased events on the story level is the repetition of an event that occurs only once (in the fabula/in "reality") but is represented a number of times. Bush's *Address* exemplifies this by repeatedly describing the plane crashes. They are (1) "a series of deliberate and deadly terrorist *acts*" (2) "evil, despicable acts of terror," (3) "acts of mass murder," (4) "terrorist attacks," (5) "these acts [that] shattered steel," and (6) "these evil acts."[31] Repetition stresses the importance of an event and calls attention to its "correct" meaning. Repeated description can serve to change the meaning of an event, such that the past has a new significance: "The same event is presented as more, or less, pleasant, innocent, or important than we had previously believed it to be. It is both identical and different: the fabula elements are the same, but their meaning has changed" (Bal 1997: 92). In Bush's *Address,* it is the repeated emphasis on the might of the United States at the end of several paragraphs in a row that brings out this aspect: "Our country is strong," "They cannot dent the steel of American resolve," and "No one will keep that light from shining." In addition, repetition solidifies meaning, which is brought about by specifying a broader claim over time. This is evident when Bush notes, "Our military is powerful, and it's prepared" and "Our financial institutions remain strong, the American economy will be open for business as well" thus specifically saying what the might consists of. He also says, "Terrorist attacks can shake the foundations of our biggest buildings, but they cannot touch the foundation of America. These acts shattered steel, but they cannot dent the steel of American resolve" (Bush 2001b).

Here, particular concepts are repeated in particular combinations on several levels. For one, we have the repetition of "foundations" once "of our biggest buildings" and then "of America." Although these are clearly two different types of foundations, they become symbolically connected in the narrative. Juxtaposing the "real" event of the literal shaken building foundations with the figurative untouchable foundations of America is a powerful reinscription of meaning. Similarly, the first mention of "steel" in the second sentence, in the context of images of the rubble of the WTC, refers to steel of the buildings demolished by the plane crashes, whereas "the steel of American resolve" is again symbolic. Placing them side by side in the manner of this statement works to redefine the events as a test (which has been passed). Finally, repetition is also evident in the placing of two sentences with an almost identical sentence structure next to each other, the effect being a mutual reinforcement of the views expressed as self-evident. Overall, the effect of the repetition is that Bush can reclaim the authority to construct meaning from the terrorists who, or so he says, "intended to frighten our nation into chaos and retreat." He then goes on to assert his own interpretation: "They have failed; our country is strong."

The *Address* also uses yet another form of repetition in the characterization of the actors. Bush begins by noting "the search is underway for those who are behind these evil acts [...] those responsible" and stressing that "we will make no distinction between the terrorists who committed these acts and those who harbor them." In the next paragraph, he contrasts this description of those terrorists with those on the other side by thanking members of Congress and world leaders who have condemned the attacks, offered condolences, and pledged support. He ends this repetition by saying, "America and our friends and allies join with all those who want peace and security in the world," thus further specifying, by implication, what characterizes the other side, that is, all that "we" are not. This sets the stage for a binary framing that is typical not only of security narratives but also of identity politics in broader terms. This piling up of data, in addition to repetition, has a function in the narrative. "The accumulation of characteristics causes odd facts to coalesce, complement each other, and then form a whole: the image of a character" (Bal 1997: 125). The construction of characters, achieved by providing actors with distinct traits, is one of the fundamental processes of narrative and is evident in the *Address* which, arguably, has the task of (re)affirming the "us"/United States after a terrorist attack. As Der Derian (1992: 81) outlines, "international terrorism simulates a legitimation crisis of the international order; conversely, counter-terrorism is a counter-simulation, an attempt to engender a new disciplinary order which can save the dominant legitimacy principle of international relations."[32]

The *Address*, in this reading, is part of a (security) narrative tradition that always also produces the subject it purports to serve.[33] Bush's *Address to the Nation* is an attempt to impose an authoritative narrative on the events of 9/11. This narrative frames the events broadly as an evil attack on innocent, freedom loving America for which those responsible will be sorry, not only because contrary to their expectations it can only make the United States stronger but also because all that is good is on the side of the war against terrorism.

In the recollection of experiences through narratives, a sequence of events is configured into a unified happening. A single event might be incorporated into different stories—as in the case of the events on September 11, 2001. The resulting narratives can change over time (cf. Andrews 2007; Brittain 2006); they are inevitably contradictory and multiple. What is more, they often are uncomfortable for the audience because of different preferences with regard to form, function, or ethics. One might think of a kaleidoscope, where lots of little pieces are constantly being reshuffled to form a new picture. However, any particular social, symbolic, economic, and political order has standards according to which narratives will be selected.

> Every society has its *régime* of truth, its 'general politics' of truth: that is, the types of discourse which it accepts and makes function as true; the mechanisms and instances which enable one to distinguish true and false statements, the means by which each is sanctioned; the techniques and procedures accorded value in the acquisition of truth; the status of those who are charged with saying what counts as true.
>
> (Foucault 1980: 131)

The traditional goal, and perceived outcome, of the narrative selection process has been the achievement of order, unity, and coherence in support of a particular modern social, symbolic, political order. To achieve this goal, some narratives are relegated to the margins and others silenced. Selected narratives, those that conform to and confirm the existing order because they can occupy a space within its confines, are re/circulated. It is a violent process of controlling and securitizing meaning because narratives arrest meaning. These processes rarely become apparent among everyday activities—they seem normal, and there is little resistance to them. However, every time "we reference an object in an available discourse, we reproduce it unreflectively" (Shapiro 1988: 19). In the modern imaginary, the re/production of meaning is depoliticized through its framing as a search for knowledge and truth. Politics is relegated to another place and time. However, every instance of selection is also a political moment. Every privileging of one narrative over another re/establishes "that very social order which sets out particular, historically specific accounts of what counts as politics and defines other areas as not politics" (Edkins 1999: 2). This is the political moment, the moment of decision, the act of constitution, the unfounded founding moment, as various thinkers have phrased it.[34] Narratives are inherently political; they always mark/mask a political moment, and they simultaneously investigate and invent an order. When the politics of creating a singular version of normality, based on a supposedly shared understanding, is not recognized, points of resistance inherent in it cannot be seized.

4 Security as narrative

> To be secure is to be safe is to be sure.
> (Constantinou 2000: 288)

> The main purpose is to render problematic what is taken for granted, namely that
> security practices order social life in a particular way.
> (Huysmans 1998: 233)

Narrative, if only temporarily, arrests meaning. The fixing of meaning by security narratives is of particular interest for International Relations (IR), primarily because it tells us much about the conflict that can occur at the sites of contesting identity claims (cf. Stern 2005). If one scrutinizes the meaning of any concept, one cannot fail to note that it is only within a certain context or tradition that meaning can be produced. Examining the social construction of patriarchy, Nancy Hirschmann notes how rules and behaviors, once constructed, take on a life of their own—constituting a (new) reality. "These rules become constitutive not only of what women are allowed to *do*, but to *be* as well: how women are able to think and conceive of themselves, what they can and should desire, what their preferences are" (1996: 57). Similarly, security narratives limit how we can think security, whose security matters, and how it might be achieved.

What is more, by focusing on the needs of (nation) states, traditional security narratives make it almost impossible to think differently of security, such as from the perspective of variously located women, where multiple allegiances lead to intersecting and mutually reinforcing insecurities (cf. Stern 2005). The meaning of security remains vague nonetheless—an ambiguity that is particularly useful for governments invoking security, because it allows them to frame any issue or event in terms of security and to generate extraordinary measures in response (cf. Buzan *et al.* 1998). Thus, debates about security are fundamentally political. Acknowledging the politics of security can provide an opening to debate and to contest security meanings that are currently assigned within a particular narrative framework.

Entering into the processes of framing security in narrative allows for a fundamentally different approach to issues of security. This approach pays attention to how subjects and meanings are constructed through security narratives and how these processes are gendered. Narratives are profoundly influential because they shape our understanding of the world, that is, the framing of events in narrative is fundamental to developing a response to them. Narrative theory, transgressing the practice/theory distinction of modern science, investigates how acts and events are framed in the telling of narratives and are thus constructed through and by them. Adopting such an approach for security studies means that one "interprets security practices by means of interpreting the meaning of security, that is, the signifying and thus ordering work of security practices" (Huysmans 1998: 233). Dominant approaches to security in IR tend to leave out critical questions, instead assuming a fairly closed narrative structure consisting of four main elements: threats locating danger, referents to be secured, agents to provide security, and means to contain danger. They are also characterized by the belief that by identifying and coordinating these elements, a comprehensive agenda can be developed to deal with security challenges. What is more, once the elements of security are known, the assumption being that we can, indeed, know them, traditional security narratives fix their meaning. Security narratives that do not conform to this structure, and might challenge these epistemological assumptions, are not recognized as security talk (cf. Huysmans 1998, 2006). Besides questioning the structure of this narrative framework, some of the normative claims implicit or explicit in much of the security studies literature need attention; most importantly, the assumption that security is something to strive for (cf. Wæver 1995a).

Narrating cold war security

Within security studies, the production of meanings cannot be addressed as long as certain a priori assumptions remain in place. Most of these hail from the early days of postwar security studies and were more fully articulated during the Cold War (cf. Klein 1994). The development of a national security structure in the United States is of particular importance because of the dominance of US strategic style in IR. Once an isolationist country, in the postwar period "the United States recognized that its vast economic resources, conventional military capabilities, and nuclear monopoly could be used to inscribe a new kind of transnational order upon Europe and Asia" (Luke 1991: 316). As the United States strove to develop its international profile, it needed to articulate its global vision. This is evident in the 1950 US National Security Council document number 68 (NSC-68), which proposes that the aim of postwar US foreign policy should be "to assure the integrity and vitality of our free society, which is founded upon the dignity and the worth of the individual" (quoted in Campbell 1998b: 23). Indeed, in his analysis of numerous foreign policy documents, David Campbell finds these texts

> are replete with statements about the fulfillment of the republic, the fundamental purpose of the nation, God-given rights, moral codes, the principles

of European civilization, the fear of cultural and spiritual loss, and the responsibilities and duties thrust upon the gleaming example of America.

(1998: 31)

These texts articulate what is worth securing—and security turns out to be "a derivative value, being meaningful only insofar as it promotes or maintains other values which have been or are being realized and are thought worth securing" (Brodie, quoted in Baldwin 1995: 122).

Traditional security narratives emerge in a world dominated by two superpowers divided into "us" and "them," where dissent is seen as unpatriotic and where multiplicity is suppressed until no grey remains in between. In this context, narratives identify the Soviet Union as posing the major threat to "the security, free institutions, and fundamental values of the United States" (Campbell 1998: 29). The Soviet Union is presented as a radical, dangerous other, which seeks to impose its authority on the rest of the world—a threat not only to the United States but also to civilization in general. This assessment became the justification for a security narrative that still resonates in security studies today. Accordingly, "the Western military build-up was an inevitable response to the Soviet occupation of Eastern Europe in the early 1940s and the communist takeovers in the later 1940s" (Kaldor 1991: 315).[1] The formation of the North Atlantic Treaty Organization (NATO) and its counterpart, the Warsaw pact, which provided a "fixed frame of international conflict and competition" (Luke 1991: 316), can be seen as a particular actualization of the traditional security narrative. This narrative consists of a shifting, yet enduring, combination of key elements (threats, referents, agents, and means) that, by linking events in a particular order, give meaning to security.

The identification of threats, rather than being a simple listing of dangers and insecurities, involves the active scripting of danger. In security studies, threats are generally described as being existential, and they encompass what is seen to threaten the survival of the referent; the implication is that this referent would cease to exist where the threat to be actualized. Although one might assume, and this would make sense in regard to a human referent, that survival refers to physical survival, in IR, it turns out to be the safeguarding of values associated with the referent (generally the state). As Wolfers formulates it, "security, in any objective sense, measures the absence of threats to acquired values, in a subjective sense, the absence of fear that such values will be attacked" (Wolfers 1962: 150).[2] However, the identification of values actually produces the very subjects it is said to describe. Jenny Edkins makes this point explicit when she writes,

> the referent objects of security are not the state, the economy, ethnic group of environment, but rather "state sovereignty," "economic wealth," "ethnic group identity," or "environmental sustainability." It is the latter that have to be securitized. Sovereignty, identity and so on represent what is worth preserving about the subjects themselves. There is no ethnic group

without identity, no state without sovereignty. These signifiers have a crucial part in the constitution of subjects they appear to merely describe.

(Edkins 2002a)[3]

Edkins' argument resonates with, and refines, Dillon's observation that security is probably the most important constitutive narrative of political order. He
notes, "Securing something requires its differentiation, classification and definition. It has, in short, to be identified" (1990: 114). This implies that security is
not only concerned with the values associated with a given subject but by naming those values as being in need of securing, and thus, by definition, existential
to the subject being secured, security narratives (re)produce the subjects' existence. Campbell (1998: 8) works with this conception in *Writing Security* where
he is concerned with "reorienting analysis from the concern with the intentional
acts of pregiven subjects to the problematic of subjectivity." In doing so, he links
security and subjectivity, which is of fundamental importance to feminist
challenges, at the heart of which is a gendered subject.

Threat identification, numerous scholars have noted, is an impulse born of fear
(cf. Constantinou 2000; Der Derian 1995; Huysmans 1998). Threat construction
is a way to manage that fear through externalization and containment. The fear in
this context is a double fear: a fear of death, as well as of not knowing, of uncertainty. "A safe life requires safe truths. The strange and the alien remain unexamined, the unknown becomes identified with evil, and evil provokes hostility—
recycling the desire for security" (Der Derian 1995: 34).[4] This point is of particular
interest for Feminist Security Studies (FSS) because the desire for mastery, which
underlies the quest to become all-knowing, is revealed to be typically male as well
as tied to an outdated epistemology (cf. Chapter 1). Feminists tend to recognize
safety as an illusion and place stress on strategies for dealing with vulnerability.
Gloria Anzaldúa (1999: 60) writes of *la facultad*, "an instant 'sensing,' a quick perception without conscious reasoning," which is latent in all of us, but is a skill
more likely to be possessed by "those pushed out of the tribe for being different
[. . .] those who do not feel psychologically or physically safe in the world." The
less privileged, the most affected by intersecting oppressions, develop *la facultad*, so
that they are better able to avoid the next blow. "It is a kind of survival tactic that
people, caught between the worlds, unknowingly cultivate" (ibid.: 61). However,
although this shift in perception allows us to sense more, "we lose something in
this mode of initiation, something is taken from us: our innocence, our unknow-
ing ways, our safe and easy ignorance" (ibid.).

Another aspect of the containment of fear is found within foreign policy,
which includes a range of practices that commute danger. They serve as "an
art of domesticating the meaning of man by constructing his problems, his dangers, his fears" (Ashley, quoted in Campbell 1998b: 62).[5] In the process, an
unspecific fear gets transformed into an identifiable danger. We "objectify death.
The abstract notion of death becomes concrete through identifying the objects
to be feared" (Huysmans 1998: 235). However, all threats are identified from
"our" perspective only. A security narrative, thus, usually begins by identifying

a threat to us, our means to counter it, as well as ourselves as referent and agent of security. Little attention is paid to "their" security, which might be threatened by the moves made to provide security for "us." However, "they" will likely respond with their own threat identification and mobilization, so that eventually a full-fledged security dilemma develops. This situation can be read as

> one of individuals seeking an impossible security from the most radical 'other' of life, the terror and death which, once generalized and national-ized, triggers a futile cycle of collective identities seeking security from alien others—who are seeking similarly impossible guarantees.
>
> (Der Derian 1995: 32–3)

Security and identity (subjectivity) are, in this narrative, tightly linked.

Not taking this dilemma seriously risks ignoring potentially crucial space for negotiations that lies somewhere in between and is often closed down through the identification of us as separate from them. For the state, Campbell (1998b: 68) writes, "identity can be understood as the outcome of exclusionary practices in which resistant elements to a secure identity on the 'inside' are linked through a discourse of 'danger' with threats identified and located on the outside." It is crucial to note that this choice is not arbitrary; the location of threats in the external, anarchic realm serves a particular function in security narratives. Most importantly, it provides internal cohesion and diverts attention away from possible misgivings about domestic politics. It also reinforces assumptions that locate "the good life" inside states, notwithstanding feminist (and other) analyses that point to the state as a source of insecurity for citizens and nonciti-zens alike (in the context of the "war on terror" see Rygiel 2006; Sharma 2006). Developing an understanding of how threats are identified and externalized—two processes that are inherently political—provides an opening for feminist challenges that are themselves, by definition, political.

Security practices are creative; rather than describing the world, they have a performative force, and they organize social relations. Security narratives are also constitutive of "us as subjects with discernable identities, possessing characteris-tics, interests, responsibilities, and histories" (Dillon 1990: 101). As Campbell (1998b) illustrates, narratives of US foreign policy constitute, produce, and maintain US political identity by focusing on particular dangers rather than others. Although, in principle, the options are unlimited, not all stories are acceptable here. Indeed, they are recognizable only if they are organized in a way that is similar enough to established security narratives. The option of multiple, coexisting meanings, none of which can be captured, is removed by the establishment of particular meanings in authorized narratives. These author-itative narratives conform to and confirm the economic, social, symbolic, and political order: "It is because the events described conduce to the establishment of social order or fail to do so that they find a place in the narrative attesting to their reality" (White 1980: 22).[6] This process is gendered in that "our very cat-egories of meaning become barriers [. . .] our epistemology itself is restraint because our ways of knowing and categories of knowledge themselves encode and derive from patriarchal constructions" (Hirschmann 1996: 57). Which narratives then become security narratives? How do these narratives function? Jef Huysmans (1998: 232) proposes "security is not just a signifier performing an ordering function. It also has a 'content' in the sense that the ordering it performs in a particular context is a specific kind of ordering." This ordering reflects the wider parameters of meaning within a particular order, including epistemological assumptions, political choices, and disciplinary confines.

In IR, sovereignty is a key organizing principle; it limits the way (international) politics are understood (cf. Walker 1990a, 1993, 1995, 1997). This also implies that the meanings and practices of security "are fixed primarily in relation to the military requirements of supposedly sovereign states" (Walker 1990a: 3). The state as the subject of security, although not often discussed, is implied in traditional security narratives that assume it is enough to identify the importance of the state in international affairs through observation. The resulting account of the state fails to recognize how historical processes have shaped states—primarily the pressures of war, but also economic forces and other factors. Steve Smith voices concern about the privileged position accorded to the state in security studies. He takes issue with Buzan's choice of the states as "the most convenient focal point" in the second edition of *People, States and Fear*, worrying "that he sees the state as ontologically prior to other candidates. As a result the state gets undertheorized and privileged" (Smith 1991: 334). More specifically, three aspects of Buzan's treatment of the state are irksome: the privileging of the state's external environment over domestic concerns, the assumption that strong states provide better security, and the account of the state itself is a historical and underdeveloped (Smith 1991).

The emergence of the modern state system is associated with the Peace of Westphalia in 1648, ending the Thirty Years War. Prior to this momentous event, "the post-roman myth of empire still played an important role," according to Eric Ringmar (1996: 10), "just as there was only one religious community governed by one church, there was, according to this mythology, only one political community governed by one ruler." The Thirty Years War shattered this mythology, and a subsequent reimagination of political community lead to the institution of the state as the only legitimate political entity; "states were governed by rulers who declared themselves 'sovereign', acknowledging no rival authorities above them and none below" (ibid.). This development made possible the world that IR takes for granted. The realist version of IR, which views modern states as the result of inevitable progression out of the medieval world, takes these developments as given and does not pay attention to the indeterminacy of each founding moment. What is more, mainstream IR's conception of politics, which focuses on supposedly rational actors and relies on a narrow, positivist conception of science, specifically excludes any appeal to identities besides the sovereign state.[7] According to Michael Williams (1998a), this was an attempt to avoid a repeat of conflict over religious identity claims that lead to the devastation of the Thirty Years War.

However, these narrow conceptions might be problematic for two reasons. For one, the idea that interests alone guide actions is an oversimplification and impoverishes the explanatory power of theories based on it. "It is only *as-some-one* that we can want *some-thing*, and it is only once we know who we *are* that we can know what we *want*," writes Ringmar (1996: 13), "it follows that to the extent that questions regarding identities remain unsettled, rationalist, inter-est-driven, explanations will fail." Furthermore, if it were, indeed, the question of identity that was at stake during the Thirty Years War, this would imply that the Peace of Westphalia was designed specifically to deal with the problem of identity. Consequently, it is necessary to recognize that at the root of the mod-ern state system lays the question of "who we are." Instead of being a natural progression, political communities emerge in response to specific historical cir-cumstances and, as these circumstances change, so should our conception of political community. However, "in the modern world, states have managed to more or less monopolize our understanding of what political life is and where it occurs" (Walker 1990a: 5–6), making it hard, some argue impossible, to con-ceive of other forms of identity.

States, as the dominant framing of political community, have fundamentally shaped the way we think about politics. Consequently, it is important to emphasize that in IR, the state is a specific solution to the tension between par-ticularity and universality or fragmentation and centralization. This tension is resolved through sovereignty; sovereignty specifies the relationship by prioritiz-ing citizenship and instituting the principle of spatial exclusion (Walker 1990a). "Authentic politics" are now located inside states, whereas the external realm is that of mere relationships of anarchy. Furthermore, Maria Stern (2001: 25) notes, "faith in a sovereign [masculine] subject delimits the possible solutions to the inevitable ambiguity and a sense of uncertainty that the contingency of life entails." Although the state initially emerged out of an emancipatory impulse, replacing the hierarchical subordination associated with empire and a cosmology centered on God, its structure requires "some apparatus of mea-surement, a specification of the norm, a means of identifying the exception [and] a detailed economy of punishment" (Dillon 1990: 107). Drawing on Carl Schmitt, Michael Dillon contends "that sovereignty is ultimately con-cerned to specify in each and every circumstance, who the enemy is" (ibid.). In other words, emphasis is placed on the identification of the exception as in security narratives. The narrative clarifies "who and what are within, as well as who and what are outwith" (ibid.). It is such that the claims of people, as part of humanity, are subordinated to the claims of citizens of particular states.[8] Because "the state is a political category in a way that the world, or the globe, or the planet, or humanity is not," notes Rob Walker (1990a: 5), "the security of states is something we can comprehend in political terms in a way that, at the moment, world security cannot be comprehended."

To imagine alternative understandings of security, it is, therefore, also neces-sary to displace the centrality of sovereign states. This move might produce spaces where a plethora of (security) narratives can exist alongside each other and where their intersections and contradictions are seen as enriching, rather than as a problem to be transcended. The difficulty lies in the desire for certainty—"for the inscription of [. . .] society to appear unproblematic, it is not possible for it to be understood as having the status of one interpretation among many" (Campbell 1998b: 63). Not only does contingency fail to satisfy, its exposure is also dangerous for the state that finds itself in the paradoxical situation of not possessing prediscursive, stable identities: "With no ontological status apart from the many practices that constitute their reality, states are (and have to be) always in the process of becoming" (ibid.: 12). However, although the exposure of the performative nature of statehood challenges current practices of governmentality, it also makes it possible to debate the political nature of representations and their effects. Such has been the case with regard to the construction of gender. Instead of dissolving distinctions between women and men, it has lead to a questioning of rigid categorizations and has opened up possibilities of an active (re)scripting of identities. Although this process has not been without conflicts and challenges, it is less marginalizing and violent, more able to accommodate difference without drawing and policing boundaries. A similarly conflictual, but not violent, process could be envisaged with regard to the state. To concede the state's construction in discourse is only problematic if one believes that a foundation outside discourse is possible. Indeed, to expose the necessarily performative nature of statehood is politically advantageous because it makes certain types of attacks on its legitimacy (such as terrorism) less viable, while at the same time providing avenues to address grievances.

However, thus far in IR, "the state is consistently theorized as a subject and not as a domain of practices" (Dillon 1990: 113). The activities of governments are seen as a consequence of states' essential character, and it is assumed that states' roles in international affairs can be specified. Although the state is crucial to understand the configuration of security studies, however, it "simply vanishes somewhere between the moment where we posited it as necessary and the moment when we started investigating it" (Ringmar 1996: 58). Then again, security studies do not even face this dilemma because they do not theorize the state and simply treat it as ontologically stable and unproblematically identifiable. What is more, states are seen to hold the legitimate, if contested, monopoly of violence. States employ much resources and violence—they deploy militaries, dispatch diplomats, and govern their citizens—to hold on to both this monopoly and their claim to legitimacy. As such, in traditional security narratives, states are simply assumed to be both referent and agent. Epistemological, ontological, and political questions are rarely engaged, leaving the entire subfield of strategic studies to preoccupy itself with identifying threats and with devising means to maintain the state's position (cf. Der Derian 1995). This is confirmed by David Bobrow (2001) who identifies the narrow confines of US strategic style as follows: a tabulation of continuing and emerging threats; the identification of types of capabilities and initiatives valuable for reducing, countering, or preventing the former; an assessment of current and expected US capabilities and initiatives; and, finally, recommendations for adjustments.

The idea that the most devastating violence is of a military kind and, thus, requires a military response seems to be confirmed by history and be so obvious that it is rarely challenged or elaborated on. However, the tendency of states to seek security by relying on military means cannot be translated into a law, as traditional security narratives tend to, neglecting all other means. As Michael Shapiro (1992: 456) argues, these means "are not randomly deployed. They function as an adjunct to some already determined, often historically conceived, 'threats.'" Not all states rely on military means at all times, and most states rely on other means of promoting their security most of the time. Importantly, states tend to cooperate on a wide variety of issues, generally seeing military means as a last resort. In some cases, such as that of the European Union, states have formalized cooperation on a variety of issues. In addition, states might also choose policies such as nonalignment or neutrality to avoid military confrontation. Wolfers (1962: 156) proposes that the options are almost endless: "The choice in each instance will depend on a multitude of variables, including ideological and moral convictions, expectations concerning the psychological and political developments in the camp of the opponent, and inclinations of individual policy makers." What is more, during the postwar period, when security studies emerged as a subfield of IR, the threat facing the United States was not considered to be primarily military. George Kennan, in his assessment of the situation in 1946, was convinced that "it is not Russian military power that is threatening us; it is Russian political power" (quoted in Campbell 1998b: 25–6). Although there was some concern that the Soviet Union might build up a sufficient military capability to attack the West, in 1947, the Central Intelligence Agency (CIA) argued "that the Soviets would not seek to militarily conquer Western Europe, preferring instead 'to gain hegemony by political and economic means'" (ibid.: 26). The greatest danger, therefore, was seen to be that of an economic collapse, which would provide fertile ground for an ideological invasion—at least until the Soviet Union tested its first nuclear weapon in 1949.[9]

"If it is not entirely a military threat, I doubt that it can be effectively met by military means," Kennan cautioned (quoted in Campbell 1998b: 26). The limits of applying military means in almost any conflict situation are rarely discussed, even though slogans such as "winning hearts and minds" abound, especially in situations that are clearly marked as political (e.g., terrorism). Again, it was historical events that led to the privileging of military means. First, there was the loss of the US nuclear monopoly in the late 1940s, which led to a shift in the field from a concern with domestic and nonmilitary threats to the threat of global nuclear war. Given the superpower rivalry between the Soviet Union and the United States, the central question became: "How could states use weapons of mass-destruction as an instrument of policy, given the risk of nuclear exchange?" (Walt, quoted in Baldwin 1995). Second, following Carl von Clausewitz's famous dictum that war is "a continuation of politics by other means," governments have long regarded the military as an instrument of policy. This perception still lingers, long after the symbolic move from ministries of war to ministries of defense, and the introduction of a language of security to replace that of conquest (cf. Klein 1994). "As distance, oceans and borders became less of a protective barrier to alien identities, and a new international economy required penetration into other worlds, *national interest* became too weak a semantic guide," writes Der Derian (1995: 42), "we found a stronger one in *national security*."[10]

As a consequence, discursively the military was no longer associated straightforwardly with being an instrument of policy in expansive terms but rather was seen to provide the material basis for defensive activities making a continued focus on the military more acceptable to citizens in liberal democracies.[11] However, this is problematic. It not only leaves the important (and much broader) topic of security to those concerned mainly with military strategy, but it also entails a paradox: the military is seen as being concerned with security in terms of defense, yet continues to be theorized in terms of the inherently more aggressive "instrument of policy" by which to pursue the "national interest." Finally, the privileging of military means is also connected to attempts at establishing a separate field of security studies. In the attempt to develop security studies as a distinct field of inquiry, the parameters of the field were defined in an increasingly narrow fashion. This trend was further exacerbated by the focus on the requirements of policy makers leading to specialization in particular areas (mostly on the superpower rivalry). It follows that the field has been first and foremost concerned with developing "expertise about the effects of the instruments of force on international relations" (Buzan 1987: 8).

This policy-driven framing of the field, largely in terms of military strategy, leaves little room to generalists who would explore other aspects of security. Instead, the focus on one set of means leads scholars to ignore the goal of the entire enterprise—security—and to define "the field entirely in terms of means, that is, 'the study of the threat, use, and control of military force'" (Baldwin 1995: 129, quoting Walt). A wealth of relevant concepts, notes Buzan (1987: 8), "including power, security, war, peace, alliance, terrorism and crisis" are no longer considered relevant.[12] This narrow focus limits traditional security narratives even on their own terms: "Policymakers rarely define a security problem as, we have these weapons; now what can we do with them? Rather, they ask, we have this problem; what means are available for coping with it?" (Baldwin 1995: 138). When this question is posed to traditional security scholars, the tendency is to focus on military means—even more so when taking into account the pervasiveness of the military-industrial complex that shapes much scholarship and policy.

Prior to the dominance of strategic studies, nonmilitary and military tools of statecraft were included in the security agenda. Even when the traditional security narrative (as identified here) evolved to become the prevailing narrative, not everyone agreed with the focus on military strategy. It is possible to conceive of the development of the field of peace research in the 1950s as an articulation of disagreement on the effects of nuclear weapons on the strategic environment.

These critics maintained that due to the vulnerability introduced by these weapons, their sheer destructive capability, as well as the danger of fatal escalation, it was no longer plausible to conceptualize them as instruments of policy (cf. Wallensteen 2001). Opposition to military means also draws "on the contention that it would help little to make national core values secure, if in the process the liberties and the social welfare of the people had been sacrificed" (Wolfers 1962: 157).[13] This question of the value of survival is at the heart of feminist revisions of security. Feminists, for example, point to the everyday politics of nuclear weapons and note the economic and social cost of maintaining nuclear readiness. Consequently, they see "the political and intellectual acceptance of nuclear weapons' deployment as something to be explained" (Cohn and Ruddick 2003: 10).

Failing narration

Traditional security narratives were crucial to the establishment and maintenance of the "imaginary war" (Kaldor 1991) that was the Cold War. "We behaved as though there were a war between East and West, acted out through war games, exercises, military plans, hostile rhetoric, espionage, and counterespionage," wrote Mary Kaldor (1991: 321). Although the traditional security narrative emerged in response to postwar challenges faced by the United States, the Cold War was a joint venture of the superpowers: just as the establishment of NATO was seen as a necessary response to the perceived Soviet threat, so the Soviet military buildup and the creation of the Warsaw pact were seen as a response to the perceived US threat. Their interpretations of security parallel each other more generally, including "the sense of endangerment ascribed to all the activities of the other, the fear of internal challenge and subversion, the tendency to militarize all responses, and the willingness to draw the line of superiority/inferiority between us and them" (Campbell 1998b: 33). Importantly, although it might have been an imaginary war, the Cold War "has involved real resources—workers, soldiers, armaments, money. And it has had a profound influence on the way we organize society in both East and West" (Kaldor 1991: 321). The symmetry of this imaginary war, which is instigated and mirrored by traditional security narratives, legitimizes both superpowers. On this reading, "the cold war might be understood in terms of the need to discipline the ambiguities of global life in ways that help to secure always fragile identities" (Campbell 1998b: 16).

The developments that shaped security studies throughout the Cold War continue to resonate in the field. Most importantly, they concern the primacy of military means and the idea that "the state does indeed provide satisfactory—sometimes merely adequate, sometimes laudable, sometimes simply natural and uncontestable—answers to the most fundamental questions about the character and location of political life" (Walker 1997: 62). The implosion of the Soviet Union, which marked the end of the Cold War, exploded the neat confines of threat construction in traditional security narratives. The lack of an identifiable threat produced a crisis for sovereignty. What is more, "states are not only damaged because they lose a self-defining threat but also because they seem to lose credibility as representatives of the principle of determinacy itself" (Huysmans 1998b: 240). The fear of disorder has a long tradition; by 1950, NSC-68 had found that "the absence of order is becoming less and less tolerable" (Campbell 1998: 24). More recently, the fear of not knowing, where uncertainty itself becomes a primary threat, has been taken to justify preemptive war. As US Secretary of Defense, Donald Rumsfeld, contextualized it in the "war on terror":

> Reports that say that something hasn't happened are always interesting to me, because as we know, there are known knowns; there are things we know we know. We also know there are known unknowns; that is to say we know there are some things we do not know. But there are also unknown unknowns—the ones we don't know we don't know. And if one looks throughout the history of our country and other free countries, it is the latter category that tend to be the difficult ones.
>
> (Rumsfeld and Myers 2002)[14]

What is feared most in traditional security narratives, and emerges in moments of change such as the end of the Cold War, is chaos and uncertainty.[15] This condition is exacerbated by the challenges of new approaches to security: some of these emanated from the third world, which refused to align itself with either the first or the second world and rejected the colonizer's narrative, others from the heart of Europe.[16] In the shadows of the superpower rivalry and on a potential battlefield for limited nuclear war, European peace researchers developed alternative conceptions of security that permeated the work of traditionally trained security scholars as well (cf. Booth 1979, 1991a; Buzan 1983).[17] The work of peace researchers in the neutral countries of the North of Europe, in particular, influenced Mikhail Gorbachev's "New Thinking" in foreign policy and possibly contributed directly to the changes in the Soviet Union's self-image that lead to an end of the Cold War (cf. Patomäki 2001: 728–9).[18] However, in security studies, the attempts by various scholars to develop new meanings for security (whether by broadening, deepening, or opening security) are themselves seen as threatening. When safety is synchronized with certainty, "undermining security knowledge by delegitimizing it [. . .] directly undermines the possibility of creating a safer world" (Huysmans 1998: 246; cf. Constantinou 2000).[19]

Traditional security studies, with its narrowly construed structure, "cannot recognize an ethico-political project which introduces ambivalence (or strangehood) into the agenda as a chance rather than as the ultimate danger" (Huysmans 1998: 247).[20] To salvage the field's narrow conception of security and to hold on to its preoccupation with military means, security scholars will attempt to counter the crisis by asserting certainty. To produce "cumulative knowledge about the role of military force," according to Stephen Walt (1991: 222), the field "must follow the standard cannons of scientific research." Traditional security studies' reliance on modern scientific rationality, which entails the possibility of identifying and containing threats, is at the basis of the claim that the field has "gradually evolved into an objective, scientific discipline in which the 'laws' governing the realm of security are discovered or, at least, the correct method for their discovery has been identified" (Krause and Williams 1996: 231). That these modern scientific standards are contested (cf. Chapter 2) does not prevent Walt from proclaiming that traditional (neorealist) approaches are the only legitimate heir. Privileging a particular approach as the only possible road to scientific progress, "creates an explicit hierarchy [which] allows conventional security studies to set itself up as the judge of alternative claims" (ibid. 1997b: 37). However, the neorealist claim to the throne of security studies and the preeminence of traditional security narratives is by no means self-evident. If Walt's "idea of security studies were logically and systematically applied," Edward A. Kolodziej (1992: 422) comments, "important security problems, even on neo-realist exclusionary grounds, could not be reached, and, if addressed, then only indirectly and obliquely as tributaries of international conflict and war."

Rather than seeing disorder and uncertainty as dangerous, as traditional security narratives tend to do, we might consider that "the desire to order itself has become a source of danger in our time" (Campbell 1998b: 18). Drawing on poststructuralist insights concerning the fundamental undecidability and indetermination of our existence, some critical approaches to security pose a challenge to the very possibility of ordering—"they articulate ambivalence and therefore challenge the (modern) ordering activity which relies on reducing ambiguity and uncertainty by categorizing elements" (Huysmans 1998: 241). The end of the Cold War and the ensuing attempts to reshape the international order reveal the failure of supposedly coherent narration as presented in traditional security narratives. Trying to limit changes in the discipline by sticking to the traditional security narrative is an attempt to mask this narrative failure. By simply shifting attention to a new source of threats—rogue states, terrorists, and more—while keeping the same analytical framework, the previous narrative failure remains unacknowledged, or sidelined as a special case, and a semblance of narrative coherence is maintained. However, the continuous framing of security in terms of the traditional security narrative ignores the important relationship between identity and security that "goes beyond the lack of a fixed enemy or the question of a new world order" (ibid.: 244). For Jef Huysmans, "it also seems to involve a deeper, wider, more general problem of ontological (in)security" (ibid.).

The failure of traditional security studies (and IR as a whole) to predict or to even adequately respond to the dissolution of the Soviet Union raises the question "should strategic studies survive?" (Betts 1997). As the imagined Cold War order broke down, some scholars began to rethink security more broadly. These scholars were often inspired by ideas emerging from other fields, such as peace research, when they began to broaden and deepen the reach of security. Because the scope of these critical approaches varies greatly, it can be as easy to be too euphoric about their achievements as it is difficult to pin down their problems.[21]

Their diverse origins and the different trajectories they have taken since their emergence in the 1980s and 1990s have lead some to attempt delineating boundaries, focusing only on the approaches that are "resolutely modernist" (Krause 1998: 299) or making reference to Frankfurt School critical theory as a marker of critical security studies (CSS).[22] Buzan and Wæver, collaborating as part of the "Copenhagen School," try to place themselves outside CSS by stressing their aim of simply providing a more accurate *Framework for Analysis* (Buzan *et al*. 1998: 34–5). This is unfortunate because their work on securitiza-tion provides important insights for attempts at broadening, deepening, and, importantly, opening the agenda (especially Wæver 1995b).

Many critical security narratives exchange elements of the tale only, leaving the structure of traditional narratives largely intact. This structure, which speci-fies that security is both achievable and favorable, limits not only the issues and events that can be considered relevant, but it also shapes the conceivable response to the identified security situation. The securitization approach of the Copenhagen School, developed initially by Ole Wæver (1995a, 1995b) and then refined and expanded in collaboration with Barry Buzan and Jaap de Wilde (1998), as well as others, offers some key insights here.[23] For Wæver (1995b: 50), "the label 'security' has become an indicator of a specific problem-atique, a specific field of practice." Applying speech act theory to this field of practice, Wæver coins the terms securitization and desecuritization. Securitiza-tion refers to the processes involved in producing a situation in which a particular event becomes framed in terms of security by the utterance of a speech act. Desecuritization, on the other hand, signifies the attempt to move an issue out of the realm of emergency back into the realm of "normal politics."[24] This conception of security as practice opens up space for debate, also because it alerts us to the contextual nature of security meanings. Once we realize that "it is in this practice that the issue becomes a security issue" (Buzan *et al*. 1998: 24), we can begin to debate the politics of securitization.

According to Wæver *et al*., issues are presented as security concerns in the international in the following manner: security is evoked whenever an issue is presented as an existential threat to a specific referent object (whether the threat is real or perceived is irrelevant); by declaring and emergency, the issue is removed from the political agenda into the realm of security; if, and only when, this move is accepted by the audience, the securitizing move has been suc-cessful (Buzan *et al*. 1998; Wæver 1995b). Concerned with the way in which appeals to security work—"asking what is particular to security, in contrast to non–security, modes of dealing with particular issues" (Wæver 1995b: 57)—the authors observe that any appeal to security needs to follow "the security form," that is, security agents need "to construct a plot that includes an existential threat, point of no return, and a possible way out" (Buzan *et al*. 1998: 32). This specifies a further component of traditional security narratives: a securitizing move is made when a securitizing agent presents an issue as a threat to move it out of the realm of politicization and into the realm of securitization, where extreme measures can be taken without requiring further justification (ibid.: 25). Crucially, the move requires that the security agent is seen as legitimate and authorized to speak security, that is, to frame an issue or event as a security situation. Uttering "security," Wæver (1995b: 54) notes, "the state can claim a special right [...] power holders can try to use the instrument of securitization of an issue to gain control over it." This description of how security gets narrated, and by whom, provides important insight into workings of power. Traditional security narratives, which are the subject of Wæver's analysis, are deeply conservative and work to maintain the status quo. Only those within the system already, the security experts, are able to successfully "speak security" (cf. Huysmans 2006). What is more, in "a situation where the subject of security has no, or limited possibility of speaking its security problem" (Hansen 2000: 294), the securitizing move can only fail (cf. Stern 2005).[25] The Copenhagen School reliance on the ability to speak and be heard recalls modern assumptions about political subjectivity and the workings of the (liberal) political (sphere). This poses a problem for feminists and other critical scholars trying to point to security narratives that do not match the established form and are not articulated by authorized security experts.

There is significant variance among the critical approaches to security, but it is notable that most scholars, contrary to their expressed political commitment to emancipation and challenging the status quo (instead of leaving power to work as is), are actually supporting a particular order by using the same narrative framework as those they seek to challenge (cf. McCormack 2009). Keeping many existing assumptions in place, these scholars impose the narrow confines of traditional security narratives onto more areas of life. Claiming that the military agenda of security studies (or more precisely strategic studies) is too narrow, these scholars propose the addition of new, nonmilitary threats. They also argue that these emerging threats require new, nonmilitary means. This broadening of the threat agenda is not a post–Cold War phenomenon but emanates from concerns in peace research, alternative defense thinking, or Third World security studies (e.g., see Bilgin *et al.* 1998). The dissatisfaction with the narrow conception of security, Buzan *et al.* (1998) note, "was stimulated first by the rise in economic and environmental agendas in international relations during the 1970s and 1980s and later by the rise of concerns with identity issues and transnational crime during the 1990s." However, adding new threats cannot alone change traditional security narratives.[26] If the inclusion of new threats takes place in line with the existing parameters, where a threat is profiled and then subject to control, the narrative frame remains unchallenged. To address environmental degradation in terms of traditional security narratives, where danger is located externally and contained by defensive measures, for example, is likely counterproductive (cf. Deudney 1990).

Within CSS, new threats are generally included along with a call for new means, often nonmilitary in kind, to address them properly as well as with a rethinking of the referent for security. Although there is overall agreement that these means require a common effort of some kind (identifiable in calls for collective, common, or cooperative security arrangements) and a move away from zero–sum thinking about security, how precisely this differs from the narrow focus on military means is underelaborated. Notable exceptions include Wæver's idea of "desecuritization: the shifting of issues out of emergency mode and into the normal bargaining processes of the political sphere" (Buzan and Herring 1998: 4; cf. Wæver 1995b) as well as the approach favored by the Aberystwyth School, which aims for emancipation as theorized by the Frankfurt School (cf. Booth 1991b; Wyn Jones 1995, 2005).[27] Arguably, focusing on emancipation simply defers the debate about meanings of security to yet another tale to be told (cf. Batscheider 1993).

Although the state has been the main subject of traditional security narratives, and is still accorded special importance in security studies, most critical approaches aim to at least partly move beyond the state as the referent of security. They argue for deepening of the agenda by including, on one hand, referents on the so-called system level, such as the planet, the environment, or humanity and, on the other, referents below the state level such as collectivities or individuals. Interestingly, although within peace research the former have been taken fairly seriously, within security studies it is the latter (more traditional categories of modern political thought) that dominate. Thus, although the inclusion of other referents might seem to be a major reorientation of the narrative of security, it needs to be regarded with caution because the *how* (the framing on text and story levels), and not only the *what* (the content of a fabula), make up the narrative (cf. Chapter 3). In particular, my disagreement concerns the assumption that one could straightforwardly name the referent of security. Naming or identifying the referent constitutes the subject within the confines of a particular frame. What is more, the question "Whose security?" serves a similar function as "Where are the women?" for feminist IR. Although each question offers a possible inroad for (feminist) contestations, they remain limited when the social, symbolic, economic, and political order within which they emerge remains intact, that is, the order within which "woman" or "security" get articulated restricts possible meanings—and thus possible reformulations—for each term. The idea that deepening security studies to include referents besides the state would be enough to address gender bias needs to be carefully examined. Even though a deepening makes it possible to talk of women as referents, and thus to expand meanings of security somewhat, the overall structure of the security narrative remains intact and limits how women's security can be perceived.

Although a security agent is implied in all security narratives, who it is, is usually not explicitly pointed to. In traditional security narratives, it is customarily assumed that states will be the main security agent, simply because they seem to be in the best position to provide security both in terms of military action (as they are assumed to have the legitimate monopoly of violence) and in terms of collective action on the international level whose main forums remain dominated by presumably sovereign states. In addition, most critical approaches to a greater or lesser degree support a second strategy, the "civil society strategy" (cf. Ignatieff 1995; Kaldor 2007). Bilgin *et al.* (1998: 154) note that "the activities of progressive social movements strengthen the sense of global responsibility which in turn contributes to the growth and spread of a new form of political community—'global civil society.'" This focus on civil society needs to be assessed carefully because it carries with it the hope of transforming international order through a triumph of ethics over power (cf. Chandler 2008). Emma Rothschild (1995: 79–80) cautions that "the elective institutions of civil society, [based on voluntariness,] are not enough, in any liberal theory, to ensure the security of individuals." The stark inequality of voluntariness between the agent and referent of security undermines the liberal commitment to equality—it is "as far as one can be from the self-sufficiency of the individual will that is at the heart [thereof]" (ibid.: 81).

Notably, the changes proposed by much critical security scholarship are largely additive rather than subversive. Proposals that aim at broadening and deepening security studies tinker with the content of security narratives without opening the agenda to address processes of meaning construction. Not taking the framing of security seriously, they are unable to alter the structure of security narratives fundamentally. CSS narratives that avoid an opening, therefore, are adaptations of the traditional security narrative only. They remain caught in a narrative tradition within which the meaning of security is already bound, albeit in varying degrees. Without disturbing foundational narratives of the discipline rooted in modernity, it will be impossible to open security studies for feminist voices to be heard. It is simply not enough to deepen and broaden security narratives by adding new variables and referents. Developing better security narratives requires an opening. It involves "questioning the history of the concept and practice of security in IR theory as well as in the world of policy," writes Stern (2001: 26), because anything less "risks repeating the logic of (realist) nation-state security—a logic which has led to much violence and harm."

Opening human security[28]

In the mid-1990s, human security was introduced to the debate by the 1994 *Human Development Report* of the United Nations Development Program (UNDP) as well as through its adoption as a guide for foreign policy by Canada and other middle powers (MacLean *et al.* 2006; cf. McRae and Hubert 2001; Suhrke 1999).[29] Security scholars, preoccupied with the narrative failures of traditional security studies post-Cold War, slowly began to consider the merits of human security (cf. Burgess 2004; Owen 2004). The tenor of their initial assessment mirrored the state of debates within security studies; scholars either embraced the concept on normative grounds because it matched their preexisting agenda or could be used to promote it (e.g., Tadjbakhsh and Chenoy 2007; Thomas and Wilkin 1999), or they rejected it on analytical grounds, finding its formulation too broad and ambiguous, lacking the rigor necessary to function as a guide to scholars (e.g., Buzan 2004; King and Murray 2001–2; Paris 2001, 2004).

Human security, it seems, was chosen to present a new agenda, combining security, development, and human rights, because "'no other concept in international relations packs the metaphysical punch, nor commands the disciplinary power of 'security'" (Der Derian 1995: 24–5). The strategy has worked well because "human security is the dominant framework for international regulation today" (Chandler 2008: 465). However, what are the political consequences of reconceptualizing what was previously outside the scope of security in terms of human security? What makes human security so appealing that both grassroots activists and state-based policy elites have embraced it? What does the signifier "human" add to the security narrative? Can human security create an opening in the agenda and challenge the way we think security, or is it just the latest installment in a series of reformulations that leave the basic traditional security narrative intact?

When the 1994 *Human Development Report* introduced human security to a larger audience, it specifically called for a "profound transition in thinking—from nuclear security to human security" (UNDP 1994: 22). Mabuq ul Haq, lead author of the report, went on to note that this implies both a broadening to include new issues beyond the formerly narrow interpretation of military security as well as a deepening from a focus on nation-states to people. Making specific reference to the end of the Cold War, the report wanted to reinvigorate "the legitimate concerns of ordinary people [for whom] *a feeling of insecurity* arises more from the worries about daily life than from the dread of a cataclysmic world event" (ibid.; italics added). This initial impetus for rethinking security leaves room also for feminist reformulations that are concerned precisely with ordinary people and everyday life as it impacts, and is impacted by, security thinking. What is more, the focus on feeling secure offers opportunities for an opening. On closer reading, however, this radical potential is not realized. Indeed, as human security gets more codified over time, it is notable that it is not only caught in a traditional liberal conception of the individual, but that it quite closely resembles the traditional security narrative.

The 1994 UNDP report lists seven distinct categories of security under which the admittedly long list of threats to human security can be bundled: economic security, food security, health security, environmental security, personal security, community security, and political security (UNDP 1994: 24–5). The 2003 *Human Security Now* report by the Commission on Human Security (CHS), which, together with the 1994 report, provides "perhaps the most thorough, authoritative and up-to-date statements on the concept" (MacFarlane and Khong 2006: 227), does not explicitly reference these categories but maintains an equally broad scope listing environmental pollution, infectious disease, transnational terrorism, and long-term conditions of oppression and deprivation alongside one another (CHS 2003: 6). What is more, CHS aims "to protect the core of all human lives in ways that enhance human freedoms and human fulfillment [by] protecting people from critical (severe) and pervasive (widespread) threats and situations" (ibid.: 4; cf. Owen 2004). Both reports, as well as much of the literature on human security elsewhere, argue for a shift in referent from "an exclusive stress on territorial security to a much greater stress on people's security" (UNDP 1994: 24). Crucially, although CHS supports this move, it goes to great lengths to stress that human security complements state security—as Frene Ginwala puts it "human security does not replace state security with the security of people. It sees the two as mutually dependent" (CHS 2003: 3). Mark Duffield (2007) cautions that this move, along with the focus on managing ineffective states implied in much of the literature, places the state (back) in the center of security and development efforts. Human security, then, is not so much a subversive approach as it is reformative, working for incremental change within the system (cf. Nuruzzaman 2006).

In the attempt to satisfy everyone, conflicts between what human security should mean and what it can mean in the context of nation state interaction arise (cf. Stoett 2000). This is exacerbated by the way human security is conceptualized; neither report specifies whose security would triumph when there is a conflict between state (or territorial) security and people's security, or how such a decision might be taken. When the CHS supports the creation of "an institutional system of oversight and decision-making that states voluntarily subscribe to" (CHS 2003: 12), it replicates the problems of liberal versions of CSS that rely on the voluntary institutions of civil society (cf. Rothschild 1995)—it fails to account for power differentials that are the result of intersecting inequalities.

Proposing that security is best achieved by shifting "from security through armaments to security through sustainable human development" (UNDP 1994: 24), proponents of human security place great emphasis on empowering people "to fend for themselves" (CHS 2003: 4). Indeed, they claim "empowerment strategies enable people to develop their resilience to difficult situations" (ibid.: 10). This empowerment, according to the CHS, flourishes at the same time as "people are to be shielded from menaces" (ibid.). This is potentially problematic because simultaneous protection and empowerment can lead to a quagmire that feminists are all too familiar with (cf. Chapter 1): the protector/protected dynamic involves an unequal power relation in which the protected has limited room to maneuver, so that any action designed to protect might, in fact, act counter to the simultaneous goal of emancipation.[30]

Aiming for a people-centered definition, the UNDP report proposes a participatory model where people take care of themselves, lest they become a burden on society. Empowerment, in this context, means that "people can contribute directly to identifying and implementing solutions to the quagmire of security" (CHS 2003: 6). This empowerment is to be achieved though "providing education and information so that they can scrutinize social arrangements and take collective action [. . .] building a social space that tolerates opposition, encourages local leadership and cultivates public discussion" (ibid.: 11). States, although not displaced, are downplayed as security agents and "regional and international organizations, nongovernmental organizations and civil society are all involved in managing security issues" (ibid.: 6). The proposed strategies are reminiscent of liberal assumptions about the political: that identities and interests do not shift and slide, that progress is possible (through education), and that individual and collective action complement each other. Most proponents of these strategies do not, however, consider how these are gendered or how they are shaped by other power differentials such as class, nation, or race. As such, there is little to no elaboration of how these various actors might divide the labor among themselves and how people are expected to become agents of their own security, given that most security situations, especially those that might fall in the "critical and pervasive" category are those where the affected might have very limited capacity to change their life situation. Responsibility and accountability become ever more difficult as the variety and the number of agents charged with providing security increases.

Kristen Timothy (2004) has argued that the adoption of the human security framework by the United Nations can be seen as an attempt to integrate its many seemingly disparate missions under one broad concept.[31] Indeed, the all-encompassing aspect of human security thinking could be another departure from attempts at closing down debates about political choices inherent in promoting one agenda over another. Most human security advocates do not shy away from pointing to the interdependence of the various components that make up the concept. However, debates about the politics of human security rarely happen (for exceptions see Bellamy and McDonald 2002; Glasius 2008; Grayson 2003, 2007). Mostly human security approaches embrace the diverse perspectives of both grassroots activists and state-based policy makers. Consequently, actions carried out in the name of human security might be diametrically opposed to each other. In this sense, "human security is like 'sustainable development'—everyone is for it, but few people have a clear idea of what it means" (Paris 2001: 88).

What is more, although the language of human security has proliferated widely, there is little evidence of actual change on the ground: Robert Muggah and Keith Krause (2006) examine two UN missions in Haiti (UNMIH 1993–5 and MINUSTAH 2003–5), the latter of which supposedly applied a human security framework, only to find little difference between the two. In their analysis of the 1999 Timor Crisis, T.S. Hataley and Kim Richard Nossal (2004: 10) find that, despite the role that Canada's foreign minister Lloyd Axworthy played in the promotion of the human security agenda during his 1996–2000 tenure, "the Canadian government's position was marked by a distinct lack of enthusiasm to take action." The reasons, Hataley and Nossal propose, are the great difficulties in putting human security into practice given, in particular, the emphasis on deprioritizing state security. Governments that have embraced the human security agenda are confronted with a sweeping, open-ended agenda requiring that policy makers develop their own list of priorities, which often leads them to simply revert to existing policies: "it is easier to embrace the rhetoric of human security than it is to actually transform the human security agenda into concrete policy initiatives" (ibid.: 17). The embrace of the human security agenda, thus, often "reflects a lack of strategic contestation and the disorientation of Western elites" (Chandler 2008: 468).

Human security narratives, on this reading, do little to change the traditional security narrative beyond the now widely accepted axes of broadening and deepening. All the while, the broadening implicated here goes further than most security scholars, critical or not, are comfortable. The securitization of human development and human rights as well as the proliferation of added signifiers (economic, food, health, environmental, personal, community, and political) should worry anyone. The constitution of a specific issue area such as human security (and also human rights or human development) always also involves the constitution of corresponding subjects (Edkins 2002). What is more, it is the signifier attached to it—humanity—that is to be securitized; it is the very idea of humanity that is considered worth preserving. This idea, however, is already exclusionary. Tracing the genealogy of humanity, Costas Douzinas (2009b) points out that the word *humanitas* initially referred to an educational standard: "Humanity was not a quality shared but, as Cicero put it, a standard of behavior used to separate the *homines humani* (the educated Romans) from the *homines barbari* (the rest)."[32] In the early modern period, in the *Déclaration des droits de l'homme et du citoyen*, humanity was assigned to citizens only—and citizenship was granted only to certain humans (*de facto* limiting it to the well-off, White, Christian, urban, male). It has been a fairly recent phenomenon that others (e.g., women) were included as being human, but ever since these early formulations "full 'humanity' is constructed against a backdrop of preconditions (citizenship, class, gender, race, religion, and sexuality)" (ibid.).

Consequently, human rights do not belong to humans but are given to some; "they help construct who and how one becomes human" (Douzinas 2009a). Similarly, specifying what human security refers to tells us whose humanity is worth preserving; specifying what human development encompasses tells us which lives are worthy of attention (cf. Duffield 2007). This means that human rights are statements of prescription—"human rights are moral claims" (Douzinas 2009a)—and a call for action. Appeals to human security are no different, as Andrew Mack (2002: 3), lead author of the Human Security Report, proposes: human security "is less an analytical concept than a signifier of shared political and moral values." Taking the human security agenda seriously, therefore, implies a rigorous debate about the political and material implications of how we think security. Were this to become the focus of human security debates, it could indeed provide an opening. As is, however, human security "supports the global and national status quo rather than challenges it" (Nuruzzaman 2006: 299) because it focuses on incremental reform of the existing system.

5 Feminist security narratives

If we continue to speak in this sameness, if we speak to each other as men have spoken for centuries, as they have taught us to speak, we will fail each other. Again ... words will pass through our bodies, above our heads, disappear, make us disappear.

(Luce Irigaray quoted in Gross 1986: 190)

Approaching security as narrative changes what one sees and what security means. A key component of the narrative approach—and the larger methodological choices advocated here—is that the differences among stories and storytellers, which characterize personal narratives, are explicitly acknowledged, rather than ironed out as they are in traditional social science approaches. What is more, they are interrogated for what they can tell us about the storytellers' conflicts, the multiple strategies that might be employed to address them, and the multiplicity of perspectives that exist in relation to them. Narratives are always contextual; securities are likewise.

Toward the end of my stay in Mozambique in 1991, I read a short piece of prose by Mozambican writer and poet Mia Cuoto. It begins: 'Suddenly, the ox exploded. It bursts without so much as a moo. In the surrounding grass a rain of chunks and slices fell, as if the fruit and leaves of the ox. Its flesh turned into red butterflies. Its bones were scattered coins. Its horns were caught in some branches, swinging to and fro, imitating life in the invisibility of the wind' (1986:17). I mention that I was at the end of my stay because, even thought the young cowherd in the story 'could not contain his astonishment,' and variously wonders if Mabata-bata, the cow, was hit by lightning or, something more magical, *ndlati*, the bird of lightning, I knew when I read the first sentence that the cow had stepped on a landmine. And I knew that by the end of the story the young cowherd would meet the same fate. At the same time, I realized that when I first arrived in Mozambique I would not have 'known' these things—I too would have wondered if it were lightning or perhaps something more magical.

(Nordstrom 1997: 36)

Across Mozambique, and over time, Carolyn Nordstrom (1997: 85) encounters the same stories over and over again, but every time they are adapted to the particular circumstance. "Parable, myth, metaphor, and innuendo are the means by which people [...] talk and talk about violence and protect their safety and need for silence at the same time." These symbologues, dialogues "based on symbolic representations" (ibid.: 209), are often employed in situations where it is necessary to tell a story indirectly because to speak about war and its effects openly would be too dangerous. They "cannot be 'read' as 'texts' of the war, intransmutable across time and space" (ibid.: 85). Their meaning is relevant only within their telling because they are meant to transmit vital, life-saving knowledge about the particular situation. Nordstrom (1997: 85–6) recounts a particular parable that implicated who was dangerous and untrustworthy within the community. She initially heard it during the war but did not have time to write down. Later, when she wanted to use the story to illustrate a point in her book, she asked another friend whether she knew the story—only to find that its meaning had shifted again to accommodate the new (postwar) circumstances. This leads her to realize that, "apart from the telling and the context, the parable means little." (ibid.: 85)[1]

Drawing on several feminist writings about security, some of which specifically adopt a narrative framework and some that can be read as such, the chapter illustrates what makes feminist security narratives fundamentally different. These narratives exemplify and/or specify feminist methodological commitments and challenge ontological and epistemological assumptions of IR. They show that how asking different questions, questions that arise by focusing on (women's) everyday experience, lead to fundamentally different understandings of security.

Instrumentalizing women in the promotion of US–Korean security interests

Katharine H.S. Moon's *Sex Among Allies* (1997) examines a classic IR dilemma: the bilateral relations of a powerful international player (the United States) with a client state (South Korea). However, her analysis does so with a twist as Moon focuses on prostitution in camptowns around US military bases. She explains, "This study of US–Korea *kijich'on* [camptown] prostitution seeks to strengthen and refine feminist analysis of foreign policy by asking when, how, and why governments use women, not just gendered ideology, as instruments of foreign policy" (1997: 12). Inspired by Enloe (1983, 1988, 1990a), who first insisted that prostitution is a matter of international politics and security, Moon's study is one of the first to provide a detailed, book-length analysis. Combining foreign-policy analysis and ethnographic research, Moon shows how *kijich'on* prostitution is regulated at the highest levels of Korean–US relationships in the Status of Forces Agreement.

Not content to limit her analysis to foreign-policy outcomes, Moon pays attention to the impact of these policies on women's everyday lives and finds women to be "directly involved in international politics [...] their relationships with foreign soldiers *personify and define*, not only underlie, relations between governments" (1997: 12). Moon arrives at these insights by weaving together an on-site study of camptown life and *kijich'on* prostitution with an analysis of the Status of Forces Agreement between the United States and South Korea during the 1970s "Camptown Clean-Up Campaign." She argues that the *kijich'on* women "became integral to the efforts of the US forces in Korea and the Seoul government to secure firm US military commitment to the Republic" (ibid.). Due to South Korea's high level of military dependence on the United States that impacted almost all aspects of the economic, political, and social life of South Korea from the Korean war to the late 1970s, her question was "to what extent and at what human and social cost a state's pursuit of its military security objectives can be justified" (ibid.: 15).

Current day *kijich'on* prostitution can be placed on a continuum with the approximately 200,000 Korean Comfort Women servicing the Japanese.[2] However, Moon is adamant to point out how the system of camptown prostitution is a direct consequence of the Korean War and, in particular, the Mutual Defense Treaty between the Republic of Korea (ROK) and the United States that followed it. Like any war, the Korean War dislocated and shattered families, creating social and political chaos. Moon describes how the war "'massproduced' prostitutes, creating a large supply of girls and women without homes and livelihoods" (1997: 28). Many of these refugees became camp followers to UN/US forces in an effort to provide for themselves. A number of the military camps, especially those close to the North Korean border, developed into more permanent settlement once the war was over.

The women who live and work in these camptowns occupy an extremely marginalized position in Korean society and are practically forced out of Korean society's consciousness. Moon writes, "for many *kijich'on* women, their pariah status is due to the unique demographic and cultural constitution of the camptowns in which they live and the particular prejudices of Korean people regarding race, class and Western influence" (1997: 6). These prejudices include their adoption of Western dress, mannerisms, and language (i.e., "Konglish"— a fusion of broken English and broken Korean) and their association with Westerners more generally (especially sexual relations with *yangnom*[3]—and the inevitable consequence of Amerasian children). "There is yet another, unspoken, reason," writes Moon, "Koreans have not wanted reminders of the war lurking around them and the insecurity that their newfound wealth and international power have been built on" (1997: 8). *Kijich'on* women serve as a constant reminder, not only of the destruction wrought by the Korean War but also of the continued division of the country and South Korea's military dependence on the United States

Only when economic power shifted in the 1980s, and South Korea became more prosperous did people begin to speak out against US influence. As Korean confidence grew, it became more acceptable to inquire into *kijich'on* prostitutes' lives and question their role in US–Korean relationships. Activists and academics who long ignored *kijich'on* women's plight, believing that "they voluntarily want to lead a life of prostitution, because they are lacking in moral character" (Moon 1997: 9–10), were beginning to pay attention. "Koreans' increasing sensitivity and resistance to US dominance in camptown life reached a critical mass with the murder of a *kijich'on* prostitute, Yun Kumi, in the fall of 1992" (ibid.: 31) bringing thousands of Koreans to the streets.[4] What is more, the shift coincided with the democratization of South Korea (the first democratic elections took place in 1987) and a larger protest culture that emerged in the1980s and continues to impact Korean society today.

It is important to place Moon's analysis within the larger context of the Cold War and the shifting US policies regarding overseas military bases (Enloe 1990b, 1993). The practices of establishing bases and regulating relationships with the local population, vary around the world as presumed cultural sensitivities are taken into consideration. Though relationships with the local population in the Middle East are highly curtailed, in Korea (and elsewhere in Asia) they tend to be tolerated, if not encouraged. Differences also exist in policies regarding the posting of military personnel; whereas soldiers stationed in Germany will often bring along dependents, soldiers posted to Korea cannot bring along dependents and are consequently often young and unattached. This influences the interactions with the local community—and the reactions of the community to the existence of US bases (cf. Lutz 2009). What is more, the policies established in the Status of Forces Agreement exhibit a variety of intersecting assumptions about race, class, and culture, both by the United States and by the Republic of Korea. However, Moon (1997: 41) argues that it is not culture, but "the South Korean government's priorities for state-building, national security, and economic development, over any concern for the social welfare of women and/or the moral order of society [that] have determined policies regarding prostitution."[5] Moon's multilayered analysis thus provides interesting insights into the varied meanings of security and confirms the feminist suspicion that "the security of the state is often built on the insecurity of its most vulnerable populations" (Tickner 2005: 11).

The story of camptown prostitution around US bases in Asia is riddled with racism and sexism (cf. Kirk and Okazawa-Rey 1998, 2001). "Racist stereotypes of Asians within the American society have mixed with sexist stereotypes of Asian women to foster American participation in camptown prostitution in Asia" (Moon 1997: 33). An army chaplain interviewed by Moon reflected on the importance of the stories soldiers hear and read before coming to Asia that influence their attitudes toward women of the host society. He proposed that, due to the myths about Korean or Thai women as beautiful and subservient, soldiers would come to view them as property, things, or slaves. In his words, "the men don't see the women as human beings—they're disgusting, things to be thrown away … they speak of the women in the diminutive" (quoted in Moon 1997: 34). Related to these expressions of racism and sexism is the treatment of Amerasian children, both in the host society and by US soldiers and officials. Large number of children are abandoned by their fathers and eventually end up becoming street children, working in prostitution and other forms of "entertainment." Others are sold, with White-looking children fetching much higher prices than those fathered by Black soldiers, again exhibiting the intersectionality of race, poverty, and militarization in the lives of camptown residents.

In her detailed analysis of the Camptown Clean-Up Campaign in the 1970s, Moon specifies the role of *kijich'on* women as "personal ambassadors" in US–ROK relationships. In establishing policies around servicing Black and White soldiers equally, both governments emphasized the need to provide a "united front" against North Korea (which might exploit internal tension to its advantage). The *kijich'on* women were seen to "determine both the image of the US–ROK military relationship in the eyes of Americans, both South and North Koreans, and the ability of Communists to wage their propaganda campaign against the United States and ROK" (Moon 1997: 89–90) and were consequently accorded a special role in reducing or eliminating racial conflict. As racial segregation was prevalent in camptowns since the 1960s, a common practice for club owners was to designate the women who were to serve Black or White servicemen. "Those designated as 'black hostesses' had to contend with the social stigma and potential loss of income from white soldiers" (ibid.: 129) and received no supplementary rewards. Given that their compliance with these policies was the only way they could earn a living, they had to accept them, even though they severely limited their ability to choose their customers.

What is more, the enforcement of these policies (referred to as "education") was left to the club owners and managers, thus exacerbating the existing climate of fear. Women who did not comply would face mistreatment at the hands of the men who were already known to physically and psychologically abuse them. As a result, "demanding that these owners/ managers increase control over these women's conduct was tantamount to increasing and legitimating the former's exploitation and abuse of the latter," (Moon 1997: 91). She then recalls how the US chair of the subcommittee in charge of the Clean-Up Campaign answered her question about how the policies were enforced: "Generally, a visit to the bar owner would either get her fired or get her head screwed on straight. Give pressure to the bar owner and they usually carried through" (quoted in Moon 1997: 91). *Kijich'on* women faced increased oppression and surveillance by a variety of actors (club owners, US military police, Korean leadership, and Black and White soldiers); "to survive in the bars, the prostitutes had to 'look over their shoulders' constantly [...], balancing the wishes and punitive power of each surveillance group" (ibid.: 129). The women at the short end of the proverbial stick had no way to address the abuse. As such, the *kijich'on* women bore the brunt of efforts to allay racial tensions within the US military.

Crucially, due to the state's lack of interest in collecting the relevant information—and because most social science methodologies cannot capture the material she needed—Moon garners much of her information by collecting personal narratives of *kijich'on* women. Reflecting on her experiences doing fieldwork in South Korean camptowns, she discusses how difficult it was to find former *kijich'on* prostitutes willing (and able) to talk to her. Many of them, who refused her request for information, were in ill health or suffered from memory loss after years of abuse and exploitation. Some were clearly lying about their experience, "because they are ashamed of revealing the past and because they have grown accustomed to lying as a means to survive in the camptowns" (Moon 1997: 14). Nonetheless, the women Moon (1997: 15) was able to speak to had a wealth of experience and knowledge to share, even if they initially thought they had nothing worthwhile to say.[6] Moon's stated aim in collecting the personal stories of *kijich'on* women is to "lift the curtains of invisibility of these women's lives [...] allowing them to construct their own identities rather than having them imposed on them by societal norms and taken-for-granted definitions" (Tickner 2005: 12). Like the work of other feminists discussed in this book, her study shows how security and identity are thoroughly intertwined. By focusing on the lives of *kijich'on* women and their experience of the negotiations around identity and security, she exemplifies the types of injuries that are the result of these policies. Moon illustrates how there is not one version of security, but how the security of some is deeply implicated in, and even predicated upon, insecurity for others.

Identifying in/securities in Mayan women's lives on the eve of peace in Guatemala

Maria Stern's *Naming Security, Constructing Identity* (2005) focuses on the relationship between in/security and identity examining a classic feminist theme.[7] Exploring the life stories of poor Mayan women at the end of the civil war in Guatemala (which lasted from 1960–96), she shows how their personal experiences with in/security, which were shaped by their location in relation to the *Ladino* community, as well as the Guatemalan state, make security in the traditional sense an illusion and, in its complexity and overlapping allegiances, defy any comprehensive version of security. Stern shows how identity and security implicate each other, and how emphasizing particular identities privileges certain forms of security over others. In the case of marginalized identities like that of a poor Mayan women, this positions people in fundamentally insecure spaces.[8]

Wherever Mayan women are found, they are exploited. In their homes, they often work a triple or even quadruple workday (doing housework, working on plantations or their own plot of land, and possibly in the informal economy), and might be subject to abuse from their husbands. In their communities, which experienced the indiscriminate violence of counterinsurgency warfare, they are particularly vulnerable to sexualized violence targeted not necessarily just at them but also at their husbands and the community at large (cf. Nordstrom 1996; Skjelsbæk 2001). On *fincas* (plantations) where Mayan families who do not possess any land of their own (and cannot afford to rent any) often live and work, women find themselves in "sexualized, subordinate positions to those in power as well as to the men with whom they worked" (Stern 2005: 152). Mayan women, besides having to fulfill all the regular household duties, are subjected to sexualized violence and gendered economic exploitation (cf. Peterson

2003). Diana, one of the women interviewed by Stern (2005: 152), recounts that women earned four *quetzals* whereas men were earning seven. A child fares even worse, as another interviewee, Rosa, explains,

> we, the children, were not human beings. We had no rights, no education, poor health ... Children didn't earn a cent ... in the *finca*, we lived like animals, children died, [received] no medical attention, returned home sick.
>
> (Stern 2005: 150)

If women organize to address their situation, they face additional dangers. Diana tells of an instance where the women demanded new tasks and equal pay: "So we went to talk to the administrator and he said, ok, I'll change your task, but now you have another task: have sex with me ..." (Stern 2005:152). When women organize in their own communities, whether to demand knowledge about the whereabouts of their disappeared loved-ones, to retrieve land taken from their families, or to garner support for widows, the fact that they are organizing as women often raises suspicions. The state/army quickly questions the intent of everyday activities (e.g., why did they buy so much food, were they feeding insurgents?). Their husbands might forbid their wives to go to meetings or might question their motives and abilities because women are not considered to have anything worthwhile to say. Even if some men support the women's efforts, they might find their masculinity questioned by others, providing a strong incentive to comply with the regulatory practices of the community.

However, the women Stern (2005: 123) interviews, all of whom belong to activist organizations, note that they became politically active because they saw no other option. "Given the horrors that the alternatives promised, there was nothing left but to join an organization and resist." Not only did the women themselves suffer from injustices that their activism addresses but their lives had become unbearable and dangerous even before they organized. Diana, for example, expresses her identity as one "who would rather die from 'a bullet' than be killed by the abuse and oppression in the *finca*" (ibid.: 153). What is more, being part of an organization provides "moral support and ideas of how to resist the persecution of the army [as well as provides] a vocation, a shelter, a community" (ibid.: 130). Importantly, given the environment of distrust created through counterinsurgency measures and the existence of collaborators within families and communities, "the organization offered a united front against the oppressor and a forum for the sharing of confidences" (ibid.: 131). As part of an organization that resists, and through the companionship with others who are suffering, the women experience the comfort of a shared identity—a feeling of belonging and security.

In the process of becoming politically active, the women begin to find their own voice and, often for the first time, they create their own, empowered identity. Stern summarizes:

Through the venue of the organization, Carmen not only spoke, but she directly challenged the 'Truth' as stated by the state and thereby named her in/security and its attendant identity, Mayan woman. Her organization offered a different account of reality, both nationally and internationally which disrupted the official story. The organization provided a ground from which countering the government/ army—and being heard—was possible, though still dangerous.

(2005: 130–1)

Throughout the book, Stern emphasizes how the processes of sculpting themselves as a Mayan woman provided a feeling of security for the women she interviewed: "because of the violence and extremity of the marginalization of Mayans throughout history, it was paramount that the *pueblo* counter the harms caused by the nation-state and the *Ladino* society by rescuing and reclaiming the culture" (Stern 2005: 115). This awareness of Mayan culture that had been buried by a history of suffering since the arrival of the Spanish some 500 years ago, and the assertion of a Mayan subject position in the 1980s and 1990s, are part of a global movement where discourses of identity politics and indigenous rights pervade. Refuting the then-dominant inscriptions of Mayan identity, Mayan activists "reinscribed sites of subordination to become sites of pride and cultural promotion" (ibid.: 53).[9] The (re)discovery of Mayan-ness evolved over time as the differences between indigenous and *Ladinos* was revalued not as simple difference but as a source of strength for the Mayan *pueblo*. "Being Mayan thus carried with it not only a history of suffering, but also a fledgling notion of privilege" (ibid.: 115). Recognizing Mayan-ness as valuable provided both cultural worth and political power, and ties together the concepts of being Mayan and being *campesina*—"their class-based identity [which] also underpinned the spiritual and cultural connection to the land" (ibid.).

This complex formation of Mayan identity meant that any "in/security configuration that was formed in tandem with these identity constellations could neither be partitioned off into separate 'security' needs, nor for that matter, specific threats" (Stern 2005: 115). Traditional security studies (including much of critical and human security) do not provide the tools to understand the situation of Mayan women, writes Stern, because it treats security as a *thing* or condition. The conceptualization of security as practice, as in the work of the Copenhagen school, provides a useful opening, but it too is limited because even societal security provides room for only one identity through which to find security. The case of Mayan women shows that identities shift and slide; even if the marker of identity (e.g., class) is the same, its meaning differs depending on the context (being poor has entirely different meanings and consequences for a Mayan than for a *Ladino/a* in Guatemala). What is more, the intersecting aspects of poor Mayan women's identities—and their attendant insecurities— are incommensurable so that seeking security through one identity simultaneously endangers another. "Marginalization from *Ladino* society was not gender-neutral; Mayan women experienced racism differently than Mayan men," Stern (2005: 100) notes, "Mayan women occupied a particularly debased and vulnerable site at the confluence of many different systems of power relations."

As is often the case in nationalist movements (cf. Anzaldúa 1999; Cockburn 1999; Trinh 1989; Yuval-Davis 1997; Yuval-Davis and Werbner 1999), Mayan women are charged with maintaining the private and the communal practices and symbols of tradition, whereas Mayan men take on political roles in the public. "As both custodians and transmitters of a particular identity, women (and their behavior) become highly political and decisive in cultural boundary making" (Stern 2005: 111). Even though these circumscribed roles clearly limit Mayan women, they are not simply impositions from the outside but, according to Stern's interviewees, many Mayan women appreciated their "roles as 'defenders of Mayan culture': they ensured the reproduction of the culture—the language, the traditions, the cosmovision, against the barrage of both *Ladino*ization and the ethnocide on the part of the Guatemalan military-state" (ibid.: 112). Speaking one of the Mayan languages and wearing the (feminine) *traje* are of particular importance as markers of Mayan identity; whereas men can more easily adopt Western style clothing (or switch back and forth depending on the context), women's association with tradition/culture meant that "if a Mayan woman became *Ladino*ized in any significant way (such as not wearing a *traje*), she had 'lost her roots'" (ibid.: 105). As the women in the movement actively rescript their identity, they "presented these makers as primordial—a natural, given aspect of being Mayan." Yet, at the same time, "they also assigned certain social/political meaning to them within the particular historical context" (ibid.: 103).

The gender roles associated with Mayan traditions and culture also implied particular social mores to govern the behavior of Mayan women and girls. Given the context of the relationships with the Other (*Ladino* society), these gender ideologies become important in determining the differences between Mayan and *Ladino* society, and display the moral superiority of Mayan culture: "Mayans *had* culture (though they might have temporarily lost it), while *Ladinos* did not" (Stern 2005: 108). In general, in the context of struggles with the *Ladino* society and the Guatemalan state, the reconstruction of a Mayan *pueblo* provides a sense of belonging and, as such, "it allowed the narrators a clear and irrefutable sense of who they were in the midst of a seeming morass of historical and present-day subjugation and danger" (ibid.: 116). Stern finds that Mayan women's identity is deeply engrained in the rhythms of everyday life and memory. "Knowing who they, their ancestors, as well as their children were, offered a safe space, a space where uncertainty was thwarted and belonging brought both support and immortality" (ibid.: 116).[10]

The life stories of Mayan women not only ensure them a subject position but also provide counter-narratives to the dominant Guatemalan state narrative. Telling their story as a security narrative, in the process both naming and eliminating dangers, provides a way to establish "a political identity from which to make claims of protection, for security" (Stern 2005: 116). One of the most interesting strategies employed by the women Stern interviews is the move to identify the various forms of violence as the consequence of outside influence.

Five hundred years of colonialism, combined with the more recent acceleration of globalization, destroyed the Mayan *pueblo* economically and culturally, as did the machismo and racism of *Ladino* society that many of the interviewees claimed had "infected" Mayan men and led them to abuse women in their own communities. The "pervasive (foreign) sexism which placed women in particularly vulnerable positions," Stern (2005: 83) notes, are "seen as yet another divisive tactic that was attendant to the Violence and its counterpart, racism." Reclaiming the Mayan *pueblo* and "recreating a gender identity/role that empowered both women *and* the Mayan *pueblo* as a unified community" (2005: 94), serves as a site of resistance to those in power and, as such, also provides a semblance of security.

One might say that Stern takes the implications of Moon's research—that security of some is based on insecurity of others—to a new level. Not only is the insecurity of some a direct consequence of attempts to achieve security, but also most of the time, for all but a privileged few, security is entirely elusive. Stern's usage of the term in/security is entirely apt to describe the situation of Mayan women, whose lives are marked by the intersections of class, gender, racism, and sexism. What is more, given the constitutive linkage between identity and security, coupled with the realization that "the representation of the subject can never be complete or finished" (Stern 2005: 31), security too can only ever be temporarily achieved. Stern's focus on security and identity as told by Mayan women showcases how telling one's story (and retelling it to accommodate new insights, locations, and future projects) is part of the process of achieving security.

Un/making the world in the Mozambican Civil War

Carolyn Nordstrom's *A Different Kind of War Story* (1997) is a unique ethnographic account of everyday life on the frontlines of war in Mozambique. Marred with successive wars, starting with the fight for independence in the 1960s, Mozambique experienced some of the worst violence in the 1980s until a peace agreement was reached in 1992. Nordstrom (1997: xviii) spent significant amounts of time in the country between 1989 and 1996, "collecting first-hand experience and second-hand accounts of the processes of war in the villages and towns directly affected by the violence." This provides her with particular insight into the ways in which people and communities recreate their worlds in the midst of ongoing violence. When the world is shattered the way it had been in Mozambique, being itself has to be reinvented.

"The first time a Mozambican said to me that the war had taken from them everything they had, including who they were, I realized that identity, the self, and personhood were strategic targets of war" (Nordstrom 1997: 178). Because who we are is determined by our relationships with and in the world, the unmaking of the world that takes place in war is also always an unmaking of the self. "If the self is continuously constructed in thought and action, and identity forged through lived experience, then self-identity is defined by what one has lived through," writes Nordstrom. "Experience is not something that

happens to the self, but *experience becomes the self*—it is that through which identity is forged" (ibid.: 185). Traveling across Mozambique in the midst of civil
war, Nordstrom is able to observe how this unmaking of the world and the
self takes place. She finds that physical violence, though being very important,
is only part of the picture, as an interviewee explains:

> Our traditions teach us how to deal with these difficult aspects of life. This
> war has elevated death and mutilation to a terrible level, worse than anyone
> should have to live through, it is true, but these things we have seen before.
> But you want to know what I think is the worst thing about this war? It is
> sleeping in the bush at night. The Bandidos come at night and attack while
> we are sleeping, so we all sneak into our villages, our homes, during the day
> to do our work and tend our crops, and then sneak back into the bush at
> night to sleep hidden by isolation in some distant location covered only
> by the sky at night. Animals live in the bush, not humans. Forcing us to
> sleep out with the animals makes us no better than them—these Bandidos,
> they take away our humanity, our dignity, they make us like animals [...]
> This is the worst violence you can subject someone to.
>
> (quoted in Nordstrom 1997: 125)

Many of the people Nordstrom talks to express their frustration at not being
able to follow their traditions, and express the worry that not doing so will lead
them to face the wrath of their ancestors. Most Mozambicans share the belief
that the spirits of victims of violence are restless, and they tend to seek some
form of revenge (ibid.: 160ff.). Although some *curandeiros* (traditional healers)
believe that the victims' spirits might go after their attackers directly, others
believe that they move with the wind and afflict all they come in contact
with. Many *deslocados* (displaced Mozambicans) also fear that the spirits might
go after those that did not bury them properly.[11] A major impact of the violence, then, concerns "the destruction of home and humanity, of hope and
future, of valued traditions and the integrity of community" (ibid.: 123).

What is more, while physical violence has a particular impact at the moment
it is enacted, "the spectacle of violence cannot be detached from its experience,
its aftermath, its enduring reality" (Nordstrom 1997: 130). Violence stays
around long after the act. Violence does not need to be, nor can it be, defined.
"People simply *know* what violence is" (ibid.: 115). When a scholar tries to pin it
down theoretically, violence is reified and to do so means "to lose not only the
experiential force of violence lived but to endanger an adequate understanding
of complex dynamics that define this phenomenon in thought and action"
(ibid.: 116). Most importantly, Nordstrom worries that too often, especially
in the West, violence is seen as some*thing* that can be simply employed to
achieve a purpose; some*thing* that is set, enduring, concrete.[12] Treating violence
this way, one tends to posit naturalness to violence. When violence is seen as
a *thing* or a given, "there is nothing people can do other than to endure it, or
protect against it" (ibid.: 217).

Instead, on the basis of her research in Mozambique, Nordstrom (1997: 217) suggests violence is made, employed by those seeking to control others.[13] As such, "its enactment forges, in fact forces, new constructs of identity, new socio-cultural relationships, new threats and injustices that reconfigure people's life-worlds, new patterns of survival and resistance" (ibid.: 141). At the same time, she is adamant to disavow those who see in violence the fount of creativity because this too risks essentializing and naturalizing violence. Instead, she proposes that the creativity that often seems to follow or emerge alongside violence is latent at all times; yet when society "functions" we are rarely called upon to make use of it.[14] For her, "creative resistance flows not from past to present but from the present to a time of future need [and] is 'always already' in the cultural repertoire of the country" (ibid.: 70).

In much of her book, Nordstrom recounts the various creative responses that act to delegitimize violence. These include ceremonies, laughter, storytelling, and the strategic employment of the grotesque to make a spectacle of terror-warfare, thus removing it from the realm of secrecy. The grotesque, also because it is always concrete, gives form to the unspeakable. It "relies on using the metaphors of excess to delegitimize violence, whereby the victims become not the enemy but the *judges* of unjust war techniques" (Nordstrom 1997: 156). Telling one's story, realizing that speaking is always also dangerous in the context of ongoing violence, is another crucial avenue to remaking the world. Telling one's story "validates the existence of those who died and those who survived to tell their tales" (ibid.: 79). Telling one's story, while respecting the "need for silence that preserves dignity and protects the survivors" (ibid.: 80), can provide a step toward healing and a semblance of security even in the midst of fighting.[15]

In 1989, Nordstrom arrived in a village in central Zambezia, Mozambique when Mozambican emergency relief workers had just left to avoid the danger of an attack. The village administrator asked her to talk with the children who were distraught about the attack because this would, in his experience, help to calm and orient the children.

> I went to sit in a quiet spot under some shade trees with a group of children ranging from about three to ten. Mindful of Veena Das observation on the Punjab riots that children who have been exposed to severe episodes of violence have sophisticated perceptions concerning their experiences and want to talk about them (but find most adults disinclined to do so), I decided to be straightforward with the children. I simply asked them, "What is war?" They responded immediately.
>
> (Nordstrom 1997: 20–1)

Crucially, she provides a testament to the transformative potential of storytelling when she recounts how, a few days later, she runs into someone who works with the Mozambican emergency relief services: "He said he heard an attack had taken place the day I was there. I said no, in what I thought was all honesty ... It was a few moments before I 'remembered' the attack ..."

(Nordstrom 1997: 21–2). What does narrative tell us about how we make life bearable? How can narrative itself make life less dangerous?

Each of these techniques, in their way, contribute to redefining violence and thus to remake the world, to construct a new political culture. The work of *curandeiros* is often crucial in this process. A *curandeiro* interviewed by Nordstrom describes the challenge as follows:

> We have had to set up new ways of treating people in this war. This war, it teaches violence. [The soldiers] return home, but they carry the violence with them, they act it out in their daily lives, and this harms their families and communities. We have to take this violence out of these people, we have to teach them how to live nonviolent lives like they did before. The problem would be serious enough if it were only the soldiers but it is not. When a woman is kidnapped, raped and forced to work for soldiers, when a child is exposed to violence in an attack, when people are submitted to assaults and terrible injuries, this violence sticks to them. It is like the soldier carrying the souls of those he has killed back into his normal life, but here, the soul carries the violence. You can even see this with children here who have seen or been subjected to violence: they begin to act more violently. They lose respect, they begin to hit, they lose their bearings—and this violence tears at the order of the community. We can treat this, we have to. We literally take the violence out of the people, we teach them how to relearn healthy ways of thinking and acting.
>
> (quoted in Nordstrom 1997: 142–3)

This approach conceptualizes violence as an illness that can and needs to be cured. What is more, "most people want to learn peace. The violence, it tears them up inside, it destroys the world they care about. They want to return to a normal life they had before" (Nordstrom 1997: 143). Nordstrom finds beliefs and practices that delegitimize violence and force as a continuation of politics replicated across Mozambique—all *curandeiros* she spoke with "had developed methods to help people survive the war in a human fashion and to institute peacebuilding processes in doing so" (ibid.: 209). Almost everyone sought the *curandeiros'* help in reconstituting their shattered worlds, "to have the violence taken out of them" (ibid.: 211) so that violence would not reproduce itself and destroy the lives of those it came in contact with.

These various acts of resistance lay the foundation for an eventual successful peace process. "It is not people, but a will to resist, not individuals, but the existence of a counter-hegemonic that challenges repressive forces" (Nordstrom 1997: 167). This form of resistance should remind us that "violence is not a fixed entity, a 'truth' to be dealt with, but instead it is a social, political and cultural construction that noncombatants—the targets of most violence—can redefine to assert their own political will" (ibid.: 143). In this context, it is crucial that these everyday acts, the "parables, myths, songs, poetry, theater, and a host of other creative tools [...] forge and circulate knowledge about surviving and resistance, about world-making and self-affirmation" (ibid.: 204). In other words, these everyday acts are ontological and epistemological endeavors, reminding us that we should not privilege one form or representation over another, and not presume that, as scholars, "we" can speak for "them" creating a hierarchy in which our thinking is privileged (ibid.: 26–8).

In her last chapter, *Mundus Imaginalis*, Nordstrom suggests a rethinking about the assumptive need for institutions and regulatory practices. During her time in Mozambique, she finds that in the midst of war "*most* people did not create abusive systems of self-gain and power" (1997: 209). Despite the massive scale of the conflict in Mozambique—with one million deaths, four million displaced, and eight million (half of the entire population) directly affected by the war, and with no functioning traditional authority in much of the country over long periods of time—"I never encountered a community that succumbed to chaos, inertia or destructiveness," Nordstrom writes, "certain individuals, yes; but they were in the minority" (ibid.: 212). This leads her to question the idea that, in the absence of a higher authority, chaos reigns and self-interest is the guiding motif. After asking why most people responded with vibrant ways of recreation in the midst of societal breakdown, she proposes that her focus on average civilians' everyday lives is crucial. The people, in their struggles to continue everyday life in the midst of violence that is not of their own making, present a wealth of solutions that are sidelined by the focus on formal political institutions and peace-processes. The community-generated solutions that "are negotiated across the possible and the real" (ibid.: 216) became the real foundation for peace in Mozambique. "War was the enemy, and anyone fighting this enemy was a compatriot" (ibid.: 218). The unmaking of the power and potential of violence through the various creative forms of resistance coalesced into a culture against war that made it very difficult to sustain the war effort in Mozambique.

What Nordstrom adds to the accounts presented by Moon and Stern is a need not only to contextualize meanings of security but she also provides ample evidence to dispel the myth of security as a *thing* that can objectively measured. By displaying the imaginative ways in which life is remade, and violence is redefined and refuted in Mozambique, she provides a vivid account of the ways in which identity and security are linked. As Nordstrom (1997: 172) points out, "if violence seeks to crush the possible, people, far from being passive victims, re-create the possible as a tactic of survival and political agency." Security, here, is created. In addition, it is only meaningful within the context within which it is articulated. Her observations have profound implications for security studies—and they support the feminist challenge to the quest for certainty that characterizes traditional science and traditional security studies.

Constructing feminist security narratives

In their work, Moon, Nordstrom, and Stern ask questions in places where scholars rarely do, drawing on the personal narratives of those rarely listened to.[16] In the process, they explicitly (and implicitly) paint a picture of security from the perspective of those marginalized not only in IR but also by the societies they live in. These narratives of security, told from outsiders' standpoints, offer a very different account of security than the dominant state-centered security narrative. Situating meanings of security in the context of intersecting oppressions, they explode the confines of traditional security accounts that attempt to fix meanings of security and anchor them to one form of identity.

Focusing on data not often collected in IR—data derived through narrative interviews—these authors (like many other feminists) are able to capture varied meanings of security as experienced in everyday circumstances. As Mattingly and Lawlor (2000: 5) point out in their discussion of narrative interviewing in cross-cultural research, "these rich narrative descriptions are much more useful than abstract generalizations or belief statements in helping us to understand the complex and often quite tacit meanings (including dilemmas, hopes, anxieties and the like)." What is more, because these life stories are always about the person who tells them, they help to illuminate not only that person's sense of self, but, in the case of security narratives, the ways in which security and identity implicate each other. Stern (2001: 268), for one, finds "the narrator's articulations of in/security were multiple, hybrid, contradictory, contingent, crafted out of discourse and defined in relation to their subjectivity."

Narratives are profoundly referential and influential in their representations. They create phenomena and have a tendency to generalize, universalize, and decontextualize the particular. At the same time, if one does not try to gloss over or iron out the inconsistencies, narratives can capture and hold on to what might otherwise be considered incommensurable differences. From the perspective of narrative theory as outlined here, disagreement and multiplicity in narrative are not only unavoidable, they should be encouraged, as they are necessary for political processes. Jean-François Lyotard argues this point with reference to personal narrative. He refers to "*differends*—incommensurable disputes between little narratives where there are no external criteria for litigation or judgment—in the coherence of a single identity narrative" (Currie 1998: 111). Consequently, narrative approaches have a "political responsibility to highlight the co-existence and the incommensurability of different stories," writes Currie (1998: 111), "not so much in the semiotic spirit of acknowledging the constitutive role of difference in the abstract but to base political action on a view of humanity as a matrix of unresolvable narrative disputes."

This is quite different from the aim of traditional science and security narratives, which aim to establish an authoritative narrative. Feminist security narratives, based on personal narratives, challenge conventional meanings for security not just because the referent of security is different (i.e., because there is a deepening of the agenda) but because narratives have the ability to capture a variety of concerns and events. On the one hand, these security narratives capture the perspective of the individual interviewee, including how it shifts and slides over time, which is why "one needs to collect all, or at least a range of responses any individual has to offer" (Nordstrom 1997: 81). On the other hand, they provide crucial insights into an event and its larger context because "narrative ordering makes individual events comprehensible by identifying the whole to which they belong" (Polkinghorne 1988: 18). All the while we cannot assume that all narrative is intelligible to us—"listening brings with it no promises of comprehension or understanding" writes Molly Andrews, "what is important is the willingness to become part of the transmission" (2007: 38–9, quoting Apfelbaum).

Vital to the approach advocated here is that these differences, among stories and storytellers, as well as over time and between places, are not smoothed over but are explicitly acknowledged. Stern does this when she stresses "the very 'untidiness' and multiplicity of the narrators' representations of their in/security" (2005: 12). Indeed, Stern (2005: 12) explicitly and strategically emphasizes them when she "explore[s] how in multiple, often conflicting ways, Mayan women's insecurity narratives both adopt the logic of security and contest and resist the imperial moves embedded in such a logic." Doing so tells us important things about the specific conflicts, the multiple strategies to address them, and the various perspectives that exist in relation to them. Such an approach also enables us "to read the texts of practice more inclusively because we can identify 'strange' slippages, conversations, locations, and perspectives that already defy the official menu of international relations, although they often go unnoticed" (Sylvester 1994a: 317).

One might wonder then, about the relationship of the stories that are captured in feminist security narratives to traditional security narratives where these women (and men) either do not feature at all or feature only as symbols. In IR, these official narratives are constrained by practices of sovereignty (cf. Edkins *et al.* 1999; Walker 1990a, 1990b,1993; Weber 1995; Weber and Biersteker 1996), but they are also shaped by male bias (and the two are linked; cf. Stern 2005; Weber 1999). The idea that men somehow have inherently more insight on what is happening at the frontlines, especially concerning matters of war and security, needs to be challenged. Elshtain (1987: 212) notes, "men have been [...] legitimated in that role because they have 'been there' or because they have greater entrée into what it 'must be like'." Meanwhile, "thousands of groups of women around the world [...] are redefining the frontline of response to escalating militarizations and their attendant social, economic, political, and cultural dynamics" (Waller and Rycenga 2000: xiv). Given the nature of war, especially protracted war, unconventional battlefields, and the high numbers of civilian casualties, frontlines have shifted even in conventional understandings.

What is more, many men that write about war and security in IR have not "been there" in any case but receive legitimacy for their stories by simple association with masculinity. On the other hand, many feminist security scholars, including the ones featured here, have actually "been there" and, as a consequence, find themselves less able to produce the kind of abstractions that characterize traditional security studies (cf. Cohn 1988, 1989a, b). Nordstrom reflects on the difference between commenting on war in a place that she has been to as opposed to a place, Iraq in this case, that she only knows through mediated accounts:

When I sat down to write each chapter for this book, I traveled back in my mind's eye to revisit the people and places I wrote about. It is the only way I know how to write about war: being there. In some ways this kind of writing takes a toll: I cannot abstract the suffering of war nor delete the people from the front lines; but in this I hope people reading my work can, in some sense, visit places and meet people they otherwise might not. It is in this meeting that war comes to take definition. But Iraq is different. I have been asked to give interviews by the media, to speak at public venues, and to write on the Iraqi war. I find myself resisting and I realize it is because I cannot enter the war in my minds eye to speak of it. I am not there; I am in a comfortable office experiential light years away.

(Nordstrom 2004: 245)

Elshtain, whose groundbreaking study *Women and War* (1987) adopts a narrative approach to explode the traditional IR confines, makes some important points about why we produce narratives about war. "They invite us to enter a war of words, to familiarize ourselves with the text and the texture of wartime experiences" (1987: 212)—so that we may take part in the experience of war, not so much to extend our sympathy but to "appropriate *their* experience, to draw it within the familiar circle of our understanding" (1987: 220). When men are the only ones authorized to narrate it becomes obvious that the absence of women from war narratives has much to do with who gets to tell them, underscoring the feminist insight that much of the bias of traditional science is rooted in the types of questions asked. This points to "the definition of problematics as a chief culprit in creating the racism, classism, and androcentrism of science to which feminists and others objects," writes Harding (1986: 239), "in problematizing the selection of scientific problems, feminists expose a phenomenon for which no one will admit responsibility."

In *Women and War*, Elshtain considers already written accounts rather than collecting personal accounts as Moon, Nordstorm, and Stern do, in an effort to reveal contradictions, inconsistencies, and tensions within and among them. How do women and men feature in these tales? Which roles are they assigned? Which do they fulfill? What is their meaning within these narratives, how is it contested? How do women and men's roles differ and where are they similar? Elshtain expressly centers her inquiry on the role of myths, how they are constructed and what type of perceptions of war they entail. Through her strategy of marking multiple contradictions and contrasting accounts and structures, she manages to deconstruct recurrent images and establish surprising linkages. In her discussion of similarities between a soldier's and a mother's tasks and intentions, for example, she points out that war "is, for men, at some terrible level the closest thing to what childbirth is for women: the initiation into the power of life and death" (Broyles, quoted in Elshtain 1987: 200).[17]

In her exploration, Elshtain is interested in "what we continue to make of war" (1987: x) as well as to "understand the constitutive role of symbols, myths, metaphors and rhetorical strategies" (ibid.: xi). She cautions that war narratives generally do not recount the reality of women and men's experiences in war, "but function instead to re-create and secure women's location as noncombatants and men's as warriors [and] dangerously overshadow other voices, other stories" (ibid.: 4). Framing what we think about war (and peace), they constitute expressions of profoundly gendered constructs, which are continually reconstituted and reinforced. Narratives that contradict the grand narratives of war, like those presented by Moon, Nordstrom, and Stern, are ignored, regarded as exceptions, or relegated to the margins.

However, many feminist scholars specifically seek out what IR considers to be marginal stories—the stories of prostitutes, poor, indigenous, and of those far from the centers of power. Exploring the limits of multiple stories of peace and war, and the experience of women located somewhere along them, feminists reveal how the personal is political—and international (cf. Enloe 1990b). When Moon makes linkages between the private experience of security, the inter/personal experience of sexuality, and official foreign relationships in, she explodes "the accepted boundaries that separate private sexual relations from politics among nations," writes Tickner (2005: 11), and demonstrates that "prostitution can be a matter of concern in international politics and a bargaining tool for two alliance partners who were vastly unequal in conventional military power." The feminist authors highlighted here demonstrate that actual war destroys the images associated with it. "Wars create new identities or new hyphenations of old identities rather than binding us ever more closely to the tired architectures of only presumable immutable class, race, culture, and colonial experience" (Sylvester 1993: 114). When feminists insist on everyday experience (which is always already mediated) and personal narrative as the basis for knowledge, they need to be prepared that there is going to be a variety of them—and they need to be careful not to make the same mistake as traditional science does and restrict them to a few massively circulated tales.

Reducing women to idealized images restricts their actions, locks them into unwanted positions, and places them in dangerous settings. Elshtain's example of woman as "beautiful soul" serving "as the collective projection of a pure, rarefied, self-sacrificing, otherworldly and pacific Other" (1982: 342) is a case in point.[18] When women are judged by their resemblance to this image rather than by their own account, no room is left for "nonpeaceful identities to inspire war on aspects of the humanist establishment which may deny women power" (Sylvester 1987: 497). Associating women with this idealized image, then, also supports the continuation of patriarchy and militarism, which is why feminists continue to challenge the facile association of women with peace (cf. Alison 2009; MacKenzie 2009; McEvoy 2009; Parashar 2009).

When they remain unexplored, these constructions render women immobile and hinder their exploration of other possibilities—as exemplified in women's association with tradition and the accompanying restrictions on their self-expression and mobility in many societies (and, in particular, by fundamentalist groups). This inhibits ontological security for women, implying a continual violent disruption of their lives, the effects of which are multiple and often devastating. Crucially, the inability to develop a sense of self—to act in accordance with one's desires and interests, and the constant denial of one's capacities seems to be a fundamental cause of distress for women (and likely for men too). I would even venture to propose that the seeds of violence (toward oneself, as well as toward others) are sown in these confining circumstances.

In such circumstances, telling one's story by itself becomes a transformative experience. Although many of the women featured in these narratives did not consider their stories worth telling, they had important things to say and sometimes realized this during the interview. Bakery Auntie, who had worked and lived as a military prostitute in South Korea for nearly all her life, is adamant that she does not have anything worthwhile to say.

> This woman, who had been born in the early 1920s, had received very little formal education but had plenty of knowledge and wisdom to impact. During one of my visits to My Sister's Place, she mentioned that Japan got rich off the Korean War and that South Korea did the same off the Vietnam War. She also asked me once if I knew why the US had fought Iraq in the Gulf War. When I asked her to tell me she stated that it was the US military–industrial complex that wanted the war; the United States had amassed too many fancy weapons, she said, that had to be used. Immediately following such words. She would say under her breath, 'But what do I know? I have no brain. I am uneducated.'
>
> (Moon 1997: 6)

Diana, one of the Mayan women interviewed by Stern echoes these sentiments and also directly addresses the transformative potential of personal narrative. In the context of reviewing the transcript of her interview with Stern, she explains:

> In reality, I was surprised by what I said in these moments. I have never talked of my life I've only suffered … […] And according to me I have not done anything. But seeing the questions that I have written here really made me think. Really, I have lived through a difficult time in my life. [Now] … I continue living the problems maybe in a different way, [reading this text] has made me refresh my memory.
>
> (quoted in Stern 2005: 206–7)

Personal narratives are powerful, not only for the researcher trying to understand a particular situation or event in a way that other methodologies cannot but also for those we are researching. "Stories," Mattingly and Lawlor (2000: 12) write, "can also find a place for those who might find themselves stripped of a voice in the face of [an event or circumstance not of their making]." Echoing the feminist, intersectional commitment advocated here, they note how "a rediscovery of voice is especially significant for those whose ethnic or racial background leaves them feeling particularly misunderstood, voiceless or overwhelmed as they face [problems—or violence—or war]" (ibid.: 12).[19] Sharing one's experiences of war and violence transforms the conflict environment and the meanings of security in it as demonstrated in Nordstrom's (1997: 20–1) account of her time in a village in central Zambezia, talking to children about the war that made her forget that an attack was taking place on the village at the time of her visit. Speaking aloud is important because it recalls and honors lives lost.

Telling and retelling one's story transforms the self—as does listening. The fluidity of subjectivity is exemplified in the way that personal narrative constructs identity and, in turn, security. "*Who (we say) we are* matters in how we conceive of, strive for, and practice security" (Stern 2005: 7). Examining the ways in which the constitution of subjects is intertwined with the ways in which security it is imagined, feminists exemplify and specify Dillon's (1990, 1996) observation that, because securing something requires its identification, security is probably the most important constitutive narrative of political order. This is why "how we 'speak' security, name danger and threats, as well as safety and well-being, implies (and indeed informs) a particular expression of our identity, which serves to represent 'us'—or, in other words, the supposedly sovereign subject of security" (Stern 2005: 7).[20]

To the more general reflection on subjectivity and security, feminists add a methodological commitment to (self) reflexivity, also questioning listening practices. In general, "rather than attending to the variability of human emotion, staying with our speakers as they weave in out of the experiences of their lives, we are trained to keep focused on our research agenda" (Andrews 2007: 14). Feminists challenge the researcher to listen attentively not just to what would seem relevant to their preset agenda but to everything that is being said. Listening attentively, being open to entering another's world and risking one's self, is key to breaking silences, "narration […] is tragically bound to the interlocutor's capacity to hear what is said" (Apfelbaum, quoted in Andrews 2007: 36). Feminist security scholars, then, "take seriously—and critically rethink—the inter-relationship between security and identity in order to make sense of the security articulated in the narratives" (Stern 2005: 7). Whether in Korea, Guatemala, or Mozambique, they also question their own positionality and remain open to reconsidering their own assumptions as well as the impact their presence might have on what is shared (or how it is framed). This commitment to "thinking critically about our relations to the stories we hear, our social constitution as men and women, our I-to-I connections" (Sylvester 1994b: 166) is captured in what Sylvester calls "empathetic cooperation."

> The process of positional slippage that occurs when one listens seriously to the concerns, fears, and agendas of those one is unaccustomed to heeding when building social theory, taking on board, rather than dismissing, finding in the concerns of others borderlands of one's own concerns and fears.
> (1994a: 317)

Nordstrom (1997: 20–8) is particularly worried about the implications of situating oneself too firmly in narrative. Due to the ways in which narrative tries to make experience meaningful—to construct a whole to which it belongs—it is important to remember that narrative organizes experience after the event. "Raw experience is now-to-*now*, and narrative is a now-to-*then* process" (ibid.: 22). At the same time, how we experience an event is itself shaped by a tradition that is constructed and transmitted through narrative (Wibben 2003). As such, there are clear differences between capturing experiences of war as it is ongoing (as Nordstrom tries to), collecting narratives after the fact (as Moon does), and even analyzing narratives produced explicitly for consumption (as Elshtain does). What is more, the limitations of not speaking the language (or only that of the colonizer), or of spending only limited periods of time in a particular locale, shape the research in a particular way (cf. Andrews 2007; Nordstrom 1997; Stern 2005). Rather than sweeping these obstacles under a rug, feminist methodologies emphasize these limitations and specifically address their impact on the research agenda and outcomes (cf. Ackerly *et al.* 2006).

All of these elements are part of the effort to get the story "right"—not in an attempt to uncover the truth, once and for all, but because stories matter. They do things. They have political and material consequences. They function as windows into a particular time and place and "in the narratives of ordinary people's lives, we begin to see some of the major forces of history at work" (Keegan, quoted in Andrews 2007: 205). The contingency of feminist security narratives illustrated here fundamentally challenges the quest for certainty that characterizes traditional security studies. Complementing the insights of some critical scholars, feminists suggest that traditional conceptions of violence and security as an identifiable *thing* or *given* limit our imagination. A rethinking of security and violence as *made* (as well as unmade and remade), through particular but also shifting practices, opens up the possibility of a creative rethinking of securities.[21]

6   The future of feminist security studies

It is not a matter of simple entry of the excluded into an established ontology, but an insurrection at the level of ontology, a critical opening up of the questions, What is real? Whose lives are real? How might reality be remade?

(Butler 2004: 33)

All beginnings and endings of the political narratives which we recount and which we live are ones we select, and the choices we make are significant and strategic.

(Andrews 2007: 190)

For feminists, narratives of 9/11 do not begin on September 11, 2001. Although most official accounts of the events constitute it as a fundamental break with the past, feminists place emphasis on locating issues on a continuum and making connections between seemingly disparate events. Even though the events of the day do, indeed, usher in a new area for some—"most Americans have probably experienced something like the loss of their First-Worldism as a result of September 11 and its aftermath" (Butler 2004: 39)—this is not true for others who do not share the same privilege and whose everyday lives are marked by intersecting oppressions, whether in the United States or elsewhere. Where the US administration emphasized a return to normalcy as "an act of courage, a defiant refusal to live as though times had changed, that is, a refusal to show fear," Delia, Moira, and the other women interviewed by Mattingly et al. (2002: 747), "repeatedly emphasize that they know how to live with fear in a racially charged environment, this was already part of their routine." The loss experienced by some segments of the US population, "the loss of the prerogative, only and always, to be the one who transgresses sovereign boundaries of other states, but never to be in the position of having one's own boundaries transgressed" (Butler 2004: 39) is not, therefore, a shared experience even within the United States or the West. The First World is not unified. At stake then, "is not only the hegemony of Western cultures, but also their identity as unified cultures," as Trinh notes. "The West is painfully made to realize the existence of a Third World in the First World and vice versa" (Trinh 1989: 98).

In her response, the events of September 11, 2001, Edkins (2002b) identifies four possible reactions to the trauma of 9/11: securitization, criminalization, aestheticization, and politicization. Of these, only a strategy that insists on politicization of trauma could successfully "avoid a rapid return to previous forms of security, safety, and power [and produce a] response that does not enter the same cycle of security and trauma" (Edkins 2002b: 254). Emphasizing politicization, "to respond directly to the traumatic impact of what happened, refusing to insert it into pre-written stories but demanding that it be accepted on its own terms" (ibid. 253), she points to the importance of how we narrate these events. Telling a narrative of 9/11 (or any security narrative) depends crucially on where one locates its beginnings and endings.

Although the official narrative of 9/11 starts "with one sunny September morning in 2001 as the opening scene"(Andrews 2007: 107), the attacks were not unanticipated.[1] By refusing to locate continuities with prior events and policies, the events of September11, 2001 became narrated outside any historical context, producing "a narrative which is most hospitable to uncritical patriotism [...] a simple tale of good and evil [that] not only appealed to the wounded American people but also gave permission to react in a particular way" (ibid.: 107–8; cf. Zehfuss 2003). The binary framing of the events—constructing the United States as moral and virtuous—was also achieved through the appropriation of women's liberation to muster support for the war on terror, making "symbolic use of women as markers of cultural, religious, and national difference [as] a device for ranking the men of the 'other' community as inferior according to their deviation from a putatively normal Western standard" (Yuval-Davis 2001: 1–2).

A framing on binary terms limits, or at least influences, the response to a particular event. It impedes the recognition of similarities, continuities, and potential linkages between "us" and "them." It fosters a tendency to underestimate the Other, not to take themseriously as political agents, or even to dehumanize the enemy. Such assumptions lead to a mistaken assessment of an ability to inflict violence, but also to overcome conflict, to rebuild lives, and to become partners in a culture of peace. Rigid framings inhibit more imaginative approaches to conflict and restrict multifaceted forms of agency, which, in turn, allow for less violent encounters. Drawing on women's everyday experience, most feminists recognize control as an illusion. The task then becomes how to face the situation and develop mechanisms for coping with uncertainty and vulnerability, emphasizing their valuable components. Feminists should embrace attempts to capture the singularity of the event, the marginal stories, without rushing into meaning and closing down the narrative before it has begun. This is necessary to counter binary, totalizing narratives of 9/11 as presented by the Bush administration.

Overall, the framing of the events was shaped by a crisis-based ethics, which holds that certain crises constitute a fundamental break from normality and, as such, are separable from everyday life.[2] Many feminists resist such an approach, not only because their version of normality is already multilayered and the notion of a fundamental break depends on a shared version of normality but also because crisis-based ethics and politics "distract from the need for sustained resistance to the enmeshed, omnipresent systems of domination and oppression that so often function as givens in most people's lives" (Cuomo 1996: 31). A fully politicized reaction is needed to challenge these framings. Such an approach refuses the tired old labels and questions the traditional security logic that attempts to weather the crisis by strengthening the existing architecture of security. It locates different beginnings and endings for narratives of 9/11, and it reconceptualizes security narratives more generally, not as a response to crises with clear beginnings and endings, but as a presence that needs to be continually rearticulated. Such a reconceptualization validates the feminist insight that "there is a fundamental interrelationship between all forms of violence, and that violence is a major consequence of the imbalance of a male-dominated society" (Reardon 1993: 39). This violence is simply "more of the same [...] all those same issues have always been in existence" (Mattingly *et al.* 2002: 746).

A narrative always has a perspective from which it is told, and a focalizor whose subjectivity is enhanced (Bal 1997). This specifies the broader feminist insight about the mutually constitutive relationship between identity and narrative (cf. Whitebrook 2001; Yuval-Davis 2006). Feminists challenge security studies and IR at their base by bringing identity into the political arena. Doing so, notes Hekman (2004: 197), they are violating one of the most fundamental tenets of liberalism: "Liberalism's universal citizen has no identity: he is abstract, eschewing the particularity of identity. Identity politics challenges this by bringing the particular into politics." The insistence on the particular, anchored in the commitment to theorizing on the basis of (women's) everyday experience, inevitably provides for different kinds of security narratives than those traditionally told in the discipline of IR. What is more, feminists insist that questions of identity and security are fundamentally interwoven: Any security narrative is also a narrative of political identity (Peterson 1992b; Stern 2005, 2006b; Sylvester 1989; Sylvester 1993).

> Through remembering and recounting their struggles [Mayan women] constructed themselves in their narratives as political subjects who experienced vast insecurities *directly related to the identities that they articulated*. [...]. Their struggles for security (safety, and well-being) were therefore not only reactions to harmful threats, but were also borne out of who they were and strove to be.
>
> (Stern 2001: 272–3, emphasis in original)

When these linkages are drawn out and the process of constructing identity/security narratives is examined, it becomes clear that there is always more than one story to be told and the "normality" presented in the narrative is always contextual. Narratives shift and slide.[3] Understanding that multiple "realities" are created through coexisting narratives is crucial to the feminist project, which can use narrative approaches to uncover how a certain normality/reality is presumed, to challenge these supposedly shared understandings, and to develop alternative scenarios. In addition, narratives are flexible enough to capture multiplicities (e.g., the lives of women in different private/public settings) that might otherwise seem contradictory. Not all narratives do this, of course, but the point is that they could.

The narrative approach developed here, and the emphasis it places on personal narrative, is central to achieving this aim. Personal stories know no disciplinary boundaries, making them an ideal focus of feminists who often draw on multiple disciplines and whose work can be found in the borderlands of existing disciplines. What is more, personal narratives provide a window into someone else's life—their positionality and their perspective on life. It is important to consider whose personal narrative one focuses on, as well as how the narratives are collected and interpreted.

How open a researcher is to engaging in (self-)reflexive research processes, interrogating their own positionality and privilege, questioning its impact on what can be perceived, being willing and able to be surprised, and adopting a stance of curiosity—all of these matter greatly. One danger of this approach is to be seduced by the myth of an empowerment narrative, the idea that we could be "giving a voice" to someone (who am I to give a voice?). Instead, we need to "ask ourselves the hard questions about what we are doing and why we are doing it" (Andrews 2007: 44). Are we engaging in the process to find stories that can be used to provide authenticity for our preconceived ideas? Or are we willing to develop listening practices that allow one to appreciate and draw out the nuances and inconsistencies that inevitably characterize personal narrative? Rather than drawing the other's experience into our circle of understanding, could one allow oneself to be moved by difference, *per se*? Might we enter into the conversation out of friendship, as Lugones suggests?

> A non-imperialist feminism requires that you make a real space for our articulating, interpreting, theorizing and reflecting about the connections among them—a real space must be a non-coerced space—and/or that you follow us into our world out of friendship. I see the 'out of friendship' as the only sensical motivation for this following because the task at hand for you is one of extraordinary difficulty. It requires that you be willing to devote a great part of your life to it and that you be willing to suffer alienation and self-disruption.
>
> (Lugones and Spelman 1983: 576)

We tend not to be taught to develop listening skills that would allow us to hear another's story. We generally frame what we find in relation to expected storylines. "We ourselves are more prepared to hear some kinds of stories than others" (Andrews 2007: 36). This has become particularly obvious in research on trauma where survivors often find themselves "willing to speak, to bear witness. But no one was willing to listen" (Weil, quoted in ibid.: 36–7). As others refuse to listen and to consider possible connections between the trauma experienced by survivors and society at large, the survivor is silenced, isolated, and inhibited in her recovery. This illustrates the extraordinary importance of the work performed by *curandeiros* in Mozambique; at the very minimum, it exhibits a simple willingness to listen, and at its best, it provides a way to reintegrate survivors into the community and, indeed, to create a new world where the old one had been shattered (Nordstrom 1997).

The first task of a feminist security scholar should then be to develop a willingness to listen and to consider another view of the world. An empathetic listener must be willing to accept vulnerability, "to suffer alienation and self-disruption" (Lugones and Spelman 1983: 576). She must be willing to suspend her own framework of meaning, to accept silence, to "accept that some events 'resist simple, straightforward comprehension;' they 'demand witness but defy narrative expression'" (Apfelbaum, quoted in Andrews 2007: 40). Listening, then, does not necessarily lead to understanding. How does one know when one is ready to hear, to listen without hurrying to interpret? When one becomes "less concerned with what we can 'get out of' personal testimony, and more focused on how we might 'get into' all that survivors have to retell" (Greenspan, quoted in ibid.: 39).

Becoming interested in what survivors have to tell us also implies staying attentive over time. The story might evolve, depending on the location (as Stern finds when interviewing the same activist in different locales), as trust and friendship are developed (as Moon finds when she works to teach English to *kijich'on* women at My Mother's Place), and as time passes (as Nordstrom illustrates when she recounts the shifting meaning of parables in the Mozambican conflict).[4] Situating knowledge, placing events on a continuum, paying attention to where we locate beginnings and endings, how frontlines are moving are all strengths found in feminist work—and should be actively cultivated by feminist security scholars. As Enloe proposes, in her foreword to *(En)Gendering the War on Terror,*

> All of us have to stay attentive as the narratives that used to make sense of politically-motivated acts of violence aimed at civilians continue to evolve [...] if we prematurely turn away from the on-going narrative creation process, imagining that the first wave of narrative creation will be forever carved into stone, we risk missing the subtle, sometimes even sharp turn in the popular narrative, even if state officials stubbornly sick to their preferred earlier story.
>
> (Hunt and Rygiel 2006b: viii)[5]

Ideally, feminism emerges in response to a particular political moment, a particular economic, social, and symbolic order. Feminism evolves as a reaction to dissatisfaction with the way women have fared, and continue to fare, in a particular time and place and is, as such, always context specific. Emerging from feminist activism, feminist thought consistently traverses the practice/theory divide that characterizes much traditional science. As feminist thought develops out of practice, it is infused with challenges that demand a constant adjustment of strategies. Contradictions arising between feminist ideals and the practicalities of everyday feminist activism can propel the feminist movement and feminist theorizing to continually address its own bias. To this end, it is important that feminists continue to "simultaneously put women at the center and decenter everything including women" (Ferguson 1993: 3). This presupposes a certain fragmentation of subjectivity within feminist IR in order "not to replicate the oppressive categorizations and exclusions of the metanarrative [...] aping the modernist discourses that have built the discipline of IR thus far" (Jabri and O'Gorman 1999: 7), which is one of the perils of developing Feminist Security Studies (FSS) as a subfield of security studies.

The narrative approach advocated in this book, then, accommodates the feminist methodological commitments outlined by Tickner (2006: 22–9): asking feminist research questions, basing one's research on women's experiences, adopting a (self)-reflexive stance, and having an emancipatory agenda. One way to ask feminist research questions is to follow Enloe's (2004) call for curiosity about any female/male-associated division of labor. Ferguson's (1993) adoption of mobile subjectivities captures the self-reflexive, ever-changing nature of feminist research, whereas Sylvester's (1994a, b) method of empathetic cooperation embeds feminist reflexivity in the production/gathering of women's experiential knowledge. Illustrating the power of an emancipatory agenda, Patricia Hill Collins' (2000) work on intersectionality challenges feminists to take into account how women's lives are shaped by intersecting oppressions based on markers of identity, such as race and gender. She reminds us that "oppression cannot be reduced to one fundamental type, and that oppressions work together in producing injustice" (ibid.: 18). The struggle of one oppressed group cannot be separated from that of others. As such, Black feminist thought, for example, has to be "*both* Black women's empowerment *and* conditions of social justice" (ibid.: x). This feminist narrative approach provides a way in which these commitments can be combined and brought to bear on the field of security studies.

It is, above all, these feminists' methodological commitments that distinguish FSS from other approaches. This can be illustrated by reference to the scope and contents of critical security studies.[6] These tackle many of the same issues and, for the most part, embrace an emancipatory agenda. They do not, however, share some of the central feminist methodological commitments: critical security scholars tend not to ask feminist research questions (the selection of problems to research is a main source of bias in traditional science) and do not base their research on women's experiences. As a result, they find themselves with strikingly different research agendas, findings, and policy recommendations.[7] With their unique methodological choices, feminist scholars can counter the prevalence of bodiless data in security studies by highlighting personal stories.

Embracing empathetic listening techniques, and the slippage in positionality that accompanies them, is of fundamental importance to the feminist project: "If we do not feel ourselves to be personally at risk when we interrogate the lives of others, then we are not doing our jobs" (Andrews 2007: 44). Feminists are asking security scholars to abandon the search for security and acknowledge that we are always already insecure. There is no escape from our fundamental condition of vulnerability—and ultimately, from death.[8] This poses a major challenge to critical security studies, which has a tendency to exhibit an awkward do-goodism in the imperialist tradition of "saving natives." Nonetheless, critical security scholars are likely to be more open and able to accommodate feminist insights than traditional security scholars who banish vulnerability, attempting "to make ourselves secure at the expense of every other human consideration" (Butler 2004: 30). Feminist security narratives show how we continue to live our lives in light of vulnerability, an avenue foreclosed in traditional security studies, which counters uncertainty with a fantasy of mastery exhibited in the construction of "narratives—about the strength and invulnerability of the state, about the security and protection it can give, and about the way in which lives lost are lives sacrificed for a greater cause" (Edkins 2002b: 253).

Pointing to the illusion of shared experience—and shared First World privilege—is a first step toward less violent encounters for "the loss of First World presumption is the loss of a certain horizon of experience, a certain sense of the world itself as a national entitlement" (Butler 2004: 39). Security scholars need to learn to listen attentively and empathetically to begin to consider not only what the world looks like from another vantage point but also to realize that their ignorance is harmful. Many feminists, particularly in the West, also need to work on this because they often exhibit the same kind of clumsy do-goodism that homogenizes the Third World. "I do not think that you have any obligation to understand us," writes Lugones. "You do have an obligation to abandon your imperialism, your universal claims, your reduction of us to yourselves simply because they seriously harm us" (Lugones and Spelman 1983: 576). Thus are the politics of security.

Feminism is political. Consequently, FSS scholars should not be afraid to tackle the politic of security directly—including the a priori assumption that security is inherently a good thing. Noting that it is impossible to secure everything takes on new meaning in this context. It implies a radically different ontology based on an acceptance of vulnerability and uncertainty where ambiguity and strangeness are embraced or at least acknowledged. Feminist security scholars cannot let traditionalists have the uncontested say about what the concept of security refers to, especially because security is so powerful when evoked. This requires that feminist scholars seriously engage debates in security studies and they demand the policies made in their name actually honor their contributions.

This book brings feminist political and methodological commitments to bear on the field not to develop a feminist security theory (though some thoughts in this direction might have crept into the preceding chapters) but rather to make a political intervention—a plea to recognize the dangers involved in establishing FSS as a subfield of security studies when feminist aims and the scope of their concerns explode its confines at every possible turn. Feminist security scholars have a long and proud tradition of feminist writing on issues of peace, violence, and war. They draw on it, further it, and move far beyond a broadening and deepening of security studies toward an opening. Challenging the limits of existing security narratives, both content and form, they revise the politics and meanings of security as we know them. As such, similar to most feminist interventions in IR, FSS should remain uncomfortably lodged at the intersections of feminist theory, feminist IR, and security studies. Only when feminist security scholarship remains true to feminist methodological and political commitments and to continual, radical, and deliberate critique, allowing only for temporal resting points, can it fulfill the promise of an opening of security studies.

Appendix

1. Good evening.
2. Today, our fellow citizens, our way of life, our very freedom came under attack in a series of deliberate and deadly terrorist acts.
3. The victims were in airplanes, or in their offices; secretaries, businessmen and women, military and federal workers; moms and dads, friends and neighbors.
4. Thousands of lives were suddenly ended by evil, despicable acts of terror.
5. The pictures of airplanes flying into buildings, fires burning, and huge structures collapsing have filled us with disbelief, terrible sadness, and a quiet, unyielding anger.
6. These acts of mass murder were intended to frighten our nation into chaos and retreat.
7. However, they have failed; our country is strong.
8. A great people has been moved to defend a great nation.
9. Terrorist attacks can shake the foundations of our biggest buildings, but they cannot touch the foundation of America.
10. These acts shattered steel, but they cannot dent the steel of American resolve of America.
11. America was targeted for attack because we are the brightest beacon for freedom and opportunity in the world.
12. And no one will keep that light from shining.
13. Today, our nation saw evil, the very worst of human nature.
14. And we responded with the best of America—with the daring of our rescue workers, with the caring for strangers and neighbors who came to give blood and help in any way they could.
15. Immediately following the first attack, I implemented our government's emergency response plans.
16. Our military is powerful, and it's prepared.
17. Our emergency teams are working in New York City and Washington, D.C. to help with local rescue efforts.
18. Our first priority is to get help to those who have been injured and to take every precaution to protect our citizens at home and around the world from further attacks.
19. The functions of our government continue without interruption.

20. Federal agencies in Washington that had to be evacuated today are reopening for essential personnel tonight, and will be open for business tomorrow.
21. Our financial institutions remain strong, and the American economy will be open for business as well.
22. The search is underway for those who are behind these evil acts.
23. I have directed the full resources of our intelligence and law enforcement communities to find those responsible and to bring them to justice.
24. We will make no distinction between the terrorists who committed these acts and those who harbor them.
25. I appreciate so very much the members of Congress who have joined me in strongly condemning these attacks.
26. And on behalf of the American people, I thank the many world leaders who have called to offer their condolences and assistance.
27. America and our friends and allies join with all those who want peace and security in the world, and we stand together to win the war against terrorism.
28. Tonight, I ask for your prayers for all those who grieve, for the children whose worlds have been shattered, for all whose sense of safety and security has been threatened.
29. And I pray they will be comforted by a power greater than any of us, spoken through the ages in Psalm 23: "Even though I walk through the valley of the shadow of death, I fear no evil, for You are with me."
30. This is a day when all Americans from every walk of life unite in our resolve for justice and peace.
31. America has stood down enemies before, and we will do so this time.
32. None of us will ever forget this day.
33. However, we go forward to defend freedom and all that is good and just in our world.
34. Thank you.
35. Good night, and God bless America.

Notes

Introduction

1 This resonates with observations of INCITE! Women of Color Against Violence collective: The choice to privilege one perspective over another is never innocent or obvious but always intensely political. What is more, the insistence on a singular narrative is itself a form of violence.

> The challenge women of color face in combating personal *and* state violence is to develop strategies for ending violence that *do* assure safety for survivors of sexual/domestic violence and *do not* strengthen our oppressive criminal justice apparatus. Our approaches must always challenge the violence perpetrated through multinational capitalism and the state.
>
> (INCITE! Women of Color Against Violence 2006: 2)

2 Lawlor and Mattingly set up the groups initially as part of a study of African American families who cared for children with special health needs (Mattingly and Lawlor 2000; Mattingly *et al.* 2002).
3 See also her contribution to the documentary *After 9/11* (more information at http://www.watsoninstitute.org/infopeace/after911).
4 Peterson (1992b) published an early intervention as a chapter in *Gendered States*.
5 Tickner (2001) also devotes a chapter of her more recent *Gendering World Politics* to the topic, specifically pointing out some overlap with critical security studies (cf. Chapter 4).
6 The focus on social and economic justice is also a recurring theme in Collins' work on intersectionality, which is crucial to the feminism adopted here (cf. Chapter 1). Collins (2000) explicitly places Black feminist thought in the context of other movements for justice and notes their interdependence.
7 Furthermore, feminists have linked these issues to economic and environmental exploitation, thus effectively providing a broad conception of security long before IR security studies came to think of it (e.g., Boserup 1970; Oswald 1979).
8 More recently, security studies have begun to see more feminist work, for example, a special issues of *Security Studies*, also published as an edited volume (with additional contributions—Sjoberg 2009a) as well as a widely circulated piece in *International Security* by Hudson *et al.* (2008/2009). What is more, since 2008, the FSS network (http://groups.yahoo.com/group/FeministSecurityStudies/) has organized a series of panels at the ISA Annual Conventions.
9 March (1982) and Thiele (1986) offer analyses of why women and feminist research remain "invisible" in different disciplines that are quite applicable here too (cf. Wibben 2004).

10 I am here referring to a broad notion of critical security studies popularized by Krause and Williams in *Critical Security Studies: Concepts and Cases* (other work in this area includes Adler and Barnett 1998; Bilgin *et al.* 1998; Booth 1991a, 1997; Buzan 1983, 1991; Buzan *et al.* 1998; Campbell 1998b; Croft and Terriff 2000; Dillon 1996; Huysmans 2006; Katzenstein 1996; Krause 1998; Krause and Williams 1996, 1997a; Lipschutz 1995; McRae and Hubert 2001; Weldes *et al.* 1999; Wyn Jones 1995, 1999).

11 For example, Buzan's *People, States and Fear*, originally published in 1983, pre-dates the end of the Cold War as does much of the work in peace research. Azar's work on protracted social conflict (begun in the 1970s) is also an important example (e.g., Azar 1990).

12 Huysmans (1998, 2006) is one of a handful of scholars who have consistently argued for a discussion of the meaning of security. Especially poststructuralists scholars have, directly or indirectly, challenged meanings for security (cf. Hansen 2010).

13 A discussion of meanings, and a possible multiplication or complication thereof is here, in line with certain epistemological assumptions that characterize accepted security narratives (cf. Chapters 2 and 4), seen to constitute meaninglessness suggesting that there is only one correct meaning—just as there is only one correct narrative. Such an insistence by itself should be seen as a form of violence.

14 Note that sometimes the term "widening" is used to indicate a "broadening" and that Booth (2005) uses the term "deepening" to refer to something more akin to what I call "opening." I use the terms "broadening" and "deepening" following Krause and Williams (1996).

15 One might think of attempts to include the notion of structural violence (Galtung 1969) in security discussions and more recent attempts by scholars in the Aberystwyth school of security studies (e.g., Booth 1991b, 1997; Wyn Jones 1999), as well as various feminist approaches (e.g., Boulding 2000; Reardon 1985, 1993; Tickner 1992, 2001).

16 This was pointed out in an exchange between Keohane (1989) and Weber (1994) and reiterated in an exchange between Keohane (1998), Tickner (1997b, 1998) and Marchand (1998) a few years later.

17 See the outline of their involvement in peace research described earlier and consider the work of the Women's International League for Peace and Freedom, which has been active since 1915.

18 An exception to this trend has been the passing of United Nations Security Council Resolution 1325 in 2000 and the debates that have begun as a result (e.g., Cohn *et al.* 2004; Hudson 2009).

19 The number of citations is limited even when feminist scholarship is acknowledged as a possible contribution to the field of security studies (Booth 1997, 2007; Wæver 2004).

1 Feminist interventions: the politics of identity

1 For more on feminist reactions to the 'war on terror' in Afghanistan and Iraq see Caiazza 2001; Hunt and Rygiel 2006b; Wibben 2002; Yuval-Davis 2001.

2 Until otherwise noted, translations are mine and original quotes will be provided in the footnote: "Fourier stellte die These auf, daß der Grad der Befreiung der Fau der Prüfstein einer jeden Gesellschaft und allgemeiner Maßstab der menschlichen Entwicklung sei" (Fourier 1990: 188).

3 The terms "Third World" or "Western" feminism are also contested, of course, because they seem to imply a measure of coherence within these groupings, which is likely illusory—for example—middle and upper class women in the first, second, and third worlds share much privilege, and women of all classes have experiences of domestic violence.

4 According to the 2007 report on "Women and Men in OECD Countries," median wages for men are higher than those for women in all OECD countries (several countries such as Korea, Japan, Germany, Switzerland, Canada, and the United States have median earnings more than 20 percent higher). Find out more at http://www.oecd.org/gender.

5 The Combahee River Collective Statement, which presented these radical challenges in 1977, still resonates today (Combahee River Collective 2000 [1983]).

6 Sylvester (2010) also includes the 1994 conference to celebrate the 75th anniversary of the International Politics Department at the University of Wales in Aberystwyth that "reviewed all leading IR scholarships, including feminism and postmodernism." Many of the contributions from this conference were subsequently published in *International Theory: Positivism and Beyond* (Smith *et al.* 1996).

7 The gender analysis advocated here needs to have its roots in feminism because it is part of a broader set of methodological commitments discussed in detail in the next chapter (cf. Carpenter 2003, 2005; Kinsella 2003; Sjoberg 2006).

8 Not all feminists are women, of course.

9 Truth here refers to "the ensemble of rules according to which the true and the false are separated and specific effects of power attached to the true" (Foucault 1980: 132).

10 More recently, the distinction between peace research and security studies scholarship has become blurred—as the success of the securitization (Copenhagen School) approach shows (Buzan *et al.* 1998). FSS are similarly drawing together these two fields as scholars are trained in either (or both), and some interesting work has emerged in the past decade or so (e.g., Giles and Hyndman 2004; Jacobs *et al.* 2000; Lorentzen and Turpin 1998; Meintjes *et al.* 2001; Moser and Clark 2001; Waller and Rycenga 2000).

11 See also Cockburn (2007) on the contributions of feminist activists to FSS.

12 Though the controversy surrounding the account of US soldiers raping as they advanced during Second World War (Lily 2007) suggests that this norm might be changing or that at least "good soldiers" should not rape.

13 The use of rape as a genocidal tactic is not a new tactic (e.g., large-scale rapes during the Nanking Massacre of 1937–38 or the deliberate use of rape against certain ethnic groups during the 1971 war for Bangladeshi independence). What is more, in the past decade or so, an intensification of various forms of sexualized violence (rape being part of a broader spectrum) is notable, particularly in protracted conflicts in Africa (Turshen 2001): From the Rwandan genocide to Côte D'Ivoire, the Congo, and Sudan (HRW 2000, 2007; IRIN 2007).

14 For other overviews, see Blanchard (2003); Broadhead (2000); Enloe (1987); Shepherd (2010); Sjoberg and Martin (2010); Tickner (1992) as well as chapters in Terriff *et al.* (1999); Tickner (2001).

15 Illustrated recently in the c.a.s.e. controversy (c.a.s.e. collective 2006; Sylvester 2007) as well as in the lack of coverage in the top five IR security journals (with the exception of *Security Dialogue*). A notable exception is "The Heart of the Matter" (Hudson *et al.* 2008/2009) because it is presented in terms more familiar to the mainstream (and published in *International Security*).

2 Challenging meanings

1 In German, the language in which both Gadamer and Heidegger theorized, the term *Vorurteil* is used, which generally translates as prejudice. Gadamer uses the notion of *Vorurteil*, in the sense of a judgment or knowledge arrived at before attempting to find a meaning in an engagement with a text (the world). This is part of the process of understanding since the interpreters' thoughts have already merged with the subject matter of the text. Gadamer, who asserts that "it is our prejudices that constitute our being" (1976: 9), wants to restore "to its rightful place a positive concept of prejudice that was driven out of our linguistic usage by the French and the English Enlightenment" (1976: 9).

2 This is not to say that choice is free, or simply made according to some criteria. As Hirschman (1996: 69–70) notes, "the choice is never abstract, for the 'individual' making these choices exists in a particular context, which always limits choices even as it simultaneously produces them."

3 Hollis and Smith (1991: 46) carry this story into IR, noting "symbolically, [Newton] inaugurates three centuries of amazing progress in explaining how nature works and in harnessing these discoveries."

4 More specifically, "new histories of other so-called progressive moments in history constantly reveal, first, that women tend to lose status at the moments traditional history marks as progressive. More strongly, democratic social impulses appear systematically to deteriorate women's social powers and opportunities" (Harding 1986: 224). The latter claim should be examined closely in (feminist) IR.

5 Note that hermeneutics was then concerned mainly with the interpretation of the Bible. The term hermeneutics has been used, since the seventeenth century, to refer to the science or art of interpretation of meaning. Until the end of the nineteenth century, hermeneutics was mostly concerned with the normative and technical aspects of interpretation and was considered a "helping discipline" for the more established sciences. Its main idea was to provide methodical guidelines to prevent arbitrariness in the interpretational sciences. Grondin (1991: 1) maintains that "wherever there are halfway methodical guidelines for interpretation were provided one could, in the wider sense, speak about hermeneutics." "*Überall, wo halbwegs methodische Interpretationsanweisungen angeboten wurden, kann man im weitesten Sinne von Hermeneutik sprechen*" (Grondin 1991: 1).

6 This is maintained by Schleiermacher and rests with the hermeneutics school until the rejection by Heidegger and Gadamer who theorize about the finitude of Being (*Dasein*) and connected to that the impossibility to understand completely the intention of the author. Additionally, Gadamer writes that with its completion, the text acquires additional meaning the author may not have been aware of.

7 This is mainly an issue of so-called feminist empiricists (cf. Harding 1986; Sylvester 1994) but is also relevant when scholars not steeped in feminist theory use gender as a category of analysis (cf. Carpenter 2003, 2005; Kinsella 2003; Sjoberg 2006).

8 In this vein, some feminists argue that women's roles as caretakers and nurturers lead them to develop different ways of thinking—maternal thinking—and an alternative ethics (cf. Gilligan 1982; Ruddick 1989a; Tronto 1987).

9 Several authors develop the concept and history of patriarchy (cf. Lerner 1986; Mies 1986; Walby 1990). Although patriarchy is present throughout the human history (as far as we know), its shape shifts along with the broader cosmology.

10 *Dasein* is once again one of those terms that refer to much more than can be translated by using the word "Being" as the prefix "da" means "there." Directly translated, it would thus rather mean "Being there" and I have also come across the notion "Being in the world" in English texts.

11 "*Einen Text der Vergangenheit verstehen heißt ihn auf unsere Situation zu übersetzen*" (Grondin 1991: 150).

12 "*Teilhabe an einem Sinne, einer Tradition, schließlich and einem Gespräch*" (Grondin 1991: 153). A note on translation: what I translate as conversation—*Gespräch*—is often translated as dialogue instead. I prefer the notion of conversation, which is also used by Rorty who argues "that the task of philosophy is not to discover absolutes but to continue the 'conversation of mankind'" (Hekman 1990: 9).

13 "*Jedes Verstehen von einer Motivation oder von Vorurteilen her bedingt ist*" (Grondin 1991: 144).

14 Note that for Gadamer "understanding is language-bound [where] language is not a system of signals that we sent off with the aid of telegraphic key when we enter the office or transmission station. [It is] the act that is linguistically creative and world experiencing" (1976: 15).

15 "*Verstehen niemals ein subjecktives Verhalten zu einen gegebenen 'Gegenstande' ist, sondern zur Wirkungsgeschichte, und das heißt zum Sein dessen gehört was verstanden wird*" (Gadamer 1965: xvii). Further, effective history (*Wirkungsgeschichte*) refers, in literary criticism, to the study of interpretations or the historical reception of a work under examination (see Grondin 1991: 146ff).

16 In times of revolution, Slavoj Žižek writes that we encounter a political moment when a new order is not yet established and thus no morality in place that would provide an

order to fall upon. This is also a moment of subjectivity as the participants find themselves "confronted with the responsibility, the burden of decision pressing upon [their] shoulders" (quoted in Edkins 1999: 7). The genealogist inconveniences because she points to this moment of decision in which a new order emerges without authority (in its tight relation to subjectivity) to legitimize it. Phrased differently, the genealogist destabilizes the commonly accepted myth of origin, put into place to hide the contingency and violence of the political moment and its establishment of a particular social, symbolic, political order.

17 Haftendorn also notes, "in the Unites States the field of international security studies has often been equated with strategic studies" (quoted in Baldwin 1995: 125).

18 Walt claims to quote Nye and Lynn-Jones, but their report on the state of international security studies provides a quite balanced picture. They explicitly note that "the tendency to equate international security studies with strategic studies unduly narrows the scope of the field and cuts it off from its political, economic, and historical context" (1988: 26).

19 All of these questions are not unique to security studies—indeed some of them are fundamental questions that all disciplines should engage as far as feminists are concerned.

20 The meanings accorded to the term security tend to be (briefly) elaborated upon, mostly by way of an introduction (see e.g., listing in Buzan 1991: 16–17). Yet, I would maintain that (within security studies) there so far has been little focus on the contexts within which these meanings emerge and which they in turn sustain (the notable exception possibly being Der Derian, 1995 and to some extent Rothschild, 1995).

21 Conceptual analyses (e.g., Baldwin 1995; Wolfers 1962) can be problematic because sometimes, as in Baldwin's case, they aim to "clarif[y] the meaning of security by eliminating ambiguities and inconsistencies in the different uses of security" (Huysmans 1998: 231). Wolfers' attempt to "demonstrat[e] the meaning of national security, including the ambiguities it comprises" (ibid.) is preferable over the former.

22 Note: These processes of subjectification are profoundly gendered (see e.g., Batscheider 1993).

23 She also points out that, "as long as the individualist model dominates our conceptual vocabulary however, it is difficult to see this contradiction" (Hirschmann 1996: 64).

24 The dominant framing of security is heavily reliant on this liberal understanding—security is almost exclusively identified as a *thing*; a measurable entity (cf. Chapter 5). Paul Chilton (1996b: 61) explicates,

In Western culture, 'security' [in the sense of prediction and strategic control of future events] is also thought of as a commodity that can be bought, sold, or stored. [It] presupposes the ontological metaphor, 'security is a measurable mass.' One can have 'more', or 'less' security, 'increase' it, 'reduce' it, 'measure' it, 'improve' it or 'enhance' it, in socio-economic, policing and military domains. What can be measured can be given a value, priced, and sold. In domestic socio-economic domain in the West security is a commodity that may be 'provided' or 'provided for' by the state, or a commodity that can be purchased by individuals in greater or lesser quantities. In policing and military domains also security is a quantifiable and purchasable commodity.

Chilton criticizes this view, as I would (see Chilton 1996a, 1996b). Having "more or less" requires that security would be measurable, which in turn requires that there is one standard according to which one could have it "in a greater or lesser degree." Yet, any standard one might agree on will always be arbitrary and context specific.

3 Toward a narrative approach

1 An approach—"not 'analysis,' 'system,' 'methodology,' or 'model,' but an 'approach,' which recognizes the impossibility of pure coherence of thought and object, and yet draws the self into the event" (Der Derian 1992: 173).

2 A note on terminology: Currie (1998: 2) asserts, "as an *-ology*, narratology declares the value of systematic and scientific analysis by which it operated before poststructuralist critiques impacted on literary studies" and prefers narrative theory instead. I also prefer the term narrative theory but would maintain that narratology, the systematic study of narrative, should not simply be dismissed but appropriated for the new approaches.

3 What is more, the medium matters greatly. In television, for example, because of the heavy emphasis on image, form shapes content to a considerable extent. Neil Postman (1987: 7) quips, "You cannot do political philosophy on television. Its form works against the content."

4 Bal insists that trying to delineate a corpus of purely narrative texts is futile and distracts from the possible insights gained through the application of narratological tools of analysis.

> Narrative theory makes describable only the narrative aspects of a text and not all the characteristics, even of a clearly narrative text. It is therefore as impossible, as it is undesirable, to specify a specific corpus. This is an issue of relevance [...] we can use the theory to describe segments of non-narrative texts as well as aspects of any given text.
>
> (Bal 1997: 10)

5 Social and political analyses also convey meaning and value, notes Shapiro. For one, "there is a level of production in the text which operates outside of the author's explicit awareness. Even [in] those texts which explicitly disavow particular ideational commitments" (Shapiro 1988: 8). Furthermore, "within whatever discourse we are referring to, the traditional notion that ethical thinking is an autonomous form of reasoning is called in to question" (ibid.: 9).

6 First, the association between author and external focalizor cannot be assumed as easily as implied here, though I would maintain that it often is the case nonetheless. Furthermore, the idea that such a presentation is likely to be interrogated has to be complicated because an external focalizor can also present a "view from nowhere," thus invoking objectivity or "truth." I return to such specifics in the discussion of the actual analysis.

7 Note that Bal (1997: 189) uses possibility (virtuality), event (realization), and result (conclusion). I find that these distinctions are confusing and would furthermore like to reserve the term "event" to designate less specific elements of the analysis (as Bal actually uses it elsewhere).

8 Bal cautions,

> this does not imply that it makes no difference if we work at random. The structures should be built on the basis of data; the relationship between data and what is done with it is only convincing if made explicit, and some degree of relevancy will be foreseeable [...] to be interested in undertaking the analysis at all.
>
> (1997: 193–4)

9 The exact time of impact varies according to the different timelines. I use the timeline provided by CNN (2001c). Unless otherwise noted, all times used are US Eastern Standard Time.

10 Through extensive use of transcripts from media sources and eyewitness accounts, I hope to emphasize the confusion, fear, and disbelief of the moment, as well as the obvious impossibility to distinguish facts and rumors. On the other hand, I am also trying to identify a framing of events by others, noting also that any representation involves all sorts of suppositions, preferences, and restrictions.

11 The moment, at which Bush's chief of staff, Andrew H. Card Jr, whispers the news of the event in Bush's ear during a visit to a primary school in Florida, was captured on video and shows a visibly struck president.

12 See also the collection of articles and analysis on "9/11: Images, Imaging, Imagination" on the website of the Information Technology, War and Peace Project [see http://www.watsoninstitute.org/infopeace/911/]. Gabler (2001) and Heidkamp (2001) in particular produce insightful comparisons between 9/11 and movies.

13 Video footage from the attacks is available on the *New York Times* website in the "A Nation Challenged" section that, since September 18, 2001, has covered the aftermath of 9/11. For the first week after the attacks, from September 11–18, 2001, coverage of the events took the entire front-page and A-section of the *New York Times* under the rubric "A Day of Terror" [see http://www.nytimes.com/pages/national/dayofterror/ for an archive].

14 Unless otherwise noted, references at the end of a paragraph indicate that previous quotes are from one document only.

15 Consider also the various alternative explanations (generally dismissed as conspiracy theories) that have been put forward.

16 There are continuous updates and corrections on reports. One of the major concerns here includes the reports of another missing United Airlines plane. As it emerges at 11:59am, the missing flight was United Airlines Flight 175—the one that had hit the south tower of the WTC at 9:03am (times according to CNN 2001c).

17 Jackson specifically looks at "the public language of the 'war on terror' and the way in which language has been deployed to justify and normalize a global campaign of counter-terrorism" (Jackson 2005: 1).

18 The *Address to the Nation* (Bush 2001b) is included as Appendix.

19 Unless otherwise noted, all quotations in this section are of the *Address to the Nation* (Bush 2001b).

20 Of interest here is that Bush mentions the military in the same paragraph, but instead of saying that the military is patrolling the skies and shores in a defensive effort (as it was that night) or giving some other specific reference, he simply states, "Our military is powerful, and it's prepared" (Bush 2001b). This suggests that the military is not doing anything specific at that point in time. It further insinuates, and this might be more interesting, that we would know what it is doing being part of a tradition where mentioning the military is taken to mean that there will be military action.

21 I predicate this on the assumption that Bush sees the events as a process and not fixed, suggested by his remark that "None of us will ever forget this day. Yet we go forward" (Bush 2001b), which indicates a moment of instability which will be remedied in time. Note also that this is not to privilege some independent "reality" out there but as a witness to the events and their framing point to the partiality if the selection in the *Address*.

22 In retrospect, we are aware that initial fears of more than 10,000 deaths were a gross overestimation. In preparation for the 1-year anniversary of the events at the WTC site, authorities reported that "after surging as high as 6,729 in late September and dropping below 3,000 in January, the final list of victims should end up at 2,800 or just below" (Lipton 2002). According to *The 9/11 Commission Report*, "more than 2,600 people died at the World Trade Center; 125 died at the Pentagon; 256 died on the four planes" (9/11 Commission 2004). What is more, the dead hailed from more than 90 countries.

23 Edkins describes the necessary incompleteness of trauma in particular by way of a "picture of witnesses to the collapse standing with their hands over their mouths in the face of the unspeakable. They watch with their mouths covered as the impossible, the unbelievable becomes real in front of their eyes." She goes on to describe how,

the traumatic event is one that exceeds experience. It cannot be explained or recounted. It is outside the bounds of language, outside the worlds we have made for ourselves. It can be spoken about, of course, but words always in a sense fail: they are insufficient. And their failure is precisely a failure to capture what is traumatic about what has happened. The way that what happened on 11 September is referred to as 'the events' and by reference to the date is symptomatic of its traumatic aspect.[...] I would like to suggest that we hold on to that word.

(Edkins 2001)

24 Moving on to practices of remembrance before even the last plane went down is one way to restore certainty and control. "Not only did Bush and other leaders move directly to remembrance, but talk of rebuilding, not only in New York, but of world order too, began straight away. The world was being rebuilt, power and sovereignty re-installed" (Edkins 2001).

25 Anachrony refers to chronological deviations. Retroversions are anachronies that lie in the past (from the moment that is being presented in the fabula), whereas anticipations concern the future (Bal 1997: 83ff.).

26 Accumulation of detail also serves to slow down or speed up the narrative, often to produce a semblance of normalcy or to create suspense.

27 The religious imagery is used, such that the terrorists are identified as the (dark) "evil" and the United States as the "bright beacon, whose light will not be kept from shining," most strikingly in the reference to Psalm 23 at the end of the *Address* that literally refers to "the valley of the shadow of death" and "evil."

28 It is important to note the fact that this was a televised speech, an element of the narrative that would be analyzed on the text level of Bal's narratology. Although it would certainly be of interest to explore the specificity of the medium in detail, it is not directly relevant to the argument I am making here. However, I do return to the role of the media in general in later parts of this chapter.

29 It is important to consider how the Bush administration was able to ignore these questions—but it is fairly easy to answer: they simply refused to debate the issues. In the weeks after 9/11, all Fleischer ever said when the topic came up was "no comment" as par of a policy of "Information Lockdown" (Shapiro 2001) justified by a need to withhold information for security reasons (see also Shanker 2002; Wibben 2001).

30 In May 2002, *Time Magazine*'s cover story on "The Bombshell Memo," a letter by FBI agent Coleen Rowley (2002), triggered a series of inquiries. Turn also to "Imaginary Intelligence" on the website of the Information Technology, War and Peace Project (at http://www.watsoninstitute.org/infopeace/911/).

31 The persistent use of "evil" and "evildoers" by the Bush administration, as evident in this collection, deserves to be debated by itself. A PBS frontline special on "Faith and Doubt at Ground Zero" makes a tentative attempt but fails to discuss the political implications of the notion (http://www.pbs.org/wgbh/pages/frontline/shows/faith/). Edkins, drawing on Levi, cautions

that we not disregard the humanity of those who plan and organise unilateral, deliberate slaughters of innocent and defenceless people. Despite their utter contempt of life, they are nevertheless human like the rest of us. If we demonise them we are taking an easy way out. We need to refuse such a facile understanding-and the polarisation to which it can lead-and try to establish, step by step, the details of their guilt.

(2001)

32 An attempt to debate and develop some of these questions was made at the Technologies of Anti- and Counter-Terror Symposium at the Watson Institute at Brown University in June 2002 (see http://www.watsoninstitute.org/infopeace/TACTSYM/).

33 This is also the argument poststructuralist analyses of security make (cf. Chapter 4).

34 Edkins goes on to explain how this moment, this act of constitution is immediately hidden and a narrative (myth) of origins put into place. The political moment is hidden, "once the moment of decision has past (assuming, since we cannot know, that there was one) the rule that the decision appears to have followed has already been invented" (Edkins 1999: 82). Just as the political moment takes place in "the temporality of future anterior, the 'will have been'" (ibid.), a narrative is told in anticipation of a sequence and ending that will make the beginning and the unfolding of the narrative intelligible. As

such then, the narrative justifies itself and makes it seem as though it followed the rule, which, however, has only just been invented.

4 Security as narrative

1 Furthermore "an analogy is drawn with the prewar period and the failure of the League of Nations to react forcefully to Hitler's occupation of the Rhineland and Italy's invasion of Abyssinia" (Kaldor 1991: 315). Dick Cheney makes a similar link in an August 26, 2002, speech arguing for a preemptive strike against Iraq:

> We will profit as well from a review of our own history. There are a lot of World War II veterans in the hall today. For the United States, that war began on December 7, 1941, with the attack on Pearl Harbor and the near-total destruction of our Pacific Fleet. Only then did we recognize the magnitude of the danger to our country. Only then did the Axis powers fully declare their intentions against us. By that point, many countries had fallen. Many millions had died. And our nation was plunged into a two-front war resulting in more than a million American casualties. To this day, historians continue to analyze that war, speculating on how we might have prevented Pearl Harbor, and asking what actions might have averted the tragedies that rate among the worst in human history.
>
> (2002)

2 Wolfers formulation relies on the idea that security be somehow measurable (cf. Chapter 2).
3 Her comment is made with regard to the sectoral approach introduced by Buzan (1983) and fundamental to the Copenhagen School (Buzan *et al.* 1998).
4 He goes on to describe the circularity of the identification of danger: "The 'influence of timidity,' as Nietzsche puts it, creates people who are willing to subordinate affirmative values to the 'necessities' of security: 'they fear change, transitoriness, this expresses a straitened soul, full of mistrust and evil experiences'" (Der Derian 1995: 34).
5 Furthermore,

> Foreign Policy is one part of a multifaceted process of inscription that disciplines by framing man in the spatial and temporal organization of inside and outside, self and other: that is, in the 'state'. These practices do not operate in terms of the domestic society that is pregiven, nor do they signify and absolute and preexisting space from which threats to domestic society emerge. Their very operation frames the domestic society in whose name they claim to be operating through their claim to know the source of threats to domestic society and 'man'.
>
> (Campbell 1998: 62)

6 When they do not fit into the order, they "find their place," more often than not, as the irrational, emotional, or otherwise (often by association with the feminine) dismissed tale.
7 It is only at the beginning of the twentieth century that the appeal to the *nation* gained greater acceptance (especially after Woodrow Wilson's "Fourteen Points" speech to the US Congress in 1918, when he referred to the rights of nations to govern themselves in points 5–13).
8 Krause and Williams (1997a: 43) support this point when they write: "the neorealist version of security effectively makes it synonymous with citizenship. Security comes from being a citizen and insecurity from citizens of other states. Threats are directed toward individuals qua citizens (that is, towards their states)."
9 Kaldor asks:

> What would we do if faced with Hitler today? Would he be deterred by nuclear weapons? Or might the threat of unleashing war be too dangerous an approach to security

problems? How do we deal with China today? Does anyone believe that military threats can halt executions or discourage a takeover of Hong Kong? Nowadays we have to seek complex, difficult, non-military ways of managing conflicts, and, in practice, that is what governments do, not always successfully.

(1991: 317)

The implementation of the Marshall Plan is evidence that US policy makers did take non-military threats seriously (and it is noteworthy that this has not been the case to the same extent since).

10 This reconceptualization is "embodied in and institutionalised in the National Security Act of 1947, as protected by the McCarran-Walter Act of 1952, and as reconstituted by the first, and subsequent National Security Council meetings of the second, cold war" (Der Derian 1995: 42).

11 Indeed, even within the academy, these intersecting developments produced the effect that security largely became equated with military strategy.

12 No doubt strategists are inclined to think too readily in terms of military solutions to the problems of foreign policy and to lose sight of the other instruments that are available. But this is the occupational disease of any specialist and the remedy for it lies in entering into debate with the specialist and correcting his perspective.

(Bull, quoted in Baldwin 1995: 138)

13 It might be of interest to note that classical realists devoted much more attention "to the relationship between national security and domestic affairs, such as the economy, civil liberties, and democratic political processes" (Baldwin 1995: 122) something that has been revived in particular at the end of the Cold War and in critical security narratives.

14 This statement also inspired poetry (Seely 2003) as well as music (Kong 2004).

15 A more recent example is the event of September 11, 2001.

16 See also the Brandt Report (Independent Commission on International Development Issues 1980), the Palme Report (Independent Commission on Disarmament and Security Issues 1982), and the Brundtland Report (World Commission on Environment and Development 1987), which all called for a reonceptualization of security.

17 Boulding urges us to remember that women scholars played an important role in the development of these redefinitions of security. She cites,

the work of Randall Forsberg (1984) and Carolyn Stevenson (1982) on alternative security, Scilla and McLean (1988) and Sheila Tobias (1985) on women and security decision making, Riitta Wahlstrom (1986) on enemy images, Eva Senghaas-Knobloch (1986, 1988), Corinne Kumar d'Souza (1986, 1988) and Diana Russel (1989) on feminist analyses of power and women's ways of knowing, and Carol Cohn (1988) on the role of male language in shaping security strategy divorced from experienced reality

(1992: 57)

The list has expanded significantly since, with feminists venturing into all kinds of areas of security thinking as this book shows.

18 Kaldor (1991: 313–14) cautions, "'New Thinking' in the Soviet Union came about not because the West was tough but for internal reasons. If there was any influence from the West, it came from Western 'new thinking' in peace movement or alternative defence circles."

19 Furthermore,

the multiplication of threat experiences in everyday life could translate into an experience of chaos and *Angst*. As a consequence, the legitimacy of the political agencies which identified themselves as the mediators of life and death, as the managers of *Angst*—the state and some international organizations in the case of security policy—could face a 'fundamental' political crisis.

(Huysmans 1998: 243)

I would argue that the crisis is ongoing and attempts by states to reassert their role, or rather, to reinvent themselves in tune with current challenges abound.

20 Der Derian (1995) elegantly elaborates this point by a four-part reading of security, drawing on Hobbes, Marx, Nietzsche, and Baudrillard.

21 A variety of tales are told about the emergence of CSS and its content (e.g., Bilgin *et al.* 1998; Buzan and Wæver 1997; Buzan *et al.* 1998; Ceyhan 1998; Eriksson 1999a, 1999b; Krause 1998; Krause and Williams 1996, 1997a; McSweeney 1996, 1998; Mearsheimer 1994/1995; Neocleous 2000; Tickner 1995, 2001; Walt 1991).

22 Note that Krause (1998: 299) explicitly states, this tradition "does not include the radically different ideas that emerge from post-structuralist or post-modernist projects." The "Aberystwyth School," in an attempt to specify its intellectual heritage, emphasizes the Frankfurt School conception of critical theory and argues for a big "C"—big "T"— conception of Critical Theory in CSS (Wyn Jones 1999).

23 The Copenhagen School framework is not without its problems, of course, as was pointed out in two major debates, first in the *Review of International Studies* (Buzan and Wæver 1997; McSweeney 1996, 1998; Williams 1998b) and then in *Cooperation and Conflict* (Eriksson 1999a, 1999b; Goldmann 1999; Wæver 1999; Williams 1999).

24 Note the particular conception of the political underlying the *New Framework*:

In theory, any public issue can be located on the spectrum ranging from nonpoliticized (meaning the state does not deal with it and it is not in any other way made an issue of public debate and decision) through politicized (meaning the issue is part of public policy, requiring government decision and resource allocations or, more rarely, some other form of communal governance) to securitized (meaning an issue is presented as an external threat, requiring emergency measures and justifying actions outside the normal bounds of political procedure).

(Buzan *et al.* 1998: 23–4)

In other words, the political here is the realm of bureaucratic management of the state, revealing also the state-centric nature of the Copenhagen School framework.

25 However, as Spivak (1988, 1996) points out in her essay "Can the Subaltern Speak?" this is certainly not as straightforward as one might believe.

26 This is similar to the feminist strategy of adding women, which leaves underlying structures of oppression intact even while it locates their effects on women (cf. Harding 1986).

27 It is possible that this move toward emancipatory research has been inspired by a similar move in peace research in the 1970s (cf. Patomäki 2001: 726–8).

28 Parts of this argument were previously published in Wibben (2008).

29 For continued efforts, see: http://humansecuritynetwork.org/; http://www.humanse curitygateway.info/; http://www.hsrgroup.org/

30 Several feminists (e.g., Chenoy 2005; Hamber *et al.* 2006; Hoogensen and Stuvøy 2006; Hudson 2005) have argued that human security could benefit from the addition of a gender perspective (or, alternatively, feminist insights), but I would contend that a simple addition is not enough.

31 For a broader intellectual history of the concept at the United Nations, see MacFarlane and Khong (2006).

32 Christianity also used humanity as a distinction, dividing between the faithful (which were considered human) and the heathen (designated barbarian).

5 Feminist security narratives

1 Beyond this, it is useful to remind ourselves that the imagined reader (or listener) never fully coincides with the actual reader and that, as such, every reading (and telling) of a narrative will be different—and will contain elements beyond the intention of its author.

2 Indeed, Moon (1997: 39) points out that "Korea has a long-standing tradition of governmental utilization of women and their sexuality for political ends" dating back to the Koryo period (918–1392).

3 "*Yang*" means Western, and "*Nom*" figuratively means bastard. *Yangnom* is a pejorative term used to describe White people. It was coined around the eighteenth century to describe Western visitors. The word *Yang* does not carry a racial connotation but the combination of the two words does (thanks to Doowan Lee for this explanation).

4 Parallels to events in Okinawa (Japan) are noticeable here (Kirk and Okazawa-Rey 2001).

5 This is exemplified in the ways that the Korean government began to integrate (and promote) women's sexual services into its tourism industry in the 1970s, specifically targeting Japanese tourists who could no longer frequent Taiwan as a result of Japan's diplomatic normalization with the People's Republic of China. This policy was a resounding success. "By 1989," writes Moon (1997: 45), "the entertainment industry—the world of night clubs, bars, and prostitution—was estimated to reach a total sales of more than 4 trillion won, or 5% of the total GNP."

6 What is more, many *kijich'on* women interviewed by Moon were unfamiliar with the concept of a research interview and thought they had little knowledge worth sharing with "educated people." Consequently, Moon (1997: 15) used her own position as a young Korean American woman to encourage them to share their stories "and avoided settings and mannerisms that would seem formal, academic, and alien to them." This included offering English lessons at My Sister's Place and other organizations runs by *kijich'on* women in the camptowns.

7 She uses the notion in/security to indicate how insecurity and security are mutually constitutive—there is no security without corresponding insecurities and vice versa.

8 Many spaces remain insecure for Mayan women also because supporters in some locations are villains in others (e.g., Mayan men). This is a common theme when oppressed women find themselves in liberation movements or marginalized communities (e.g., such as African American women). The question becomes whether their own liberation (as women) is less/more important than the liberation of the group (e.g., do you speak out about the violence experienced at the hands of African American men, thus playing into discourses about the violent Black male that circulate in wider US society and are part of the oppressive mechanism used against all African Americans—or do you relegate that fight to another day?).

9 The celebration of Mayan identity both as "a source of pride and a basis for political action" (Stern 2005: 50) also leads to some tensions within the movement between culturally focused groups (which often aimed to mainly preserve Mayan traditions) and popular groupings that articulated broader demands in terms of ethnicity, arguing that "salvaging the culture must occur within the context of the immediate political and economic situation of the pueblo" (Stern 2005: 52).

10 This identity also encompasses an association of women with the earth, and the particular traditions of cultivating their plots of land—many of the women interviewed by Stern (2005: 158) expressed that without land "the Mayan people were existentially at risk." Not only due to "the inseparability of the Mayan culture, spirituality, and the land" (ibid.157) but also because access to land also means access to food for today and the future (e.g., for their grown-up children and their families).

11 Interestingly, the belief held by these different groups coincide with their overall preoccupations—*deslocados*, who often were displaced by horrific violence, are wrecked with survivor's guilt and often find that the violence they were not able to prevent or that they had to witness has continuing effects on them. For *curandeiros*, who play an

important role in maintaining the traditions and providing hope and healing for the community, emphasizing the impact of engaging in violence on the perpetrator serves the double function of relieving the victim from the burden of guilt of not having performed traditional ceremonies and warning those engaged in violence of the consequences of their actions. As such, the stories they tell and the beliefs they expressed are profoundly shaped not only by their experience, but also by their need to give meaning to their current situation—as are all life stories (cf. Stern 2005: 160ff.).

12 Compare this with Stern's observation of security as some*thing*—as well as larger critiques of security studies that point to the attempt to clearly identify something (cf. Chapter 4).

13 Militaries clearly operate with the notion of violence as a means to an end. Nordstrom (1997: 114–5) takes this seriously in her definition of war when she writes that war comes into existence when violence is employed. For her, "it is in the act of violence [...] that the definition of war is found. Militaries operate on a single truth: the strategic employment of violence."

14 This parallels Sylvester's (1993: 114) observation that wars tend to create new or changed identities and that "surely peaces do likewise since they are, after all, constituted with reference to war."

15 This need to recognize the crucial importance of silence is noted by many feminist scholars who work in conflict zones, and it is especially acute in long-term conflicts (cf. Cockburn 1999, 2007; Sharoni 1999).

16 For the sake of consistency throughout the book I use the term personal narrative where Stern uses the term life stories, Lyotard writes of identity narratives, and others use a variety of other terms.

17 What is more, the structure of their experience is similar. They both involve duty and guilt; "The soldier and the mother do their duty, and both are racked with guilt at not having done it right or having done it wrong as they did what they thought was right" (Elshtain 1987: 222). They both worry that a different action might have saved someone or spared some negative influence. Another set of parallels concerns "a slippery slide toward forgetting, on one end, toward remembering in nostalgic and sentimental ways, on the other" (ibid.: 223). Finally, the experiences of mothering and soldiering both involve boundary experiences, which "forever alter the identities of those to whom they happen, or through whom they take place" (ibid.).

18 Elshtain (1982, 1987) also discusses the corresponding image of the "just warrior," which presents a particular image of men's roles that is equally confining.

19 Importantly, "rediscovery of voice" is not the same as "giving voice" (cf. Conclusion).

20 Actually, it serves to represent both "them" and "us" and has implications for the research itself.

21 As mentioned, such an opening is hinted at in the securitization literature (Wæver 1995a, b), but firmly closed down by the continued reference to just one form of identity and security, and the realist emphasis on the state, its institutions, and militarized approaches (Buzan *et al.* 1998).

6 The future of feminist security studies

1 In 2000, Chalmers Johnson had warned about the consequences that would inevitably follow the imperial actions of the United States in the preceding decades:

> given its wealth and power, the United States will be a prime recipient in the foreseeable future of all of the more expectable forms of blowback, particularly terrorist attacks in and out of the armed forces anywhere on earth, including within the United States.
>
> (quoted in Andrews 2007: 107)

2 Such a framing is exemplified starkly in just war approaches, which, by making a distinction between *jus ad bellum* and *jus in bello* fixate the distinction of war as a crisis or event with clearly identifiable beginnings and endings.

3 The advantages of focusing on personal stories and taking a longer view by not singling out events, but considering an ongoing presence, are illustrated strikingly in the story of Wilton Sekzer in the acclaimed documentary *Why We Fight*. Sekzer's son was killed in New York City on September 11, 2001, and he became a strong supporter of the invasion of Iraq, even asking that a bomb with his son's name written on it be dropped. On hearing President Bush proclaim that he does not know from where people got the idea that there was a link between Saddam Hussein and the 9/11 attacks, Sekzer became angry at being mislead and uncertain if he should regret his actions (Dwyer 2008). Making Sekzer's reflections a central part of his *Why We Fight*, the film's director, Eugene Jarecki, illustrates how narratives shift and slide.

4 In her discussion of the ethics of *Doing Research On/With Women in Conflict Zones*, Sharoni suggests that "there are two basic principles—collaboration and accountability—that must be present for a project to be legitimate" (1999). She specifies these further in her discussion of many of the things pointed to here: situating knowledge, building trust, as well as the relationships between researcher and the community they work in.

5 In one of the book chapters, contrasting the "Lynndie England story" with the "Jessica Lynch story" while also remaining attentive to how both stories evolve over time, Brittain is able to pinpoint a significant directional change in US public opinion on the war in Iraq. She is also able to show that, despite the seemingly opposing representation of both women (Lynch as the "victim-of-rape-in-need-of-rescue" and England as the "depraved-villain-in-need-of-reform"), "both significations co-opt the category of white femininity as a way of relieving white masculinity from the burden of signifying as anything but a just and civilizing force" (Brittain 2006: 92).

6 Arguably, feminists can also be considered critical security scholars, but the point here is to draw out what distinguishes feminist approaches to security.

7 I must thank the participants at two of the workshops where I presented my work over the past years for prompting me to clarify these distinctions. In 2007, I presented ideas "Toward feminist security theory" to a research group in International Politics at the University of Wales in Aberystwyth and was asked by an audience member why I did not simply pursue a general critical security studies agenda because all the issues I was addressing could be presented under that umbrella. Initially puzzled by this assertion, in a conversation with my host, Jenny Edkins, later that evening some of the reasons began to crystallize. When I presented on "The politics of feminist security studies" at the Watson Institute for International Studies in 2009, I was again prompted by my colleague Nina Tannenwald to answer the question "what makes feminist approaches to security studies different from other non-mainstream approaches?" leading me to further specify my reasons for pursuing FSS (see http://www.watsoninstitute.org/news_detail.cfm?id=1074).

8 How security narratives are shaped by the fear of death and the mastery of uncertainty is discussed by some security scholars (e.g., Burke 2007; Der Derian 1995; Huysmans 1998) whose work promotes an opening of security studies (cf. Chapter 4). Scholars working with a poststructuralist agenda, as I do here, even if they are not feminists, tend to be working toward an opening of security studies already and be more familiar with these types of arguments (cf. Hansen 2010).

Bibliography

ABC News (2001a) *Special Report 8:53AM*, September 11th, 2001.

ABC News (2001b) *Special Report: America Under Attack 10:00AM,* September 11, 2001.

Ackerly, B.A., Stern, M. and True, J. (eds) (2006) *Feminist Methodologies for International Relations,* Cambridge: Cambridge University Press.

Adler, E. and Barnett, M.N. (1998) *Security Communities,* Cambridge: Cambridge University Press.

Albrecht-Heide, A. and Bujewski-Crawford, U. (eds) (1991) *Frauen-Krieg-Militär: Images und Fantasien (Women–War–Military. Images and Fantasies),* Tübingen: Verein für Friedenspädagogik Tübingen.

Alison, M. (2009) *Women and Political Violence: Female Combatants in Ethno-National Conflict,* London: Routledge.

Andrews, M. (2007) *Shaping History: Narratives of Political Change,* Cambridge: Cambridge University Press.

Anzaldúa, G. (1999) *Borderlands/La Fronterra: The New Mestiza,* 2nd edn, San Francisco, CA: Aunt Lute Books.

Ardener, S., Holden, P. and Macdonald, S. (1987) *Images of Women in Peace and War: Cross Cultural and Historical Perspectives,* London: Macmillan.

Aron, R. (1967) *Peace and War: A Theory of International Relations,* London: Weidenfeld & Nicolson.

Azar, E.E. (1990) *The Management of Protracted Social Conflict: Theory and Cases,* Aldershot: Dartmouth.

Bal, M. (1997) *Narratology: Introduction to the Theory of Narrative,* 2nd edn, Toronto: University of Toronto Press.

Baldwin, D.A. (1995) 'Security studies and the end of the Cold War', *World Politics,* 48(1), 117–41.

Batscheider, T. (1993) *Friedensforschung und Geschlechterverhältnis: Zur Begründung feministischer Fragestellungen in der kritischen Friedensforschung (Peace Research and Gender Relations: On the Need for Feminist Inquiry in Critical Peace Research),* Marburg: BdWi Verlag.

Bayard de Volo, L. (1998) 'Drafting motherhood: Maternal imagery and organizations in the United States and Nicaragua', in: Lorentzen, L.A. and Turpin, J. (eds) *The Women and War Reader,* New York: New York University Press, 240–53.

Behnke, A. (2007) 'Presence and creation: A few (meta-)critical comments on the c.a.s.e manifesto', *Security Dialogue,* 38(1), 105–11.

Bellamy, A.J. and McDonald, M. (2002) '"The utility of human security": Which humans? What security? A reply to Thomas and Tow', *Security Dialogue,* 33(3), 373–7.

Benet, S. (2001) 'US feminists voice post-Taliban concerns', *Women's Enews*. Online. Available HTTP: http://www.womensenews.org/article.cfm?aid=750 (accessed 20 March 2002).

Betts, R.K. (1997) 'Should strategic studies survive?', *World Politics*, 50(1), 7–33.

Bilgin, P., Booth, K. and Wyn Jones, R. (1998) 'Security studies: The next stage?', *Nação e Defesa*, 84(2), 131–57.

Blanchard, E.M. (2003) 'Gender, international relations, and the development of feminist security theory', *Signs: Journal of Women in Culture and Society*, 28(4), 1289–312.

Bleicher, J. (1980) *Contemporary Hermeneutics: Hermeneutics as Method, Philosophy, and Critique*, London: Routledge & Kegan Paul.

Bobrow, D.B. (2001) 'Visions of (in)security and American strategic style', *International Studies Perspectives*, 2(1), 1–12.

Booth, K. (1979) *Strategy and Ethnocentrism*, New York: Holmes & Meier.

Booth, K. (1991a) *New Thinking About Strategy and International Security*, London: Harper Collins Academic.

Booth, K. (1991b) 'Security and emancipation', *Review of International Studies*, 17(4), 313–26.

Booth, K. (1997) 'Security and the self: Reflections of a fallen realist', in: Krause, K. and Williams, M.C. (eds) *Critical Security Studies: Concepts and Cases*, Minneapolis: University of Minnesota Press, 83–119.

Booth, K. (2005) 'Critical explorations', in: Booth, K. (ed.) *Critical Security Studies and World Politics*, Boulder, CO: Lynne Rienner, 1–18.

Booth, K. (2007) *Theory of World Security*, Cambridge: Cambridge University Press.

Boserup, E. (1970) *Woman's Role in Economic Development*, London: Allen & Unwin.

Boulding, E. (1978) 'Women and social violence', *International Journal of Social Science*, 30(4), 801–15.

Boulding, E. (1981) 'Perspectives of women researchers on disarmament, national security and world order', in: Haavelsrud, M. (ed.) *Approaching Disarmament Education*, Guildford: Westbury House.

Boulding, E. (1988) 'Warriors and saints: Dilemmas in the history of men, women and war', in: Isaksson, E. (ed.) *Women and the Military System*, London: Harvester-Wheatsheaf, 225–46.

Boulding, E. (1992) 'Women's experiential approaches to peace studies', in: Kramarae, C. and Spender, D. (eds) *The Knowledge Explosion: Generations of Feminist Scholarship*, New York: Teachers College Press.

Boulding, E. (2000) *Cultures of Peace: The Hidden Side of History*, Syracuse, NY: Syracuse University Press.

Brittain, M. (2006) 'Benevolent invaders, heroic victims and depraved villains: White femininity in media coverage of the invasion of Iraq', in: Hunt, K. and Rygiel, K. (eds) *(En)gendering the War on Terror: War Stories and Camouflaged Politics*, Aldershot: Ashgate, 73–96.

Broadhead, L.-A. (2000) 'Re-packaging notions of security: A sceptical feminist response to recent efforts', in: Jacobs, S., Jacobson, R. and Marchbank, J. (eds) *States of Conflict: Gender, Violence and Resistance*, London: Zed Books, 27–44.

Brockhaus (1990) *Brockhaus Enzyklopädie (Brockhaus Encyclopedia)*, 19 edn, Mannheim: FA Brockhaus.

Brock-Utne, B. (1985) *Educating for Peace: A Feminist Perspective*, New York: Pergamon Press.

Brock-Utne, B. (1989) *Feminist Perspectives on Peace and Peace Education*, 1st edn, New York: Pergamon Press.

Brown, J. (2001a) 'Terror's first victims'. Salon.com. Online. Available HTTP: http://www.salon.com/mwt/feature/2001/09/24/taliban_women/ (accessed 4 October 2001).

Brownmiller, S. (1975) *Against our Will: Men, Women, and Rape*, New York: Simon & Schuster.

Bumiller, E. and Sanger, D.E. (2001) 'A somber Bush says terrorism cannot prevail', *The New York Times*, 12 September 2001, p. A1 and A4.

Burgess, J.P. (2004) 'Special issue on human security', *Security Dialogue*, 35(3), 275–396.

Burguieres, M.K. (1990) 'Feminist approaches to peace: Another step for peace studies', *Millennium: Journal of International Studies*, 19(1), 1–18.

Burke, A. (2002) 'Aporias of security', *Alternatives*, 27, 1–27.

Burke, A. (2007) *Beyond Security, Ethics and Violence: War Against the Other*, London: Routledge.

Bush, G.W. (2001a) Remarks by the President after two planes crashed into World Trade Center, 9:30am. White House. Online. Available HTTP: http://www.whitehouse.gov/news/releases/2001/09/20010911.html (accessed 4 April 2002).

Bush, G.W. (2001b) Statement by the President in His Address to the nation, 8:30pm. White House. Online. Available HTTP: http://www.whitehouse.gov/news/releases/2001/09/20010911-16.html (accessed 4 April 2002).

Bush, L. (2001) Radio Address by Laura Bush to the nation. White House. Online. Available HTTP: http://www.whitehouse.gov/news/releases/2001/11/20011117.html (accessed 22 March 2002).

Butler, J. (1990) *Gender Trouble: Feminism and the Subversion of Identity*, New York: Routledge.

Butler, J. (2004) *Precarious Life: The Powers of Mourning and Violence*, London: Verso.

Buzan, B. (1983) *People, States, and Fear: The National Security Problem in International Relations*, Chapel Hill: University of North Carolina Press.

Buzan, B. (1987) *An Introduction to Strategic Studies: Military Technology and International Relations*, New York: St Martin's Press.

Buzan, B. (1991) *People, States, and Fear: An Agenda for International Security Studies in the Post-Cold War Era*, 2nd edn, New York: Harvester-Wheatsheaf.

Buzan, B. (2004) 'A reductionist, idealist notion that adds little analytical value', *Security Dialogue*, 35(3), 369–70.

Buzan, B. and Herring, E. (1998) *The Arms Dynamic in World Politics*, Boulder, CO: Lynne Rienner.

Buzan, B. and Wæver, O. (1997) 'Slippery? Contradictory? Sociologically untenable? The Copenhagen school replies', *Review of International Studies*, 23(2), 241–50.

Buzan, B., Wæver, O. and Wilde, J. D. (1998) *Security: A New Framework for Analysis*, Boulder, CO: Lynne Rienner.

Caiazza, A. (2001) *Why Gender Matters in Understanding September 11: Women, Militarism, and Violence*, Washington, DC: Institute for Women's Policy Research #1908.

Campbell, D. (1998a) *National Deconstruction: Violence, Identity, and Justice in Bosnia*, Minneapolis: University of Minnesota Press.

Campbell, D. (1998b) *Writing Security: United States Foreign Policy and the Politics of Identity*, 2nd edn, Minneapolis: University of Minnesota Press.

Carpenter, R.C. (2003) 'Gender theory in world politics: Contributions of a non-feminist standpoint', *International Studies Review*, 4(3), 153–65.

Carpenter, R.C. (2005) 'Women, children and other vulnerable groups: Gender, strategic frames, and the protection of civilians as a transnational issue', *International Studies Quarterly*, 49(2), 295–334.

Carver, T., Cochran, M. and Squires, J. (1998) 'Gendering Jones: Feminisms, IRs, masculinities', *Review of International Studies*, 24(2), 283–97.

c.a.s.e. collective (2006) 'Critical approaches to security in Europe: A networked manifesto', *Security Dialogue*, 37(4), 443–87.

Ceyhan, A. (1998) 'Analyser la sécurité: Dillon, Wæver, Williams et les autres' ('Analyzing security: Dillon, Wæver, Williams and the others'), *Cultures et Conflits*, 31(32), 39–62.

Chandler, D. (2008) 'Human security II: Waiting for the tail to wag the dog—a rejoinder to Ambrosetti, Owen and Wibben', *Security Dialogue*, 39(4), 463–9.

Chapkis, W. (1988) 'Sexuality and militarism', in: Isaksson, E. (ed.) *Women and the Military System*, London: Harvester-Wheatsheaf, 106–13.

Cheney, D. (2002) Vice President Speaks at VFW 103rd National Convention. White House. Online. Available HTTP: http://www.whitehouse.gov/news/releases/2002/08/print/20020826.html (accessed 2 September 2002).

Chenoy, A.M. (2005) 'A plea for engendering human security', *International Studies*, 42(2), 167–79.

Chilton, P.A. (1996a) 'The meaning of security', in: Beer, F.A. and Harriman, R. (eds) *Post-Realism: The Rhetorical Turn in International Relations*, East Lansing: Michigan State University Press, 193–216.

Chilton, P.A. (1996b) *Security Metaphors: Cold War Discourse from Containment to Common House*, New York: P. Lang.

CHS (2003) *Human Security Now*, New York: Commission on Human Security.

CNN (2001a) 'American Morning with Paula Zahn (9:15am)'. *CNN, Transcript # 090411CN.V74*.

CNN (2001b) 'Breaking News: America under Attack (10:30am), September 11, 2001'. *CNN, Transcript # 091104CN.V00*.

CNN (2001c) 'September 11: Chronology of Terror'. *CNN*, Online. Available HTTP: http://www.cnn.com/2001/US/09/11/chronology.attack/index.html (accessed 15 April 2002).

Cockburn, C. (1999) *The Space Between Us: Negotiating Identities in Conflict*, London: Zed Books.

Cockburn, C. (2004) 'The continuum of violence: A gender perspective on war and peace', in: Giles, W. and Hyndman, J. (eds) *Sites of Violence: Gender and Conflict Zones*, Berkeley: University of California Press, 24–44.

Cockburn, C. (2007) *From Where We Stand: War, Women's Activism and Feminist Analysis*, London: Zed Books.

Cockburn, C. and Zarkov, D. (eds) (2002) *The Postwar Moment: Militaries, Masculinities, and International Peacekeeping*, London: Lawrence & Wishart.

Cohn, C. (1988) 'A feminist spy in the house of death: Unravelling the language of strategic analysis', in: Isaksson, E. (ed.) *Women and the Military System*, London: Harvester-Wheatsheaf, 288–317.

Cohn, C. (1989a) 'Emasculating America's linguistic deterrent', in: Harris, A. and King, Y. (eds) *Rocking the Ship of State: Toward a Feminist Peace Politics*, Boulder, CO: Westview Press, 153–70.

Cohn, C. (1989b) 'Sex and death in the rational world of defense intellectuals', in: Forcey, L.R. (ed.) *Peace: Meanings, Politics, Strategies*, New York: Praeger, 39–71.

Cohn, C. and Enloe, C. (2003) 'A conversation with Cynthia Enloe: Feminists look at masculinity and the men who wage war', *Signs: Journal of Women in Culture and Society*, 28(4), 1187–207.

Cohn, C. and Ruddick, S. (2003) *A Feminist Ethical Perspective on Weapons of Mass Destruction*, Boston: Boston Consortium on Gender, Security and Human Rights. Working Paper No. 104.

Cohn, C. and Ruddick, S. (2004) 'A feminists ethical perspective on weapons of mass destruction', in: Lee, S. and Hashmi, S.H. (eds) *Ethics and Weapons of Mass Destruction: Religious and Secular Perspectives*, Cambridge: Cambridge University Press, 405–35.

Cohn, C., Kinsella, H. and Gibbings, S. (2004) 'Women, peace, security: Resolution 1325', *International Feminist Journal of Politics*, 6(1), 130–40.

Colebrook, C. and Buchanan, I. (2000) *Deleuze and Feminist Theory*, Edinburgh: Edinburgh University Press.

Collins, P.H. (1999) 'Producing the mothers of the nation: Race, class and contemporary US policies', in: Yuval-Davis, N. and Werbner, P. (eds) *Women, Citizenship and Difference*, London: Zed Books, 118–29.

Collins, P.H. (2000) *Black Feminist Thought: Knowledge, Consciousness, and the Politics of Empowerment*, 2nd edn, New York: Routledge.

Combahee River Collective (2000 [1983]) 'The Combahee River Collective statement', in: Smith, B. (ed.) *Home Girls: A Black Feminist Anthology*, New Brunswick, NY: Rutgers University Press, 264–74.

Connell, R.W. (2000) *The Men and the Boys*, Berkeley: University of California Press.

Constantinou, C. (2000) 'Poetics of security', *Alternatives: Social Transformation and Humane Governance*, 25(3), 287–306.

Croft, S. and Terriff, T. (2000) *Critical Reflections on Security and Change*, London: Frank Cass.

Culler, J.D. (1997) *Literary Theory: A Very Short Introduction*, Oxford: Oxford University Press.

Cuomo, C.J. (1996) 'War is not just an event: Reflections on the significance of everyday violence', *Hypatia*, 11(4), 30–45.

Currie, M. (1998) *Postmodern Narrative Theory*, New York: St Martin's Press.

D'Amico, F. (1998) 'Feminist perspectives on women warriors', in: Lorentzen, L.A. and Turpin, J. (eds) *The Women and War Reader*, New York: New York University Press, 119–25.

D'Costa, B. (2006) 'Marginalized identity: New frontiers of research for IR?', in: Ackerly, B.A., Stern, M. and True, J. (eds) *Feminist Methodologies for International Relations*, Cambridge: Cambridge University Press, 129–52.

Declaration of the Essential Rights of the Afghan Women. Dushanbe, Tajikistan. Online. Available HTTP: http://www.kabultect.org.declarat.htm (accessed 15 October 2010).

Deibert, R.J. (1997) *Parchment, Printing, and Hypermedia: Communication in World Order Transformation*, New York: Columbia University Press.

DeLillo, D. (2001) 'In the ruins of the future: Reflections on terror and loss in the shadow of September', *Harper's Magazine*, December, 33–40.

Der Derian, J. (1992) *Antidiplomacy: Spies, Terror, Speed, and War*, Cambridge: Blackwell.

Der Derian, J. (1995) 'The value of security: Hobbes, Marx, Nietzsche, and Baudrillard', in: Lipschutz, R.D. (ed.) *On Security: New Directions in World Politics*, New York: Columbia University.

Deudney, D. (1990) 'The case against linking environmental degradation and national security', *Millennium: Journal of International Studies*, 19(3), 461–76.

Dillon, G.M. (1990) 'The alliance of security and subjectivity', *Current Research on Peace and Violence*, 13(3), 101–24.

Dillon, M. (1996) *Politics of Security: Towards a Political Philosophy of Continental Thought*, London: Routledge.

Douzinas, C. (2009a) 'What are human rights?'. *The Guardian*, Comment is free (18 March 2009). Online. Available HTTP: http://www.guardian.co.uk/commentisfree/libertycentral/2009/mar/18/human-rights-asylum (accessed 14 August 2009).

Douzinas, C. (2009b) 'Who counts as "human"?'. *The Guardian*, Comment is Free (1 April 2009). Online. Available HTTP: http://www.guardian.co.uk/commentisfree/libertycentral/2009/apr/01/deconstructing-human-rights-equality (accessed 14 August 2009).

Duffield, M. (2007) *Development, Security and Unending War: Governing the World of Peoples*, Cambridge: Polity Press.

Dwyer, J. (2008) 'Mourning after 9/11, outrage ever since'. *New York Times*, Online. Available HTTP: http://www.nytimes.com/2008/03/15/nyregion/15about.html (accessed 19 May 2010).

Eagleton, M., (ed.) (1986) *Feminist Literary Theory: A Reader*, Oxford: Basil Blackwell.

Edkins, J. (1999) *Poststructuralism and International Relations: Bringing the Political Back In*, Boulder, CO: Lynne Rienner.

Edkins, J. (2001) 'The Absence of Meaning: Trauma and the Events of 11 September'. Information Technology, War, and Peace Project. Online. Available HTTP: http://www.watsoninstitute.org/infopeace/911/article.cfm?id=27 (accessed 4 September 2002).

Edkins, J. (2002a) 'After the subject of international security', in: Valentine, J. and Finlayson, A. (eds) *Politics and Post-Structuralism: An Introduction*, Edinburgh: Edinburgh University Press, 66–80.

Edkins, J. (2002b) 'Forget trauma? Responses to September 11', *International Relations*, 16(2), 243–56.

Edkins, J. (2003) *Trauma and the Memory of Politics*, Cambridge: Cambridge University Press.

Edkins, J., Persram, N. and Pin-Fat, V. (1999) *Sovereignty and Subjectivity*, Boulder, CO: Lynne Rienner.

Ehrenreich, B. (1999) 'Men hate war too', *Foreign Affairs*, 78(1), 118–22.

Ehrenreich, B. (2001) 'A mystery of mysogyny', *The Progressive*, 65(12), 12–13.

Elshtain, J.B. (1982) 'On beautiful souls, just warriors and feminist consciousness', *Womens Studies International Forum*, 5(3/4), 39–57.

Elshtain, J.B. (1987) *Women and War*, New York: Basic Books.

Enloe, C. (1983) *Does Khaki Become You? The Militarisation of Women's Lives*, London: Pluto Press.

Enloe, C. (1987) 'Feminist thinking about war, militarism and peace', in: Hess, B.B. and Ferree, M.M. (eds) *Analyzing Gender: A Handbook of Social Science Research*, Newbury Park: Sage, 526–47.

Enloe, C. (1988) 'Beyond "Rambo": Women and the varieties of militarized masculinity', in: Isaksson, E. (ed.) *Women and the Military System*, London: Harvester-Wheatsheaf, 71–93.

Enloe, C. (1990a) 'Bananas, bases and patriarchy', in: Elshtain, J.B. and Tobias, S. (eds) *Women, Militarism, and War: Essays in History, Politics and Social Theory*, Totowa: Rowman & Littlefield.

Enloe, C. (1990b) *Bananas, Beaches & Bases: Making Feminist Sense of International Politics*, 1st US edn, Berkeley: University of California.

Enloe, C. (1993) *The Morning After: Sexual Politics at the End of the Cold War*, Berkeley: University of California Press.

Enloe, C. (1996) 'Margins, silences and bottom rungs: How to overcome the underestimation of power in the study of international relations', in: Smith, S., Booth, K. and Zalewski, M. (eds) *International Theory: Positivism and Beyond*, Cambridge: Cambridge University Press, 186–202.

Enloe, C. (1998) 'All the men are in militias and all the women are victims: The politics of masculinity and femininity in nationalist wars', in: Lorentzen, L.A. and Turpin, J. (eds) *The Women and War Reader*, New York: New York University Press, 50–62.

Enloe, C. (2000) *Maneuvers: The International Politics of Militarizing Women's Lives*, Berkeley: University of California Press.

Enloe, C. (2004) *The Curious Feminist: Searching for Women in a New Age of Empire*, Berkeley: University of California Press.

Enloe, C. (2007) *Globalization & Militarism: Feminists Make the Link*, Lanham, MD: Rowman & Littlefield.

Eriksson, J. (1999a) 'Debating the politics of security studies: Response to Goldman, Wæver, and Williams', *Cooperation and Conflict*, 34(3), 345–52.

Eriksson, J. (1999b) 'Observers or advocates? On the political role of security analysts', *Cooperation and Conflict*, 34(3), 311–30.

Fairlamb, H.L. (1994) *Critical Conditions: Postmodernity and the Question of Foundations*, Cambridge: Cambridge University Press.

Farrel, S. (2001) 'West's feminists under fire from female general', *The Times*, 28 November 2001, p. 9. Online. Available HTTP: http://www.hartford-hwp.com/archives/51/131.html (accessed 25 September 2002).

Feinman, I.R. (1998) 'Women warriors/women peacekeepers: Will the real feminists please stand up!', in: Lorentzen, L.A. and Turpin, J. (eds) *The Women and War Reader*, New York: New York University Press, 132–8.

Ferguson, K.E. (1993) *The Man Question: Visions of Subjectivity in Feminist Theory*, Berkeley: University of California Press.

Flax, J. (1987) 'Postmodernism and gender relations in feminist theory', *Signs: Journal of Women in Culture and Society*, 12(4), 621–43.

Fleischer, A. (11 September 2001a) 'Press briefing to the pool by Ari Fleischer, 1:47pm'. White House. Online. Available HTTP: http://www.whitehouse.gov/news/releases/2001/09/20010911-6.html (accessed 4 April 2002).

Fleischer, A. (11 September 2001b) 'Press briefing to the pool by Ari Fleischer, 5:30pm'. White House. Online. Available HTTP: http://www.whitehouse.gov/news/releases/2001/09/20010911-8.html (accessed 4 April 2002).

Fleischer, A. (11 September 2001c) 'Press gaggle by Ari Fleischer, 8:13pm'. White House. Online. Available HTTP: http://www.whitehouse.gov/news/releases/2001/09/20010911-13.html (accessed 4 April 2002).

Florence, M.S., Marshall, C. and Ogden, C.K. (1987) *Militarism Versus Feminism: Writings on Women and War*, London: Virago Press.

Forcey, L.R. (1989) *Peace: Meanings, Politics, Strategies*, New York: Praeger.

Foucault, M. (1980) *Power/Knowledge: Selected Interviews and Other Writings, 1972–1977*, Brighton: Harvester Press.

Fukuyama, F. (1998) 'Women and the evolution of world politics', *Foreign Affairs*, 77(5), 24–40.

Gabler, N. (2001) 'This time, the scene was real', *New York Times*, 16 September 2001, Online. Available HTTP http://www.nytimes.com/2001/09/16/weekinreview/16GABL.html (accessed 5 October 2001).

Gadamer, H.G. (1965) *Wahrheit und Methode (Truth and Method); Grundzüge einer philosophischen Hermeneutik*, 2. Aufl. edn, Tübingen: Mohr.

Gadamer, H.G. (1976) *Philosophical Hermeneutics*, Berkeley: University of California Press.

Galtung, J. (1969) 'Violence, peace, peace research', *Journal of Peace Research*, 6(3), 167–91.

Giles, W. and Hyndman, J. (eds) (2004) *Sites of Violence: Gender and Conflict Zones*, Berkeley: University of California Press.

Gilligan, C. (1982) *In a Different Voice: Psychological Theory and Women's Development*, Cambridge: Harvard University Press.

Gioseffi, D., (ed.) (2003) *Women on War: An International Anthology of Writings from Antiquity to the Present*, New York: Feminist Press at the City University of New York.

Glasius, M. (2008) 'Human security from paradigm shift to operationalization: Job description for a human security worker', *Security Dialogue*, 39(1), 31–54.

Goldman, N.L., (ed.) (1982) *Female Soldiers—Combatants or Noncombatants?*, Westport, CT: Greenwood Press.

Goldmann, K. (1999) 'Issues, not labels please!', *Cooperation and Conflict*, 34(3), 331–3.

Grant, R. (1991) 'The sources of gender bias in international relations theory', in: Grant, R. and Newland, K. (eds) *Gender and International Relations*, Bloomington: Indiana University Press, 8–26.

Grant, R. and Newland, K. (1991) *Gender and International Relations*, Bloomington: Indiana University Press.

Grayson, K. (2003) 'Securitization and the boomerang debate: A rejoinder to Liotta and Smith-Windsor', *Security Dialogue*, 34(3), 337–43.

Grayson, K. (2007) 'Persistence of memory? The (new) surrealism of American security policy', in: Dauphinee, E. and Masters, C. (eds) *The Logics of Biopower and the War on Terror*, New York: Palgrave Macmillan, 82–107.

Grondin, J. (1991) *Einführung in die philosophische Hermeneutik (Introduction to Philosophical Hermeneutics)*, Darmstadt: Wissenschaftliche Buchgesellschaft.

Gross, E. (1986) 'Conclusion: What is feminist theory?', in: Pateman, C. and Gross, E. (eds) *Feminist Challenges: Social and Political Theory*, Sydney: Allen & Unwin, 190–204.

Gross, E. (1990) 'Contemporary theories of power and subjectivity', in: Gunew, S.M. (ed.) *Feminist Knowledge: Critique and Construct*, London: Routledge, 59–120.

Hall, S. (1996) 'Introduction: Who needs "identity"?', in: Hall, S. and Du Gay, P. (eds) *Questions of Cultural Identity*, London: Sage, 1–17.

Hamber, B., Hillyward, P., Maguire, A., McWilliams, M., Robinson, G., Russell, D. and Ward, M. (2006) 'Discourses in transition: Re-imagining women's security', *International Relations*, 20(4), 487–502.

Hamilton, C. (2007) 'Political violence and body language in life stories of women ETA activists', *Signs: Journal of Women in Culture and Society*, 32(4), 911–32.

Hansen, L. (2000) 'The little mermaid's silent security dilemma and the absence of gender in the Copenhagen school', *Millennium: Journal of International Studies*, 29(2), 285–306.

Hansen, L. (2001) 'Gender, nation, rape: Bosnia and the construction of security', *International Feminist Journal of Politics*, 3(1), 55–75.

Hansen, L. (2010) 'Poststructuralism and security', in: Denemark, R. A. (ed.) *The International Studies Encylopedia*. Blackwell Publishing. Online. Available HTTP: http://www.isacom pendium.com/subscriber/tocnode?id=g9781444336597_chunk_g978144433659716_ss1-17 (accessed 9 April 2010).

Haq, F. (2007) 'Militarism and motherhood: The women of the Lashkar-i-Tayyabia in Pakistan', *Signs: Journal of Women in Culture and Society*, 32(4), 1023–46.

Harding, S.G. (1986) *The Science Question in Feminism*, Ithaca, NY: Cornell University Press.

Hataley, T.S. and Nossal, R.K. (2004) 'The limits of the human security agenda: The case of Canada's response to the Timor crisis', *Global Change, Peace and Security*, 16(1), 5–17.

Heidkamp, B. (2001) 'Now rolling'. PopPolitics.com. Online. Available HTTP: http://www.poppolitics.com/articles/2001-09-12-wtc.shtml (accessed 5 October 2001).

Hekman, S.J. (1990) *Gender and Knowledge: Elements of a Postmodern Feminism*, Boston: Northeastern University Press.

Hekman, S.J. (1999) *Feminism, Identity, and Difference*, London: Frank Cass.

Hekman, S.J. (2004) 'Feminist identity politics', in: Taylor, D. and Vintges, K. (eds) *Feminism and the Final Foucault*, Chicago: University of Illinois, 197–213.

Herbert, M.S. (1998) *Camouflage isn't Only for Combat: Gender, Sexuality and Women in the Military*, New York: New York University Press.

Hirschmann, N.J. (1996) 'Revisioning freedom: Relationship, context, and the politics of empowerment', in: Hirschmann, N.J. and Di Stefano, C. (eds) *Revisioning the Political: Feminist*

Reconstructions of Traditional Concepts in Western Political Theory, Boulder, CO: Westview Press, 51–74.

Hite, M. (1989) *The Other Side of the Story: Structures and Strategies of Contemporary Feminist Narrative*, Ithaca, NY: Cornell University Press.

Hollis, M. and Smith, S. (1991) *Explaining and Understanding International Relations*, Oxford: Oxford University Press.

Hoogensen, G. and Stuvøy, K. (2006) 'Gender, resistance and human security', *Security Dialogue*, 37(2), 207–28.

hooks, b. (1984) *Feminist Theory: From Margin to Center*, Cambridge: South End Press.

HRW (2000) 'Rwanda: Women speak', in: Barstow, A.L. (ed.) *War's Dirty Secrets: Rape, Prostitution, and Other Crimes Against Women*, Cleveland, OH: The Pilgrim Press, 93–5.

HRW (2007) '*My Heart is Cut': Sexual Violence by Rebels and Pro-Government Forces in Côte d'Ivoire*, New York: Human Rights Watch.

Hudson, H. (2005) '"Doing" security as though humans matter: A feminist perspective on gender and the politics of human security', *Security Dialogue*, 36(2), 155–74.

Hudson, N.F. (2009) *Gender, Human Security and the United Nations: Security Language as a Political Framework for Women*, London: Routledge.

Hudson, V.M., Caprioli, M., Ballif-Spanvill, B., McDermott, R. and Emmett, C.F. (2008/2009) 'The heart of the matter: The security of women and the security of states', *International Security*, 33(3), 7–45.

Hunt, K. (2006) '"Embedded feminism" and the war on terror', in: Hunt, K. and Rygiel, K. (eds) *(En)gendering the War on Terror: War Stories and Camouflaged Politics*, Aldershot: Ashgate, 51–71.

Hunt, K. and Rygiel, K. (2006a) '(En)gendered war stories and camouflaged politics', in: Hunt, K. and Rygiel, K. (eds) *(En)gendering the War on Terror: War Stories and Camouflaged Politics*, Aldershot: Ashgate, 1–24.

Hunt, K. and Rygiel, K. (2006b) *(En)gendering the War on Terror: War Stories and Camouflaged Politics*, Aldershot: Ashgate.

Huysmans, J. (1998) 'Security! What do you mean? From concept to thick signifier', *European Journal of International Relations*, 4(2), 226–55.

Huysmans, J. (2006) *The Politics of Insecurity: Fear, Migration and Asylum in the EU*, London: Routledge.

Ibáez, A.C. (2001) 'El Salvador: War and untold stories—women guerrillas', in: Moser, C.O.N. and Clark, F.C. (eds) *Victims, Perpetrators or Actors? Gender, Armed Conflict and Political Violence*, London: Zed Books, 117–30.

Ignatieff, M. (1995) 'On civil society', *Foreign Affairs*, 74(2), 135–36.

INCITE! Women of Color Against Violence (ed.) (2006) *Color of Violence: The INCITE! Anthology*, Cambridge: South End Press.

Independent Commission on Disarmament and Security Issues (1982) Common Security: A Programme for Disarmament (Palme Report), London: Pan Books.

Independent Commission on Disarmament and Security Issues (1980) North–South: A Programme for Survival (Brandt Report), London: Pan Books.

IRIN (2007) *The Shame of War: Sexual Violence Against Women and Girls in Conflict*, Kenya: United Nations Office for the Coordination of Humanitarian Affairs.

Isaksson, E., (ed.) (1988) *Women and the Military System*, London: Harvester-Wheatsheaf.

Jabri, V. and O'Gorman, E. (1999) *Women, Culture, and International Relations*, Boulder, CO: Lynne Rienner.

Jackson, R. (2005) *Writing the War on Terrorism: Language, Politics and Counter-Terrorism*, Manchester: Manchester University Press.

Jacobs, S., Jacobson, R. and Marchbank, J. (eds) (2000) *States of Conflict: Gender, Violence and Resistance*, London: Zed Books.

Jacoby, T. (2006) 'From the trenches: Dilemmas of feminist IR fieldwork', in: Ackerly, B.A., Stern, M. and True, J. (eds) *Feminist Methodologies for International Relations*, Cambridge: Cambridge University Press, 153–73.

Jancar, B. (1988) 'Women soldiers in Yugoslavia's national liberation struggle, 1941–1945', in: Isaksson, E. (ed.) *Women and the Military System*, London: Harvester-Wheatsheaf, 47–67.

Jehlen, M. (1990) 'Gender', in: Lentricchia, F. and McLaughlin, T. (eds) *Critical Terms for Literary Study*, Chicago: Chicago University Press, 263–73.

Jones, A. (1996) 'Does "gender" make the world go round? Feminist critiques of international relations', *Review of International Studies*, 22(4), 405–29.

Jones, A. (1998) 'Engendering debate', *Review of International Studies*, 24(2), 299–303.

Kaldor, M. (1991) 'Rethinking Cold War history', in: Booth, K. (ed.) *New Thinking About Strategy and International Security*, London: Harper Collins Academic, 313–31.

Kaldor, M. (2001) 'Wanted: Global politics', *The Nation*,

Kaldor, M. (2007) *New and Old Wars: Organized Violence in a Global Era*, 2nd edn, Stanford, CA: Stanford University Press.

Katzenstein, P.J. (1996) *The Culture of National Security: Norms and Identity in World Politics*, New York: Columbia University Press.

Kaufman, L.A. (2001) 'The anti-politics of identity', in: Ryan, B. (ed.) *Identity Politics in the Women's Movement*, New York: New York University Press, 23–34.

Keohane, R. (1989) 'International relations theory: Contributions of a feminist standpoint', *Millennium: Journal of International Studies*, 18(2), 245–54.

Keohane, R. (1991) 'International relations theory: Contributions of a feminist standpoint', in: Grant, R. and Newland, K. (eds) *Gender and International Relations*, Bloomington: Indiana University Press, 41–50.

Keohane, R. (1998) 'Beyond dichotomy: Conversations between international relations and feminist theory', *International Studies Quarterly*, 42(1), 193–8.

King, G. and Murray, C.J.L. (2001–2) 'Rethinking human security', *Political Science Quarterly*, 116(4), 585–610.

Kinsella, H. (2003) 'For careful reading: The conservatism of gender constructivism', *International Studies Review*, 5(2), 294–97.

Kirk, G. and Okazawa-Rey, M. (1998) 'Making connections: Building an East Asia–US women's network against US militarism', in: Lorentzen, L.A. and Turpin, J. (eds) *The Women and War Reader*, New York: New York University Press, 308–22.

Kirk, G. and Okazawa-Rey, M. (2001) 'Demilitarizing security: Women oppose US militarism in East Asia', in: Waller, M.R. and Rycenga, J. (eds) *Frontline Feminisms: Women, War, and Resistance*, New York: Routledge, 159–71.

Klein, B.S. (1994) *Strategic Studies and World Order*, Cambridge: Cambridge University Press.

Kleinfield, N.R. (2001) 'A creeping horror: Buildings burn and fall as onlookers search for elusive safety', *The New York Times*, 12 September 2001, p. A1 and A7. Online. Available HTTP: http://www.nytimes.com/2001/09/12/nyregion/12SCEN.html (accessed 5 October 2001).

Kolodziej, E.A. (1992) 'Renaissance in security studies? Caveat lector!', *International Studies Quarterly*, 36(4), 421–38.

Kong, B. (2004) *'The poetry of Donald Rumsfeld, set to music'*, *Morning Edition*, USA: National Public Radio.

Krause, K. (1998) 'Critical theory and security studies: The research programme of "critical security studies"', *Cooperation and Conflict*, 33(3), 298–333.

Krause, K. and Williams, M.C. (1996) 'Broadening the agenda of security studies: Politics and methods', *Mershon International Studies Review*, 40, 229–54.

Krause, K. and Williams, M.C. (eds) (1997a) *Critical Security Studies: Concepts and Cases*, Minneapolis: University of Minnesota Press.

Krause, K. and Williams, M.C. (1997b) 'From strategy to security: Foundations of critical security studies', in: Krause, K. and Williams, M.C. (eds) *Critical Security Studies: Concepts and Cases*, Minneapolis: University of Minnesota Press, 33–59.

Lanser, S. (1991) 'Towards a feminist narratology', in: Warhol, R.R. and Price Herndl, D. (eds) *Feminisms: An Anthology of Literary Theory and Criticism*, New Brunswick, NJ: Rutgers University Press.

Lerner, G. (1986) *The Creation of Patriarchy*, New York: Oxford University Press.

Lily, R.J. (2007) *Taken by Force: Rape and American GIs in Europe During WWII*, 2nd edn, New York: Palgrave Macmillan.

Linge, D.E. (1976) *'Editor's introduction', Philosophical Hermeneutics*, Berkeley: University of California Press, xi–lviii.

Lipschutz, R.D. (1995) *On Security: New Directions in World Politics*, New York: Columbia University Press.

Lipton, E. (2002) 'Struggle to tally all 9/11 dead by anniversary', *The New York Times*, 1 September 2002. Online. Available HTTP: http://www.nytimes.com/2002/09/01/nyregion/01COUN.html (accessed 2 September 2002).

Lorde, A. (1984) *Sister Outsider: Essays and Speeches*, Trumansburg, NY: Crossing Press.

Lorentzen, L.A. and Turpin, J. (eds) (1998) *The Women and War Reader*, New York: New York University Press.

Lugones, M.C. and Spelman, E.V. (1983) 'Have we got a theory for you! Feminist theory, cultural imperialism and the demand for "the woman's voice"', *Women's Studies International Forum*, 6(6), 573–81.

Luke, T. (1991) 'The discipline of security studies and the codes of containment: Learning from Kuwait', *Alternatives: Social Transformation and Humane Governance*, 16(3), 315–44.

Lutz, C. (2009) *The Bases of Empire: The Global Struggle Against US Military Posts*, New York: New York University Press.

McCormack, T. (2009) *Critique, Security and Power: The Political Limits to Critical and Emancipatory Approaches*, London: Routledge.

McEvoy, S. (2009) 'Loyalist women paramilitaries in Northern Ireland: Beginning a feminist conversation about conflict resolution', *Security Studies*, 18(2), 262–86.

MacFarlane, N.S. and Khong, Y.F. (2006) *Human Security and the United Nations: A Critical History*, Bloomington: University of Indiana Press.

Mack, A. (2002) *The Human Security Report Project: Background Paper*, Vancouver: Human Security Center, Liu Institute for Global Studies, University of British Columbia.

McKelvey, T. (2007) *One of the Guys: Women as Aggressors and Torturers*, Emeryville, CA: Seal Press.

MacKenzie, M. (2009) 'Securitization and de-securitization: Female soldiers and the reconstruction of women in post-conflict Sierra Leone', *Security Studies*, 18(2), 241–61.

MacLean, S.J., Black, D.R. and Shaw, T.M. (eds) (2006) *A Decade of Human Security: Global Governance and New Multilateralisms*, Aldershot: Ashgate.

McRae, R.G. and Hubert, D. (2001) *Human Security and the New Diplomacy: Protecting People, Promoting Peace*, Montreal: McGill-Queen's University Press.

McSweeney, B. (1996) 'Identity and security: Buzan and the Copenhagen school', *Review of International Studies*, 22(1), 299–54.

McSweeney, B. (1998) 'Durkeim and the Copenhagen school: A response to Buzan and Wæver', *Review of International Studies*, 24(1), 137–40.

March, A. (1982) 'Female invisibility in androcentric sociological theory', *Insurgent Sociologist*, 11(2), 99–107.

Marchand, M.H. (1998) 'Different communities/different realities/different encounters: A reply to J. Ann Tickner', *International Studies Quarterly*, 42(1), 199–204.

Masters, C. (2005) 'Bodies of technology: Cyborg soldiers and militarized masculinities', *International Feminist Journal of Politics*, 7(1), 112–32.

Mathews, J.T. (1989) 'Redefining security', *Foreign Affairs*, 68(2), 162–77.

Mattingly, C. and Lawlor, M. (2000) 'Learning from stories: Narrative interviewing in cross-cultural research', *Scandinavian Journal of Occupational Therapy*, 7, 4–14.

Mattingly, C., Lawlor, M. and Jacobs-Huey, L. (2002) 'Narrating September 11: Race, gender, and the play of cultural identities', *American Anthropologist*, 104(3), 743–53.

Mearsheimer, J.J. (1994/1995) 'The false promise of international institutions', *International Security*, 19(3), 5–49.

Meijer, M. (1993) 'Countering textual violence—on the critique of representation and the importance of teaching its methods', *Womens Studies International Forum*, 16(4), 367–78.

Meintjes, S., Pillay, A. and Turshen, M. (eds) (2001) *The Aftermath: Women in Post-Conflict Transformation*, London: Zed Books.

Mies, M. (1986) *Patriarchy and Accumulation on a World Scale: Women in the International Division of Labour*, London: Zed Books.

Miller, J.H. (1990) 'Narrative', in: Lentricchia, F. and McLaughlin, T. (eds) *Critical Terms for Literary Study*, Chicago: Chicago University Press, 66–79.

Mohanty, C.T. (1992) 'Feminist encounters: Locating the politics of experience', in: Barrett, M. and Phillips, A. (eds) *Destabilizing Theory: Contemporary Feminist Debates*, Stanford, CA: Stanford University Press, 77–92.

Molloy, P. (1995) 'Subversive strategies or subverting strategy? Toward a feminist pedagogy for peace', *Alternatives*, 20(2), 225–42.

Moon, C. (2008) *Narrating Political Reconciliation: South Africa's Truth and Reconciliation Commission*, Lanham, MD: Lexington Books.

Moon, K.H.S. (1997) *Sex Among Allies: Military Prostitution in US–Korea Relations*, New York: Columbia University Press.

Moraga, C. and Anzaldúa, G. (1983 [1979]) *This Bridge Called my Back: Writings by Radical Women of Color*, New York: Kitchen Table, Women of Color Press.

Moser, C.O.N. and Clark, F.C. (eds) (2001) *Victims, Perpetrators or Actors? Gender, Armed Conflict and Political Violence*, London: Zed Books.

Muggah, R. and Krause, K. (2006) 'A true measure of success? The discourse and practice of human security in Haiti', in: MacLean, S.J., Black, D.R. and Shaw, T.M. (eds) *A Decade of Human Security: Global Governancee and New Multilateralisms*, Aldershot: Ashgate, 113–26.

Naaman, D. (2007) 'Brides of Palestine/angels of death: Media, gender, and performance in the case of Palestinian female suicide bombers', *Signs: Journal of Women in Culture and Society*, 32(4), 933–55.

Nacos, B.L. (2005) 'The portrayal of female terrorists in the media: Similar framing patterns in the news coverage of women in politics and in terrorism', *Studies in Conflict and Terrorism*, 28, 435–51.

Narayan, U. (2001) 'The scope of our concerns: Reflections on "women" as the subject of feminist politics', in: DesAutels, P. and Waugh, J. (eds) *Feminists Doing Ethics*, Lanham, MD: Rowman & Littlefield, 15–31.

Neocleous, M. (2000) 'Against security', *Radical Philosophy*, 100, 7–15.

Nicholson, L.J. (1994) 'Interpreting gender', *Signs: Journal of Women in Culture and Society*, 29(1), 79–105.

Nikolic-Ristanovic, V. (1998) 'War, nationalism, and mothers in the former Yugoslavia', in: Lorentzen, L.A. and Turpin, J. (eds) *The Women and War Reader*, New York: New York University Press, 234–39.

Nikolic-Ristanovic, V. (ed.) (2000) *Women, Violence and War: Wartime Victimization of Refugees in the Balkans*, Budapest: Central European University Press.

9/11 Commission (22 July 2004) *The 9/11 Commission Report—Executive Summary. National Commission on Terrorist Attacks Upon the United States*. Online. Available HTTP: http://www.c-span.org/pdf/911finalreportexecsum.pdf (accessed 1 July 2009).

Nordstrom, C. (1996) 'Rape: Politics and theory in war and peace', *Australian Feminist Studies*, 11(23), 147–62.

Nordstrom, C. (1997) *A Different Kind of War Story*, Philadelphia: University of Pennsylvania Press.

Nordstrom, C. (2004) *Shadows of War: Violence, Power, and International Profiteering in the Twenty-First Century*, Ewing: University of California Press.

Nuruzzaman, M. (2006) 'Paradigms in conflict: The contested claims of human security, critical theory and feminism', *Cooperation and Conflict*, 41(3), 285–303.

Nye, J.S. and Lynn-Jones, S.M. (1988) 'International security studies: A report of a conference on the state of the field', *International Security*, 12(4), 5–27.

O'Gorman, E. (1999) 'Writing women's wars: Foucauldian strategies of engagement', in: Jabri, V. and O'Gorman, E. (eds) *Women, Culture, and International Relations*, Boulder, CO: Lynne Rienner, 91–116.

Oswald, U. (1979) 'Agribusiness, green revolution, and cooperation', in: Herrera, L. and Väyrynen, R. (ed.) *Peace, Development and the New International Order*, Tampere: IPRA.

Owen, T. (2004) 'Human security—conflict, critique and consensus: Colloquium remarks and a proposal for a threshold-based definition', *Security Dialogue*, 35(3), 373–87.

Parashar, S. (2009) 'Feminist international relations and women militants: Case studies from Sri Lanka and Kashmir', *Cambridge Review of International Affairs*, 22(2), 235–56.

Paris, R. (2001) 'Human security: Paradigm shift or hot air?', *International Security*, 26(2), 87–102.

Paris, R. (2004) 'Still an unscrutable concept', *Security Dialogue*, 35(3), 370–2.

Patomäki, H. (2001) 'The challenge of critical theories: Peace research at the start of the new century', *Journal of Peace Research*, 38(6), 723–37.

Peterson, V.S. (1992a) *Gendered States: Feminist (Re)visions of International Relations Theory*, Boulder, CO: Lynne Rienner.

Peterson, V.S. (1992b) 'Security and sovereign states: What is at stake in taking feminism seriously?', in: Peterson, V.S. (ed.) *Gendered States: Feminist (Re)Visions of International Relations Theory*, Boulder, Co: Lynne Rienner, 31–64.

Peterson, V.S. (1992c) 'Transgressing boundaries: Theories of knowledge, gender and international relations', *Millennium: Journal of International Studies*, 21(2), 183–206.

Peterson, V.S. (1996) 'The gender of rhetoric, reason, and realism', in: Beer, F.A. and Hariman, R. (eds) *Post-Realism: The Rhetorical Turn in International Relations*, East Lansing: Michigan State University Press, 257–75.

Peterson, V.S. (2003) *A Critical Rewriting of Global Political Economy: Integrating Reproductive, Productive and Virtual Economies*, London: Routledge.

Peterson, V.S. (2004) 'Feminist theories within, invisible to, and beyond IR', *Brown Journal of World Affairs*, 10(2), 35–45.

Peterson, V.S. and Runyan, A.S. (1993) *Global Gender Issues*, Boulder, CO: Westview Press.

Pettman, J. (1996) *Worlding Women: A Feminist International Politics*, St Leonards: Allen & Unwin.

Pierson, R.R. (1986) *'They're Still Women After All': The Second World War and Canadian Womanhood*, Toronto: McClelland Steward.

Polkinghorne, D. (1988) *Narrative Knowing and the Human Sciences*, Albany: State University of New York Press.

Pollit, K. (1999) 'Father knows best', *Foreign Affairs*, 78(1), 122–5.

Postman, N. (1987) *Amusing Ourselves to Death: Public Discourse in the Age of Showbusiness*, London: Methuen.

Rancière, J. (1999) *Disagreement: Politics and Philosophy*, Minneapolis: University of Minnesota Press.

Reardon, B. (1985) *Sexism and the War System*, New York: Teachers College Press.

Reardon, B. (1993) *Women and Peace: Feminist Visions of Global Security*, Albany: State University of New York Press.

Ringmar, E. (1996) *Identity, Interest and Action: A Cultural Explanation of Sweden's Intervention in the Thirty Years War*, Cambridge: Cambridge University Press.

Rothschild, E. (1995) 'What is security?', *Daedalus*, 124(3), 53–98.

Rowley, C. (2002) 'Coleen Rowley's Memo to FBI Director Robert Mueller'. *Time Magazine*, Online. Available HTTP: http://www.time.com/time/covers/1101020603/memo .html (accessed 4 September 2002).

Ruddick, S. (1983) 'Pacifying the forces: Drafting women in the interest of peace', *Signs: Journal of Women in Culture and Society*, 8(3), 471–89.

Ruddick, S. (1989a) *Maternal Thinking: Toward a Politics of Peace*, Boston: Beacon Press.

Ruddick, S. (1989b) 'Mothers and men's wars', in: Harris, A. and King, Y. (eds) *Rocking the Ship of State: Toward a Feminist Peace Politics*, Boulder, CO: Westview Press, 75–92.

Ruddick, S. (1998) '"Woman of peace": A feminist construction', in: Lorentzen, L.A. and Turpin, J. (eds) *The Women and War Reader*, New York: New York University Press, 213–26.

Rumsfeld, D. and Myers, R. (2002) *DoD News Briefing—Secretary Rumsfeld and Gen. Myers*, Washington, DC: Office of the Assistant Secretary of Defenses. Online. Available HTTP: http://www.defenselink.mil/transcripts/transcript.aspx?transcriptid=2636 (accessed 7 August 2009).

Rygiel, K. (2006) 'Protecting and proving identity: The biopolitics of waging war through citizenship in the post-9/11 era', in: Hunt, K. and Rygiel, K. (eds) *(En)gendering the War on Terror: War Stories and Camouflaged Politics*, Aldershot: Ashgate, 145–67.

Scheper-Hughes, N. (1998) 'Maternal thinking and the politics of war', in: Lorentzen, L.A. and Turpin, J. (eds) *The Women and War Reader*, New York: New York University Press, 227–33.

Schmemann, S. (2001) 'Hijacked jets destroy twin towers and hit Pentagon', *The New York Times*, 9 September 2001, p. A1 and A14. Online. Available HTTP: http://www. nytimes.com/2001/09/12/nyregion/12PLAN.html (accessed 5 October 2001).

Seely, H. (2003) 'The poetry of D.H. Rumsfeld: Recent works by the secretary of defense'. Slate.com. Online. Available HTTP: http://slate.msn.com/id/2081042 (accessed 5 August 2009).

Shanker, T. (2002) 'Rumsfeld's search for a way to fight a new type of foe', *New York Times*, 4 September 2002. Online. Available HTTP: http://www.nytimes.com/2002/09/04/international/04RUMS.html (accessed 4 September 2002).

Shapiro, B. (2001) 'Information lockdown'. *The Nation*, Online. Available HTTP: http://www.alternet.org/story.html?StoryID=11816 (accessed 4 November 2001).

Shapiro, M.J. (1988) *The Politics of Representation: Writing Practices in Biography, Photography, and Policy Analysis*, Madison: University of Wisconsin Press.

Shapiro, M.J. (1992) 'That obscure object of violence: Logistics, desire, war', *Alternatives: Social Transformation and Humane Governance*, 17(4), 453–77.

Sharma, N. (2006) 'White nationalism, illegality and imperialism: Border controls as ideology', in: Hunt, K. and Rygiel, K. (eds) *(En)gendering the War on Terror: War Stories and Camouflaged Politics*, Aldershot: Ashgate, 121–43.

Sharoni, S. (1997) 'Gendering conflict and peace in Israel/Palestine and the North of Ireland', *Millennium: Journal of International Studies*, 27(4), 1061–89.

Sharoni, S. (1999) *Doing Research on/with Women in Conflict Zones: Some Ethical Considerations*, Online. Available HTTP: http://www.simonasharoni.com/Pages/publications.html (accessed 16 March 2010).

Shepherd, L.J. (2010) 'Feminist Security Studies', in: Denemark, R. A. (ed.) *The International Studies Enclopedia*. Blackwell Publishing. Online. Available HTTP: http://www.isacompendium.com/subscriber/tocnode?id=g9781444336597_chunk_g97814443365978_ss1-10 (accessed 9 April 2010).

Sheridan, S. (1990) 'Feminist knowledge, women's liberation, and women's studies', in: Gunew, S.M. (ed.) *Feminist Knowledge: Critique and Construct*, London. Routledge, 36–55.

Sjoberg, L. (2006) 'Gendered realities of the immunity principle: Why gender analysis needs feminism', *International Studies Quarterly*, 50(4), 889–910.

Sjoberg, L. (ed.) (2009a) *Gender and International Security: Feminist Perspectives*, London: Routledge.

Sjoberg, L. (2009b) 'Introduction to security studies: Feminist contributions', *Security Studies*, 18(2), 183–213.

Sjoberg, L. and Gentry, C.E. (2007) *Mothers, Monsters, Whores: Women's Violence in Global Politics*, London: Zed Books.

Sjoberg, L. and Martin, J. (2010) 'Feminist Security Theorizing', in: Denemark, R. A. (ed.) *The International Studies Encyclopedia*. Blackwell Publishing. Online. Available HTTP: http://www.isacompendium.com/subscriber/tocnode?id=g9781444336597_chunk_g97814443365978_ss1-11 (accessed 9 April 2010).

Skjelsbæk, I. (2001) 'Sexual violence and war: Mapping out a complex relationship', *European Journal of International Relations*, 7(2), 211–37.

Smith, S. (1991) 'Mature anarchy, strong states and security', *Arms Control*, 12(2), 325–39.

Smith, S. (2005) 'The contested concept of security', in: Booth, K. (ed.) *Critical Security Studies and World Politics*, Boulder, CO: Lynne Rienner, 27–62.

Smith, S., Booth, K. and Zalewski, M. (1996) *International Theory: Positivism and Beyond*, Cambridge: Cambridge University Press.

Snyder, C.A. (1999) 'Contemporary security and strategy', in: Snyder, C.A. (ed.) *Contemporary Security and Strategy*, New York: Routledge, 1–12.

Solaro, E. (2006) *Women in the Line of Fire: What you Should Know About Women in the Military*, Emeryville, CA: Seal Press.

Spivak, G.C. (1988) 'Can the subaltern speak?', in: Nelson, G. and Grossberg, L. (eds) *Marxism and the Interpretation of Culture*, Basingstoke: Macmillan, 271–313.

Spivak, G.C. (1996) 'Subaltern talk: Interview with the editors', in: Landy, D. and MacLean, G. (eds) *The Spivak Reader: Selected Works of Gayatri Chakravorty Spivak*, London: Routledge, 287–308.

Stern, M. (2001) *Naming In/Security—Constructing Identity: 'Mayan Women' in Guatemala on the Eve of 'Peace'*, Gothenburg, Sweden: Peace and Development Research Institute Gothenburg University.

Stern, M. (2005) *Naming Security—Constructing Identity: 'Mayan women' in Guatemala on the Eve of 'Peace'*, Manchester: Manchester University Press.

Stern, M. (2006a) 'Racism, sexism, classism, and much more: Reading security-identity in marginalized sites', in: Ackerly, B.A., Stern, M. and True, J. (eds) *Feminist Methodologies for International Relations*, Cambridge: Cambridge University Press, 174–97.

Stern, M. (2006b) '"We" the subject: The power and failure of (in)security', *Security Dialogue*, 37(2), 187–205.

Stiehm, J. (1983) *Women and Men's Wars*, 1st edn, Oxford: Pergamon Press.

Stiehm, J. (1996) *It's our military, too! Women and the US Military*, Philadelphia: Temple University Press.

Stiehm, J.H. (1982) 'The protected, the protector, the defender', *Womens Studies International Forum*, 5(3/4), 367–76.

Stiehm, J.H. (1988) 'The effect of myths about military women on the waging of war', in: Isaksson, E. (ed.) *Women and the Military System*, London: Harvester-Wheatsheaf, 94–105.

Stiglmayer, A. (ed.) (1993) *Mass Rape: The War Against Women in Bosnia-Herzegovina*, Lincoln: University of Nebraska Press.

Stoett, P. (2000) *Human and Global Security: An Exploration of Terms*, Toronto: University of Toronto Press.

Suhrke, A. (1999) 'Human security and the interests of states', *Security Dialogue*, 30(3), 265–76.

Swingewood, A. (1984) *A Short History of Sociological Thought*, New York: St Martin's Press.

Sylvester, C. (1987) 'Some dangers in merging feminist and peace projects', *Alternatives: Social Transformation and Humane Governance*, 12(4), 493–509.

Sylvester, C. (1989) 'Patriarchy, peace, and women warriors', in: Forcey, L.R. (ed.) *Peace: Meanings, Politics, Strategies*, New York: Praeger, 97–112.

Sylvester, C. (1993) 'Riding the hyphens of feminism, peace, and place in 4-(or more)part cacophony', *Alternatives: Social Transformation and Humane Governance*, 18(1), 109–18.

Sylvester, C. (1994a) 'Empathetic cooperation—A feminist method for IR', *Millennium: Journal of International Studies*, 23(2), 315–34.

Sylvester, C. (1994b) *Feminist Theory and International Relations in a Postmodern Era*, Cambridge: Cambridge University Press.

Sylvester, C. (2002) *Feminist International Relations: An Unfinished Journey*, Cambridge: Cambridge University Press.

Sylvester, C. (2007) 'Anatomy of a footnote', *Security Dialogue*, 38(4), 547–58.

Sylvester, C. (2010) 'Feminisms Troubling the Boundaries of International Relations', in: Denemark, R. A. (ed.) *The International Studies Encyclopedia*. Blackwell Publishing. Online. Available HTTP: http://www.isacompendium.com/subscriber/tocnode?id=g9781444433 6597_chunk_g97814443365978_ss1-5 (accessed 9 April 2010).

Tadjbakhsh, S. and Chenoy, A.M. (2007) *Human Security: Concepts and Implications*, London: Routledge.

Terriff, T., Croft, S., James, L. and Morgan, P.M. (1999) *Security Studies Today*, Malden, MA: Polity Press.

Thiele, B. (1986) 'Vanishing acts in social and political thought: Tricks of the trade', in: Gross, E. and Pateman, C. (eds) *Feminist Challenges: Social and Political Theory*, Sydney: Allen & Unwin, 30–43.

Thomas, C. and Wilkin, P. (1999) *Globalization, Human Security and the African Experience*, Boulder, CO: Lynne Rienner.

Tickner, J.A. (1988) 'Hans Morgenthau's principles of political realism—a feminist reformulation', *Millennium: Journal of International Studies*, 17(3), 429–40.

Tickner, J.A. (1992) *Gender in International Relations: Feminist Perspectives on Achieving Global Security*, New York: Columbia University Press.

Tickner, J.A. (1995) 'Re-visioning security', in: Booth, K. and Smith, S. (eds) *International Relations Theory Today*, Cambridge: Polity Press, 175–97.

Tickner, J.A. (1997a) 'Changing differences: Women and the shaping of American foreign policy, 1917–1994—Jeffreys Jones, R', *Diplomatic History*, 21(1), 157–62.

Tickner, J.A. (1997b) 'You just don't understand: Troubled engagements between feminists and IR theorists', *International Studies Quarterly*, 41(4), 611–32.

Tickner, J.A. (1998) 'Continuing the conversation . . . ', *International Studies Quarterly*, 42(1), 205–10.

Tickner, J.A. (2001) *Gendering World Politics: Issues and Approaches in the Post-Cold War Era*, New York: Columbia University Press.

Tickner, J.A. (2004) 'Feminist responses to international security studies', *Peace Review*, 16(1), 43–8.

Tickner, J.A. (2005) 'What is your research program? Some feminist answers to International Relations methodological questions', *International Studies Quarterly*, 49(1), 1–21.

Tickner, J.A. (2006) 'Feminism meets international relations: Some methodological issues', in: Ackerly, B.A., Stern, M. and True, J. (eds) *Feminist Methodologies for International Relations*, Cambridge: Cambridge University Press, 19–41.

Timothy, K. (2004) 'Human security discourse at the UN', *Peace Review*, 16(1), 19–24.

Tobias, S. (1985) 'Toward a feminist analysis of defense spending', *Frontiers*, 8(2), 65–8.

Trinh, T.M.-H. (1989) *Woman, Native, Other: Writing Postcoloniality and Feminism*, Bloomington: Indiana University Press.

Tronto, J.C. (1987) 'Beyond gender difference to a theory of care', *Signs: Journal of Women in Culture and Society*, 12(4), 644–63.

Turshen, M. (2001) 'The political economy of rape: An analysis of systematic rape and sexual abuse of women during armed conflict in Africa', in: Moser, C.O.N. and Clark, F.C. (eds) *Victims, Perpetrators or Actors? Gender, Armed Conflict and Political Violence*, London: Zed Books, 55–68.

Ullman, R.H. (1983) 'Redefining security', *International Security*, 8(1), 123–9.

UNDP (1994) *Human Development Report*, New York: United Nations Development Program.

Wæver, O. (1995a) *Concepts of Security*, Copenhagen, Denmark: University of Copenhagen.

Wæver, O. (1995b) 'Securitization and desecuritization', in: Lipschutz, R.D. (ed.) *On Security: New Directions in World Politics*, New York: Columbia University Press.

Wæver, O. (1999) 'Securitizing sectors? Reply to Eriksson', *Cooperation and Conflict*, 34(4), 334–40.

Wæver, O. (2004) 'Aberystwyth, Paris, Copenhagen—New "schools" in security theory and their origins between core and periphery', *International Studies Association Annual Convention*, Montreal, Quebec, Canada.

Walby, S. (1990) *Theorizing Patriarchy*, Oxford: Basil Blackwell.

Walker, R.B.J. (1990a) 'Security, sovereignty, and the challenge of world politics', *Alternatives: Social Transformation and Humane Governance*, 15(1), 3–27.

Walker, R.B.J. (1990b) 'Sovereignty, identity, community: Reflections on the horizons of contemporary political practice', in: Walker, R.B.J. and Mendlovitz, S. (eds) *Contending Sovereignties: Redefining Political Community*, Boulder, CO: Lynne Rienner, 159–85.

Walker, R.B.J. (1993) *Inside/Outside: International Relations as Political Theory*, Cambridge: Cambridge University Press.

Walker, R.B.J. (1995) 'History and structure of international relations', in: Der Derian, J. (ed.) *International Theory: Critical Investigations*, New York: New York University Press, 308–39.

Walker, R.B.J. (1997) 'The subject of security', in: Krause, K. and Williams, M.C. (eds) *Critical Security Studies: Concepts and Cases*, Minneapolis: University of Minnesota Press, 61–81.

Wallensteen, P. (2001) *The Growing Peace Research Agenda: Kroc Institute Occasional Paper #21:OP:4*, San Diego, CA: University of San Diego.

Waller, M.R. and Rycenga, J. (eds) (2000) *Frontline Feminisms: Women, War, and Resistance*, New York: Routledge.

Walt, S. (1991) 'The renaissance of security studies', *International Studies Quarterly*, 35(2), 211–39.

Walters, M. (2005) *Feminism: A Very Short Introduction*, Oxford: Oxford University Press.

Weber, C. (1994) 'Good girls, little girls, and bad girls: Male paranoia in Robert Keohane's critique of feminist international relations', *Millennium: Journal of International Studies*, 23(2), 337–49.

Weber, C. (1995) *Simulating Sovereignty: Intervention, the State and Symbolic Exchange*, Cambridge: Cambridge University Press.

Weber, C. (1999) *Faking it: US Hegemony in a Post-Phallic Era*, Minneapolis: University of Minnesota Press.

Weber, C. and Biersteker, T.J. (eds) (1996) *State Sovereignty as Social Construct*, Cambridge: Cambridge University Press.

Weedon, C. (1987) *Feminist Practice and Poststructuralist Theory*, Oxford: Basil Blackwell.

Weldes, J., Laffey, M., Gusterson, H. and Duvall, R. (1999) *Cultures of Insecurity: States, Communities, and the Production of Danger*, Minneapolis: University of Minnesota Press.

White, A.M. (2007) 'All the men are fighting for freedom, all the women are mourning their men, but some of us carried guns: A raced-gendered analysis of Fanon's psychological perspectives on war', *Signs: Journal of Womens in Culture and Society*, 32(4), 857–84.

White, H. (1980) 'The value of narrativity in the representation of reality', in: Mitchell, W.J.T. (ed.) *On Narrative*, Chicago: University of Chicago Press, 1–23.

Whitebrook, M. (2001) *Identity, Narrative and Politics*, London: Routledge.

Whitworth, S. (2004) *Men, Militarism & UN Peacekeeping*, Boulder, CO: Lynne Rienner.

Whitworth, S. (2005) 'Militarized masculinities and the politics of peacekeeping', in: Booth, K. (ed.) *Critical Security Studies and World Politics*, Boulder, CO: Lynne Rienner, 89–106.

Wibben, A.T.R. (1998) *Narrating Experience: Raymond Aron and Feminist Scholars Revis(it)ed— A Subversive Conversation*, Tampere: University of Tampere.

Wibben, A.T.R. (2001) *Lies & (Self) Analysis*, Information Technology, War and Peace Project. Online. Available HTTP: http://www.watsoninstitute.org/infopeace/911/atrw_lies.html (accessed 24 April 2002).

Wibben, A.T.R. (2002) *Security Narratives in International Relations and the Events of September 11, 2001: A Feminist Study*, Ph.D. University of Wales, Aberystwyth, UK.

Wibben, A.T.R. (2003) 'Whose meaning(s)?! A feminist perspective on the crisis of meaning in international relations', in: Mandaville, P.G. and Williams, A.J. (eds) *Meaning and International Relations*, London: Routledge, 86–105.

Wibben, A.T.R. (2004) 'Feminist international relations: Old debates and new directions', *Brown Journal of World Affairs*, 10(2), 97–114.

Wibben, A.T.R. (2008) 'Human security: Toward an opening', *Security Dialogue*, 39(4), 455–62.

Wibben, A.T.R. and Turpin, J. (2008) 'Women and war', in: Kurtz, L. (ed.) *The Encyclopedia of Violence, Peace, and Conflict*, 2nd edn, Amsterdam: Elsevier Academic Press, 2456–67.

Williams, M.C. (1998a) 'Identity and the politics of security', *European Journal of International Relations*, 4(2), 204–25.

Williams, M.C. (1998b) 'Modernity, identity and security: a comment on the "Copenhagen controversy"', *Review of International Studies*, 24(3), 435–9.

Williams, M.C. (1999) 'The practices of security: Critical contributions', *Cooperation and Conflict*, 34(3), 341–4.

Williams, M.C. (2005) *The Realist Tradition and the Limits of International Relations*, Cambridge: Cambridge University Press.

Wolfers, A. (1962) *Discord and Collaboration: Essays on International Politics*, Baltimore, MD: Johns Hopkins Press.

Woollacott, A. (1998) 'Women munition makers, war, and citizenship', in: Lorentzen, L.A. and Turpin, J. (eds) *The Women and War Reader*, New York: New York University Press, 126–31.

World Commission on Environment and Development (1987) *Our Common Future (Brundtland Report)*, Oxford: Oxford University Press.

Wyn Jones, R. (1995) '"Message in a bottle?": Theory and praxis in critical security studies', *Contemporary Security Policy*, 16(3), 299–319.

Wyn Jones, R. (1999) *Security, Strategy, and Critical Theory*, Boulder, CO: Lynne Rienner.

Wyn Jones, R. (2005) 'On emancipation: Neccessity, capacity, and concrete utopias', in: Booth, K. (ed.) *Critical Security Studies and World Politics*, Boulder, CO: Lynne Rienner, 213–35.

Young, I.M. (2003) 'Feminist reactions to the contemporary security regime', *Hypatia*, 18(1), 223–31.

Young, I.M. (2007) 'The logic of masculinist protection: Reflections on the current security state', in: Fergunson, M.L. and Marso, L.J. (eds) *W Stands for Women: How the George W. Bush Presidency Shaped a New Politics of Gender*, Durham, NC: Duke University Press, 115–39.

Yuval-Davis, N. (1994) 'Identity politics and women's ethnicity', in: Moghadam, V.M. (ed.) *Identity Politics and Women: Cultural Reassertions and Feminisms in International Perspective*, Boulder, CO: Westview Press, 408–24.

Yuval-Davis, N. (1997) *Gender & Nation*, London: Sage.

Yuval-Davis, N. (2001) 'The binary war'. *openDemocracy*, Online. Available HTTP: http://www.opendemocracy.net/forum/document_details.asp?CatID=98&DocID=760&DebateID=150 (accessed 4 November 2001).

Yuval-Davis, N. (2006) 'Belonging and the politics of belonging', *Patterns of Prejudice*, 40(3), 196–213.

Yuval-Davis, N. and Werbner, P. (eds) (1999) *Women, Citizenship and Difference*, London: Zed Books.

Zehfuss, M. (2003) 'Forget September 11', *Third World Quarterly*, 24(3), 513–28.

Zengotita, T. d. (2001) 'Since then: Real, surreal, virtual', *Harper's Magazine*, December.

Index

Address to the Nation see 9/11, as security narrative
Andrews, M. 101, 105, 107, 108, 110, 112
Anzaldùa, G. 14, 68
Aron, R. 17

Bal, M. 19, 46–9, 59–61
Boulding, E. 23–4
Burguieres, M.K. 24
Bush administration 10, 54, 108
Butler, J. 4, 20, 25, 107
Buzan, B. 38, 41, 65, 70, 74, 78–80, 81

Campbell, D. 39, 66–9, 72–3, 75–7
Chandler, D. 81, 82, 84
Cockburn, C. 23, 94
Cohn, C. 21, 22, 24, 75, 101
Collins, P.H. 22, 112
colonialism 13, 18, 33, 95
Commission on Human Security (CHS) 82–3
Constantinou, C. 6, 40–1, 65, 68, 76
Copenhagen School 6, 78, 79, 93
critical security studies: concepts of security and 38, 77–8; feminism and 5, 7, 112; narrative frameworks within 79–81; role of the state in 80; threat identification in 79
Culler, J.D. 45, 51–2
cultural identity, Mayan women and 94
Currie, M. 43, 44–5, 100

deconstruction 33, 34, 45, 102
decontextualization 19, 27, 36, 44, 84, 100, 108; *see also* subjectivity *vs.* objectivity
Der Derian, J. 6, 40, 41, 42, 63, 68–9, 72, 74, 82

desecuritization *see* securitization
Dillon, M. 6, 39, 40, 45, 60, 68, 69, 71, 72
Douzinas, C. 85
Duffield, M. 83, 85

Edkins, J. 6, 41, 47, 64, 67–8, 85, 101, 108, 113
Elshtain, J.B. 19, 21, 22, 101–3, 106
empathetic cooperation 105, 111, 112
empowerment: feminism and 5, 18, 92–3, 95, 112; human security and 83; narrative of 110; political activism and 92–3; protector/protected dynamic and 83
Enlightenment thought *see* hermeneutics; science, modern; subjectivity *vs.* objectivity
Enloe, C. 4–5, 12, 17, 21, 22, 23, 25, 34, 87, 89, 103, 111, 112
epistemology *see* science, modern
everyday experience *see also* intersecting oppressions: feminism's grounding in 1–3, 5, 12–13, 15, 44, 103; Feminist Security Studies and 21, 25, 82, 87–8, 99, 100; identity and 94, 95, 98–9; International Relations and 18, 25–6; intersecting oppressions and 42; narrative and 64, 109; narrative theory and 45; science and 34

fabula 46–52
feminism: embedded 10–11; everyday experience and (*see* everyday experience); evolution of 11–12, 111–12; gender stereotypes within (*see* gender conceptions/roles, in feminism); and hermeneutics *vs.* scientific method 32–3, 37; identity politics and 15–16 (*see also*

security narrative, identity in);
International Relations and 4–5, 11–12,
16–21, 25–6, 109; intersecting oppressions
and (*see* intersecting oppressions); liberal
13–14, 15; multiplicity/contradiction in
11, 24–5, 86, 109–12; personal/specific *vs.*
abstract/general focus in 2, 12–15, 19, 20,
36, 108; political project of 12, 52;
reflexive nature of 11, 18, 105–6, 110,
112; security studies and (*see* Feminist
Security Studies)

Feminist Security Studies: everyday
experience and (*see* everyday experience);
fragmented subjectivity in 111–12;
listening skills in 111; narrative
reformulation by 80, 86, 87, 106; origins
of 4–5, 21; personal narrative, importance
to 3, 100, 101–3; political nature of
113–14; security studies *vs.* 112–14 (*see
also* security studies, opening of *vs.* reform
of); study of gender roles in security
studies (*see* gender conceptions/roles);
study of violence in 23, 25, 106, 109; war
and militarism in 24, 25, 87–91

Ferguson, K.E. 20, 36–7, 112

Flax, J. 19, 24, 35

focalizor 47–50, 109

Foucault, M. 28, 30, 34, 64

Frankfurt School 78, 80

FSS *see* Feminist Security Studies

Gadamer, H-G. 34–6, 45

gender bias: in human security 84, 85; in
security narratives 69–70

gender conceptions/roles: in feminism 22–4;
science and 34; in security studies, study by
Feminist Security Studies 23, 68, 101–2

Hansen, L. 6, 21, 23, 79

Harding, S. 7, 18, 27, 29–31, 34, 37, 102

Hekman, S. 15, 32, 33, 45, 109

hermeneutics: narrative meaning and 27–8,
35, 45; *vs.* scientific method 31–3, 34–6

Hirschmann, N.J. 16, 27, 28, 41, 65, 70

Hollis, M. 31–2

hooks, b. 13–14, 15

human security *see* security, human

humanity, exclusive nature of 85

Hunt, K. 10, 111

Huysmans, J. 5, 6, 7, 25, 38–9, 45, 65, 66,
68, 76, 77, 79

identity *see also* security narrative, identity in;
subjectivity: contingent nature of 83, 93;
everyday experience and (*see* everyday
experience); intersectionality of 2, 3, 20,
89, 93 (*see also* intersecting oppressions);
markers 2, 15, 17, 27, 94, 108, 112;
violence and 95–6, 103

imperialism 33, 61, 101, 110, 113; *see also*
postcolonial analysis

in/security *see* insecurity; security

insecurity *see also* security: identity and 109;
sources of 82, 93–5; state role in creating
22, 69, 89–90; women and 65, 88–95

International Relations: agents in 6–7, 41, 60,
66–7, 72; everyday experience and (*see*
everyday experience); feminism and (*see*
feminism, International Relations and);
hermeneutics *vs.* scientific method in 31–2;
male bias in 17–18, 101–3; military power in
73–4; referents in 6–7, 66–9, 72; security as
defined in (*see* security); sovereignty in 70–2,
101; terrorism and 63; threat identification in
6–7, 38, 66–9; womens' presence in 17

intersecting oppressions 9, 13–14, 20, 23, 25,
42, 68, 95, 100, 107, 112; everyday
experience and (*see* everyday experience)

IR *see* International Relations

Jabri, V. 18, 26, 112

Kaldor, M. 4, 21, 67, 75, 80

Kennan, G. 73

Keohane, R. 12

Krause, K. 6–7, 31, 77, 78, 84

liberalism, assumptions in 11, 13, 15, 24, 41,
74, 79, 81–3, 109

Lugones, M.C. 14, 110, 111, 113

Mattingly, C. 1–3, 41–2, 104, 107, 109

Meijer, M. 43, 49–50

methodology *see* hermeneutics; science,
modern

militarization: prostitution and 87–91;
sexualized violence and 91; women's roles
in 21–3, 103

mobile subjectivity *see* subjectivity, mobile
Moon, K.H.S. 5, 17, 45, 47, 87–91, 95, 99,
    103, 104, 111
Morgenthau, H. 31

Narayan, U. 15–16
narrative: 9/11 and (*see* 9/11); construction
    and/or restriction of meaning through 2–4,
    27–8, 43–4, 100–1, 106, 108; contextual/
    contingent nature of 27–8, 39–40, 100,
    109–11; counternarratives and 56–7;
    everyday experience and (*see* everyday
    experience); listening to 52, 101, 105,
    110–11, 112–13; personal 90–1, 94–5, 97,
    98–102, 104–6, 110; political nature of 64;
    security studies reform and 7, 101
narrative theory *see also* fabula; focalizor;
    poststructuralist analysis; subjectivity:
    applicability, limits of 46, 51–2; as challenge
    to traditional security narratives 44, 65–6,
    100, 102–3; definition and history of 44–5;
    everyday experience and (*see* everyday
    experience); feminist approaches to 51–2,
    61, 112 (*see also* narrative; security
    narrative); layers of analysis in 46–7;
    ordering processes in 47–8, 59–60, 70, 101;
    poststructuralist thought and 51; specific
    applications of 49–50, 56–7; truth in 64
narratology 44–5
naturalness, concept of 12, 13, 18, 29, 34, 71,
    75, 94, 96–7
neorealism: and IR 7, 31, 77, 81; male bias
    in 17
9/11: accounts of 1–4, 53–6, 61; feminist
    views of 107–9; First World identity and
    107; as security narrative 2–4, 41–2, 54–8,
    60–3, 108–9; as security narrative,
    complications to 58–9; as security
    narrative, omissions from 61–2
Nordstrom, C. 21, 86–7, 91, 95–9, 100,
    101–2, 105, 106, 111
normality, concepts of 1–2, 3, 8, 12–13, 64,
    109–10
normality *vs.* trauma 41, 107–9

ontology *see* hermeneutics; science, modern

peace research 4, 5, 74, 76, 79
personal narrative *see* narrative, personal

Peterson, V.S. 6, 16, 17, 18, 21–2, 91–2, 109
politicization of trauma 108–9
postcolonial analysis 13, 18, 61; *see also*
    imperialism
poststructuralist analysis 18, 19, 33, 39, 77;
    see also narrative theory

Realism 31; *see also* neorealism
Reardon, B. 4, 5, 21, 22, 23, 109
Rothschild, E. 5, 6, 40, 41, 81, 83
Ruddick, S. 5, 22, 24, 25, 75
Rumsfeld, D. 76
Rygiel, K. 69, 111

science, modern: everyday experience *vs.*
    (*see* everyday experience); feminism,
    historical parallels with 29–30; gender
    conceptions in (*see* gender conceptions/
    roles, science and); hermeneutics *vs.* 32–3
    (*see also* International Relations,
    hermeneutics *vs.* scientific method in);
    humanism in 32, 34; as narrative 28–9,
    33–4, 43–4; objectivity of (*see* subjectivity
    vs. objectivity); political nature of 30–1,
    34; positivism in 29, 31, 32–3; practice/
    theory divide 66, 111; value-neutrality of
    30–1, 34; violence of 33–4
securitization: desecuritization *vs.* 78, 80; of
    humanity 85; as means of creating
    certainty 26; as speech act 78–9
security *see also* insecurity; securitization;
    security, human: agents of 6, 7, 60, 66, 69,
    72, 78–81, 83–4; alternative definitions of
    41–2, 66, 68, 71–2, 75, 76–7, 87, 105;
    contextual/contingent nature of 8, 78, 99,
    100; historical definitions of 40; identity
    and 93–5, 100; insecurity as predicate for
    4, 45, 91; as made *vs.* natural 106; politics
    of 113; prostitution as instrument of 87–
    91; referents of 6, 7, 66–7, 69, 72, 78–81,
    82–3, 100; security studies' definition of
    38–9, 113
security, human: gender bias in (*see* gender
    bias, in human security); limits of 84–5;
    notions of security in 5, 41, 82–3; origins
    of 6, 81–2; role of state in 83; security
    narratives in 82
security narrative *see also* 9/11: agents of 80–
    1; contextual/contingent nature of 71–2,

86–7; critical (*see* critical security studies, narrative frameworks within); feminist 25–6, 101, 106 (*see also* narrative, personal); gender bias in (*see* gender bias, in security narratives); human (*see* security, human); identity in 75, 77, 91, 100, 105, 109; performative/creative function of 39, 69, 72, 75, 78 (*see also* securitization); politicization of trauma as challenge to 108–9; referents of 80; role of the state in 72, 113; threat identification in 69, 75–6; traditional 25–6, 41, 65–80, 66–7, 76
security studies (traditional) *see also* critical security studies: Cold War failures of 77; feminism and (*see* Feminist Security Studies); military strategy bias in 74–5, 76–7; as narrative (*see* security narrative); opening of *vs.* reform of 5–7, 25–6, 37–8, 78, 80–1, 84–5, 106, 113–14; origins of 37; role of modern science in 76–7; role of the state in 72, 80–1; vulnerability in 113
Shapiro, M.J. 33, 43, 46, 64, 73
Smith, S. 7, 31–2, 70
Spelman, E.V. 14, 110, 111, 113
Stern, M. 18, 45, 65, 71, 79, 81, 91–5, 99, 100, 101–5, 109, 111
subjectivity: identity and (*see* identity); mobile 20–1, 36, 112; modern science and 29, 32, 36; narrative theory's analysis of 47–8, 50, 105, 109; security narratives and 39, 68–9, 79, 100, 105, 112; women's 2, 12–13, 20, 24, 100

subjectivity *vs.* objectivity 18–19, 28–9, 36
Sylvester, C. 115, 16, 21, 22, 24, 25, 34, 101, 103, 105, 109, 112

terrorism: women's rights and 10–11
threat construction *see under* critical security studies; international relations; security narrative
Tickner, J.A. 4, 12, 21, 24, 31, 89, 91, 103, 112

United Nations Development Program 81–3

violence: lasting effects of 96; as made *vs.* natural 96–7, 98, 106; male-dominated society and 109; narrative resistance to 97–9

Wæver, O. 5, 6, 25, 38, 40, 66, 78–80
Walker, R.B.J. 70, 71, 75
war: Cold War as security narrative 66–7; narratives of women in 102–3, 104–5 (*see also* narrative, personal)
Weber, C. 7, 11–12
Weber, M. 32
Williams, M.C. 6, 7, 31, 37–8, 41, 70, 77
Wolfers, A. 41, 67, 73, 75
Women's liberation/rights: Afghan women and 10–11, 20; 9/11 and 108

Yuval-Davis, N. 16, 18, 22, 94, 108, 109

Zehfuss, M. 4, 108